The Spanish Elizabethans

The Spanish Elizabethans

THE ENGLISH EXILES
AT THE COURT OF PHILIP II

] *Albert J. Loomie,* s.j. [

FORDHAM UNIVERSITY PRESS

NEW YORK   1963

For

Leo and Edward

Contents

CONTENTS

Abbreviations and Shortened Titles

A.G.I.   Archivo General de Indias, Seville

A.G.R.   Archives Générales du Royaume, Brussels

    P.E.A. Papiers d'États et Audience

    S.E.G. Secretarie d'État et de Guerre

A.G.S.   Archivo General de Simancas

A.H.N.   Archivo Historico Nacional, Madrid

A.P.C.   *Acts of the Privy Council.* (Cited by years)

A.R.S.J.   Archivum Romanum Societatis Jesu.

A.S.V.   Archivio Segredo di Vaticano.

Birch, *Memoirs:* Thomas Birch, *Memoirs of the Reign of Queen Elizabeth from the Year 1581* . . . 2 vols. (London, 1754)

Birch, *Historical View:* Thomas Birch, *An Historical View of the Negotiations Between the Courts of England, France, and Brussels* . . . (London, 1749)

  B.M.   British Museum

Col. Doc. Ined.: Colección de Documentos Inéditos . . . *para la Historia de España* . . . 112 vols. (Madrid, 1842–95)

C.R.S.   Catholic Record Society Publications

C.S.P.   *Calendars of State Papers* (Cited by years)
    Dom.: Domestic; *For.:* Foreign; *Add.:* Addenda

    E   *Sección de Estado,* of A.G.S. (Cited with *legajo* and *carpeta*)

Foley, *Records:* Henry Foley, *Records of the English Province of the Society of Jesus,* 7 vols. (London, 1877–84)

ABBREVIATIONS

H.M.C.   *Historical Manuscripts Commission*
         Salisbury MSS: Calendar of Manuscripts at Hatfield
         House belonging to the Marquess of Salisbury . . .
         15 vols.

Knox, *Allen:* Thomas Knox, *Letters and Memorials of William*
         Allen (London, 1882)

Lechat, *Les Refugiés:* Robert Lechat, *Les Refugiés Anglais dans*
         les Pays-bas espagnols durant le règne d'Elizabeth
         (Louvain, 1914)

n.f.   No folio or page number on the original document

P.R.O.   Public Record Office
         S.P. State Papers (Cited by press number, volume
         and folio)

S.A.C.   Saint Alban's College Archive, Valladolid

Sadler Papers: Arthur Clifford, ed. *The State Papers and Letters*
         of Sir Ralph Sadler. 2 vols. (Edinburgh, 1809)

Somers Tracts: Walter Scott, ed. *A Collection of Scarce and*
         Valuable Tracts, selected . . . *of the late Lord*
         Somers. 13 vols. (London, 1809–15)

Strype, *Annals:* John Strype, *Annals of the Reformation and*
         Establishment of Religion . . . 4 vols. (Oxford,
         1820–40)

W.C.A.   Westminster Cathedral Archive, London

Winwood, *Memorials:* Edmund Sawyer, ed. *Sir Ralph Win-*
         wood, Memorials of Affairs of State in the Reigns of
         Queen Elizabeth and King James I. 3 vols. (Lon-
         don, 1725)

Note: In citing contemporary books and tracts, only the *incipit* has
been given in the footnotes for reasons of space, since the full title is
placed in the bibliography. In those instances when a document cited
was not numbered within the original bundle in the archive, its date,
or a descriptive title is placed in the text to assist identification.

Foreword

Nine years ago, I began the study of the political implications of Spain's concern about English Catholicism during the latter part of the reign of Queen Elizabeth. This led
me to probe one over-riding issue within that problem: the
relationship of the activities of the English Catholic exiles to
the political objectives of Kings Philip II and Philip III. In
the documents of the Estado collection at Simancas, the archive of St. Alban's in Valladolid, the letters and reports in
the Jesuit archives in Rome, and the "State Papers, Foreign" of the Public Record Office I found considerable new
evidence. The basic research was presented in a doctoral
dissertation at London University in 1957 entitled "Spain
and the English Catholic Exiles, 1580–1604." Since then
I have prepared an extensive revision of that original study.
I have attempted here to explore the principal ways in which
Spain tried to assist the exiles during the Anglo-Spanish war,
and the complexity of the problems that its policy raised, but
did not always solve.

Five leading personalities among the refugees in Spanish
Hapsburg lands have been selected to illustrate the basic
trends in this significant issue. They are Sir Francis Englefield, Hugh Owen, Lady Jane Dormer, Sir William Stanley
and Father Joseph Creswell, S.J. The norms for their selection were basically four. First, the abundance of original
Spanish material concerning them. Secondly, their lengthy
association with the courts at Valladolid and Brussels, which
was roughly a quarter of a century in each case. Thirdly, their
direct involvement in problems which were typical of their
compatriots in exile. Finally, their official positions, which

enabled them to make decisions affecting the lives of their fellow refugees, and, to a certain extent, the policies of both the English and Spanish courts.

I am deeply indebted to my mentors at University College, London, Sir John Neale, and his present successor as Astor Professor of History, Mr. Joel Hurstfield for their invaluable guidance in Elizabethan research. I am also grateful to the late Canon Edwin Henson, Rector of St. Alban's in Valladolid, who graciously provided access to that college's archive. Don Ricardo Magdaleno and his skilled staff at Simancas were most kind in guiding my investigation in that great depository of Spanish Hapsburg documents. At Stonyhurst College, the Librarian, Fr. Hubert Chadwick, was most helpful in making manuscript material available. No less important was the assistance I received at the Archivio Segredo di Vaticano and the Archivum Romanum Societatis Jesu, and from the Reverend Archivist at Westminster Cathedral in London. I am especially grateful to Dr. Louis B. Wright for the grant of a summer Fellowship at the Folger Library where I had an opportunity to do additional reading and research. While residing at Farm Street, London, my fellow Jesuits, Fr. Leo Hicks and Fr. Bazil Fitzgibbon, were particularly generous in sharing the results of their study of recusant history. Fr. Edwin A. Quain, Director of the Fordham University Press, has made many helpful comments for the final manuscript. However, for the mistakes that have eluded the vigilance of my friends I alone am responsible.

Fordham
May 1963

A. J. L.

The Spanish Elizabethans

CHAPTER ONE

SPAIN AND THE ENGLISH CATHOLICS

"THE PAPISTS in England, they have been accounted, ever since I was born, Spaniolized,"[1] Oliver Cromwell once observed, as he looked back upon his experiences since the dawn of the seventeenth century. That many of his contemporaries had the same impression can be traced with abundant detail in the printed collections of late Elizabethan and early Jacobean state papers, proclamations and parliamentary debates. When Cromwell was young, there was a long-standing mistrust at the English Court of what it considered to be two inimical influences: Spanish power and revived Catholicism. Why had this tension continued? Basically because the longevity of the Anglo-Spanish war had blurred these two distinct issues. For many they had become fused into one.

The struggle with Spain had originated in the Court's partisanship of the Dutch rebels, and a fear of the political consequences of a Spanish victory in the north. There was also

[1] J. Wake, *The Brudenells of Deane*, p. 103.

the deep-seated resentment of the merchant class over its official exclusion from Caribbean trade, and the mounting severity of Spanish retaliation to any contraband activities there. For many Protestants a deep conviction that Spain was, in fact, "the right arm of the Papacy," had been nurtured by the clumsy meddling in English Catholic affairs of an envoy, such as Guerau Despes.

However, by the early 1580's the anti-Catholic animus of the Court was as much a frustration as anything else. Previously during the first decade of Elizabeth's reign, there had been a facile eradication of the superficial accomplishments of the Marian "Restoration," as well as any lingering pockets of medieval Catholicism. In its enforcement of the Acts of Uniformity and Supremacy the Court had rarely encountered heroic Catholic resistence as the majority of the clergy bowed to another change. The laity had apparently shown little disapproval. But in the closing years of the second decade of Elizabeth's reign, there was a perceptible change. Recusancy was becoming more frequent as a stubborn affection for the older faith had become noticeable.[2]

Faced with this unexpected and unwanted Catholic challenge the later Elizabethan parliaments and the Privy Coun-

[2] The quality of this Catholic resurgence is being studied on the local level, where varying regional patterns can be established. See H. Aveling, *Post Reformation Catholicism in East Yorkshire*, East Yorkshire Local History Society, 1960; J. E. Paul's study of the Hampshire Recusants is in the *Proceedings of the Hampshire Field Club and Archeological Society*, vol. xxi, part 2 (1959); J. S. Leatherbarrow's survey of the Lancashire Recusants in the *Chetham Society Proceedings*, 1947; A. G. Dickens' two studies of Yorkshire recusancy are in *Yorkshire Archeological Journal*, vols. xxxv (1941) and xxxvii (1948). The enforcement procedures of the Northern commissioners are studied in Catholic Record Society, vol. liii (1961) pp. 291–307; the administration of the Recusant rolls is clarified by H. Bowler's "Some Notes on the Recusant Rolls of the Exchequer," *Recusant History*, vol. iv (1958) pp. 182–98.

cil retaliated by a formidable battery of penal laws, denunciatory proclamations and other forms of coercion. Meanwhile, a more serious disapproval of the Crown's religious policy was being expressed by the Puritans, whose disdain for the theological compromises embodied in the Acts of Supremacy and Uniformity had not as yet lead to separatism. Thus after a relatively tranquil early period the Established Church appeared to be a painful bed of Procrustes, to which an Englishman either measured his conscience or suffered the consequences. There was a serious warning to the Court in the eloquent statement of a non-conformist such as John Penry that "in the discharge of my conscience all the world must bear with me if I prefer my testimony to the truth of Jesus Christ before the favour of any creature." [3] Robert Southwell, his Jesuit contemporary, would reveal not merely the sincere refusal to conform, but the mystic's lofty desire to transcend his present condition:

"Soare up, my soule, unto thy reste, cast off this loathsome lode;
Long is the date of thy exile, too long the strikt abode."

That there were three printings of the *Moeoniae*,[4] where these lines appeared, in the year of Southwell's execution was not without its significance. While the Queen had announced that she would not open "windows in men's souls"—an outward conformity to her established church would suffice —Southwell had an appeal for many Englishmen who sought their spiritual integrity elsewhere.

What steps could the Crown take to shatter the attraction represented by Southwell and other Catholics? Gradually during the last twenty years of Elizabeth's reign an unequal struggle developed during which three particular policies

[3] D. Neal, *The History of the Puritans* (J. Toulmin, ed.) vol. i, p. 359.
[4] From "Seek Flowers of Heauen," *Moeoniae* (London, 1595) p. 32.

were proved to be supremely effective. First, there was the constant harassment of the Catholic clergy by search, imprisonment, exemplary execution or exile. There was the deliberate exclusion of the laity from the universities and public service; and lastly, an attrition of their economic resources by the exaction of various grades of fines. Inevitably there were some irregularities in the enforcement of this policy, but in the perspective of history the overall success of the Crown's counterattack can never be minimized.

The most serious loophole in the Crown's control of the Catholic resurgence was the presence of Catholic refugees abroad, particularly in the lands of the Spanish Hapsburgs. In their secure haven abroad these "Spaniolized" Englishmen posed a very nagging question. Would the might of Spain be placed at the service of their coreligionists? From their printing presses in the Low Countries came devotional books, theological tracts, *apologiae* and controversial literature. Their colleges founded in Rome, Douai and below the Pyrenees were able to send back scores of young priests, ready "to cry alarm spiritual," in Edmund Campion's vivid watchword. This alone was enough to sabotage the Crown's success over religious conformity. It was for this obvious reason that the pledge of Lord Burghley that "the seminaries" who would "content themselves with their profession and devotion" would undoubtedly be spared the gallows and "even all further bodily punishments" [5] kept the hollow ring of the propaganda ploy of the politician.

Every confident declaration from a leading refugee such as William Cardinal Allen increased the worried uncertainty of the Court. This attitude has been recalled by one modern historian in these words: "Burghley and Walsingham and the rest of the Queen's council, Lord Grey and Sir John Norris

[5] *The Execution of Justice in England*, 1583, *Somer's Tracts*, vol. i, p. 208.

and her other military advisers were almost as much afraid of a Catholic rising if the Spanish landed as Allen was confident of it. Since we know very little of the actual numbers of the English Catholics, and for obvious reasons much less of their real sentiments, and about the crypto-Catholics and 'schismatics' on whom Allen was counting, practically nothing at all, it is very difficult to say how right or wrong he was." [6]

The continuing vigor of the Court's emotions was mirrored in a speech of Lord Burghley in the House of Lords in 1593. Here, while attempting to prod the House to approve a higher subsidy for the war, he announced that Philip II and Pope Clement VIII were striving "to win a party in England to be ready to second his invasion." He feared that there was already some success among "a multitude of vulgar people" and he found that "some that are of wealth and countenance" were poised to seize the offices of the kingdom should there be opportunity.[7]

Although Burghley's rhetoric was never noted for its light touch, the underlying fears of Spain and Catholicism that this powerful courtier played upon were a safe *locus communis* in Elizabethan political tracts. It was customary in the course of these warnings to point an accusing finger at the "Spaniolized" Catholic in exile. Four special features were regularly included within the current notion of this sinister figure. The first was that the refugee's exit from England was provocatively subversive, and deserved the severe censures that the Crown decreed. The second was that the exiles' activities were part of a well-laid plan of the Papacy and Spain to alter the religious independence of England. The third was that

[6] G. Mattingly, "William Allen and Catholic Propaganda in England," *Aspects de la Propagande Religieuses* (*Travaux d'Humanisme et Renaissance*) vol. xxviii, p. 339.

[7] Strype, *Annals*, vol. iv, p. 154.

the exiles figured prominently in the Spanish consultations over an *Empresa* against England, which they were confident would be the panacea for the troubles of their coreligionists in England. In the absence of such an ominous military under-taking, the exiles were identified with lurid conspiracies di-rected to the assassination of the Queen. Fourthly, the lot of the refugees in Spanish lands was painted in tones of distaste-ful service and unrelieved poverty, if not starvation. This portrait, founded in part on authentic experiences, yet ob-viously distorted by the aims of the propagandist, can be ex-emplified in the following incidents.

A typical exile who merited English reprisals will be found in the vivid contemporary narratives concerning Dr. John Storey. He had once been a member of Bishop Bonner's tribunal in London, seconding that unpopular prel-ate's attempts to reform his clergy in the reign of Queen Mary. After living in the Low Countries for over ten years, he was kidnapped in Antwerp and brought a prisoner to Eng-land to stand trial. Denying the right of the court to try him he maintained: "God commaunded Abraham to go foorth from the land and countrey where he was borne, from his friends and kynfolks into another country." For conscience's sake, he insisted that he could follow this example and so "for-sake his countrye and the lawes of this realme" to enter "the service of a forayne governour, Kyng Philip, Kyng of Spaine." He reasoned that "every man is free borne, and he hath the whole face of the earth before him to dwell and abyde in, where he liketh best; and if he cannot lyve here he may go elsewhere." [8] His defense was considered inadmis-sible, and Storey was sentenced to death and executed.

In the following year Parliament enacted special laws de-claring Englishmen living abroad without the Queen's leave

[8] *A Declaration of the Lyfe and Death of John Storey* (1571) *Somer's Tracts*, vol. i, pp. 482, 486.

] 8 [

to be liable to severe penalties.[9] At the very time that these salutary warnings were being enacted, Sir Francis Walsingham was writing to Lord Burghley to remind him that "the house of Austria is become the Pope's champion and professed enemy of the Gospel, and daily practiceth the rooting out of the same, and therefore we that are professors of the gospel ought to propose ourselves against it." [10] The serious differences, especially in his English policy, which Philip II had with Pius V and later with Gregory XIII and Sixtus V [11] were rarely appreciated at the English Court. For roughly ten years before Philip actually wasted his fortunes in the Armada of 1588, the Privy Council was credulous of reports of that king's intentions to invade England. The exiles contributed to this misapprehension for they never abandoned their conviction that "the stoute assaylinge" of England—as Nicholas Sanders' familiar phrase advised—would settle the crisis in the Low Countries. Neither the refugees nor Elizabeth understood the priorities which Philip maintained in his policies. Because of the serious objections of his military advisers to an attack on England,[12] Philip adhered to his frontal attack on his rebels in the north, and his most sustained offensive, outside of Flanders, was to prove his later involvement in France. When the war finally broke out between England and Spain in 1586, the "stoute assaylinge" by the English fleets of the Iberian peninsula in 1587, 1589 and 1596 was far more successful than Philip's three armadas.

If there was not an armada on the horizon to rouse the country to the perils of Spain, or Catholicism, there were con-

---

[9] *Statutes of the Realm*, vol. iv, 13 Elizabeth cap. 3.

[10] Dudley Digges, *The Compleat Ambassador*, p. 121.

[11] J. Lynch, "Philip II and the Papacy," *Transactions of the Royal Historical Society*, Series V, vol. xi (1961) pp. 29ff.

[12] P. O. De Törne, *Don Juan d'Autriche et les projets de conquête de l'Angleterre, 1568–78* (Helsingfors, 1915–28) vol. i, pp. 40ff.

spiracies detected periodically which were declared to have a distinct Spanish pedigree. For example, the "Throckmorton Plot," the "Parry Plot," the "Squire Plot" and later even the "Gunpowder Plot" all had identified refugees figuring in their prelude. While the evidence in these instances was more controversial than reliable,[13] there is no doubt that these plots added to the popular dread of the "Spaniolized" fugitives.

If these malodorous dealings were not a sufficient deterrent to an Englishman planning flight, there was the doleful plight of Samuel Lewknor to be pondered. Writing late in the reign of Elizabeth of his personal experiences in Spanish service, Lewknor stressed the great uncertainties of survival. About 1580 he had traveled secretly to the Low Countries, and by the Duke of Parma's favor he had been enrolled in his army. Eventually, while serving as a captain of a company, he was seriously wounded in his arm and forced to return to his family in Antwerp, for he had married the daughter of a Brabant merchant. He had many new troubles to face. There was a law suit over his wife's dowry and he lost his pension. By 1587 he had been reduced to the sorry expedient of begging an exemption from a tax on beer and bread in order to live.[14] Finally, in June 1590 he begged a passport for England from Sir Robert Sydney, the Governor of Flushing. Five years later he authored *The Estate of English Fugitives.* The public interest in his adventures was reflected in its four

[13] J. H. Pollen was among the first to publish evidence from foreign archives. Some of his revisionist findings were summarized in "Plots and Sham Plots" in *The Month* vol. xcix, pp. 600–18, vol. c, pp. 71–87; M.A.S. Hume criticized the reliability of the "Squire Plot" in *Treason and Plot*, pp. 317–25. L. Hicks has reconstructed the actual antecedents of the "Parry Plot" in "The Strange Case of Dr. William Parry," *Studies* (Dublin, 1948) vol. xxxviii, pp. 343–62.

[14] A.G.R., P.E.A. 1830/3 n.f. depositions of 9 and 13 Feb. 1587; 23 July 1588.

printings in the next two years.[15] Passing over the real reasons for his return to England he warned that Philip's only motive in helping an Englishman was to have him "sowe sedition," or lose his life in the Spanish service. He ranted violently against the Catholic clergy within England: "They make you and other Catholics believe that what practices and drifts so ever they take in hand, are all for the zeale of religion . . . and you silly foules think all they saie to bee Gospell, whereas —God Wot—religion is the least matter of a thousand they think upon."[16]

There was impartial evidence from other witnesses that without some Prince's "Entertainment" an exile was usually helpless. For example, in the spring of 1598 five English-women asked the Archduke Albert for a safe-conduct out of Antwerp so that they could return to England. They stated that they were going, "despite the danger to their lives," since their husbands had not been paid for twenty months of service in the Spanish army. The request was granted although their husbands' names remained on the muster lists of the army until at least 1604. At the same time a John Harrison asked for a similar passport to return for he explained that he had been trying for two years, "with others of his nation" to obtain a pension, but he had given up after consistent failure.[17]

However, reconstructing this contemporary notion of the English refugees does not offer a satisfactory basis to appraise

[15] *C.S.P. Dom. Add. 1580–1625*, p. 307. It is reprinted in *Sadler's Papers*, vol. ii, pp. 208–330, with excerpts in Strype, *Annals*, vol. iii(2), pp. 85ff. Burghley's annotated copy is in B.M., Stowe MS 159 ff. 276–302. Since the work was addressed to a "good cousin" about to enter Spanish service, it is possible that it was meant for a Samuel Lewknor, son of Thomas Lewknor of Sussex, who had fled in 1593 "without his father's privity or liking." B.M., Harleian 7042 f.166ᵛ.

[16] *Sadler's Papers* vol. ii, pp. 267ff.

[17] A.G.R., P.E.A., 1869 n.f. petitions of 1 and 20 April, 22 June 1598.

the precise relationships between Spain, the Catholics and England. What really was the menace—or the benefit—in the conduct of Philip II and Philip III? A study of the sources surviving in Spain has indicated that this significant issue should be explored through the analysis of the actual interests of the exiles at that time.

First in prominence was the question of their maintenance: what was the nature of the Spanish pension system among these exiles? More ominous from the viewpoint of Elizabeth was Spanish military power: what type of military services did the Hapsburgs require of the exiles? Apparently the English refugees were afraid that their haven would be denied to them: what steps did they take against possible threats to their security? How did they probe the reaction of Elizabeth's Court to them and to Spain? The English colleges below the Pyrenees were roundly denounced in public proclamations: how did these institutions come into existence? How did they solve the problems facing any new college abroad? Lastly, it was known that the exiles tended to divide into factions: why was this so? In what way could leadership be asserted among them?

In the study of the evidence on these basic questions five personalities soon emerged prominently among the refugees: Sir Francis Englefield, Lady Jane Dormer, Sir William Stanley, Hugh Owen and Father Joseph Creswell. Because of their residence for over a quarter of a century at the center of Spanish power, each gradually assumed a paramount place in the decisions which affected the lives of their compatriots abroad. Unfortunately, a traditional biography of these figures was found to be too elusive after the scanty resources of memoirs, private letters, or even reliable portraiture were surveyed. Instead their histories remained embedded in the mass of official correspondence focusing on their careers at Court. There remained, however, a wider implication to their achievements; for their experiences were not unique, and scores of their exiled compatriots appreciated the problems they handled. It is hoped that this cluster of leading personalities might illumine the entire pattern of the lives of the English expatriates in Spanish Hapsburg lands.

CHAPTER TWO

A PENSIONER : *Sir Francis Englefield*

1522–1596

"The sudden stormes that heaue me to and froo
Had wel neare pierced faith, my guyding saile,
For I, that on the noble voyage goo
to suchor treuthe and falsehood to assaile,
constrayned am to beare my sayles ful loo
and never could attayne some pleasaunt gaile,
For unto such the prosperous winds doo bloo
as ronne from porte to porte to seek availe . . ."

Prolog to Psalm 73
HENRY HOWARD, EARL OF SURREY

ON AUGUST 1, 1593 a penniless Englishman at the Spanish
Court in Madrid, named John Doughty, wrote a short letter
to a blind and elderly compatriot named Englefield, who was
living in Valladolid. "Right woorshipful," he began in a ful-
some greeting, "and the very honour of our nation in all these
so great and extreame persecutions, my most humble dewty
remembered unto yow, with most humble thankes for all your

] 14 [

charitable goodness so bountyfully bestowed uppon mee." He then reported briefly on an interview with Don Juan de Idia-quez, a member of the Council of State, to whom he had delivered Englefield's "favourable letter." The powerful Span-ish courtier had asked him "many particular things" about his request for half an hour and then told him to return later. The grateful Doughty could not omit a prompt note of thanks to Englefield for enabling him to have such an opportunity.[1] Eventually Doughty was sent on his way with an alms. Yet the letter in its natural sincerity documents the unique position at the Spanish Court of an Englishman at the end of an im-portant and self-made career.

The early life of Francis Englefield had been the total op-posite of his declining days. The heir to a large manor which had been in his family's name for centuries, his father, Sir Thomas, had been sufficiently in the confidence of Henry VIII to be made the Master of the Court of Wards jointly with Sir William Paulet. He had held that lucrative office through the uncertain years of the King's "great matter" and first steps into schism. On his father's death in 1537 Francis possessed lands in both Oxfordshire and Berkshire and, in his first Court ap-pointment at the age of twenty-four, he was named High Sheriff of both counties. He received his knighthood a year later at the coronation of Edward VI but his own personal convictions forced him to seek a more congenial appointment in the household of "the Lady Mary," the king's sister.

It was hardly a sinecure. When the stubborn princess re-fused to dismiss her Catholic chaplains and conform to Ed-ward's Protestantism Englefield was one of her three trusted servants who were sent to the Tower in August 1551. He was to remain there for nine months until he was released with his two companions "for reasons of health." [2]

[1] S.A.C. Serie II, legajo 6, autograph.
[2] A.P.C. 1550–52, pp. 333, 352, 508.

However, over a year later, when Mary came to the throne in August 1553, Englefield was in line for a career even more prosperous than his father's. At the age of thirty-one he became a Privy Councilor and shortly after he was granted the same responsible post his father had held nearly twenty-five years before, the Mastership of the Court of Wards.[3]

The intense factional rivalry at the court of Mary Tudor did not make his further advancement easy. While following the leadership of his father's friend the astute Sir William Paulet, Englefield always showed a close sympathy for the Queen's three conservative advisers on religious matters: Gardiner of Winchester, Tunstall of Durham and Bonner of London. These aggressive prelates, each of whom had also been imprisoned previously in the Tower, were not of sufficient weight to have their way in several crucial decisions. This party favored the Queen's marriage to Courtenay and worked earnestly for the speedy arrival of Cardinal Pole in England. The opposition, abetted by the skillful Hapsburg diplomacy, was able to delay Pole's return for two years and then to turn the Queen to the fateful choice of marrying Prince Philip.

When Philip reached England in July 1554 Englefield was not high on his list of favorites. In fact, the pension of 500 crowns a year promised to him by the Spanish embassy was more likely intended to soften his attitude than to reward previous services. It was not as large as the pensions given to others, nor was it paid faithfully. However in the closing months of the Queen's unhappy reign a tacit understanding developed between Englefield and the Count of Feria whom King Philip had placed as his envoy when he left England in July 1557. After observing the earnest young councilor during the first months of Elizabeth's reign Feria concluded that Sir Francis was "a good man and a Christian."[4]

[3] E.H.R. vol. lxviii (1953), pp. 30–31.
[4] C.S.P. Spanish 1554–58, p. 455; E. H. Harbison, Rival

It was hardly a eulogy, but Feria and nearly everyone else at the English Court were mutually disenchanted, and at least Englefield had made clear his disapproval of the direction of Elizabeth's religious policy. His removal from his responsible post was to be speedily accomplished despite some futile delaying tactics on his part. When ordered to deliver up the seals of his Mastership of the Court of Wards he informed the Privy Council that he did so at the Queen's command but that he did not "relinquish his right." It was a futile gesture since the patent of his office had only extended to the Queen's pleasure. A month later, in January 1559, he was ordered to surrender "all suche records and books" belonging to the Court to his former friend, Sir William Paulet.[5]

Early in the spring of 1559 Englefield decided to live in the Low Countries. There was no intention of entering Spanish service at this time. He obviously disapproved of the activities of Elizabeth's first Parliament and he had noted Bishop Bonner's fruitless attempt to have a conservative statement of doctrine approved in Convocation. On May 8, 1559 he drew up an assignment concerning the revenues of his wife, Catherine Fettiplace, and he placed his brother John in charge of his estates. He had no trouble in leaving the country, but he was cautioned by the Queen not to reside in Rome.[6]

While he did not expect it, Sir Francis was never to return to England again. He journeyed to the university town of Louvain where he had many friends and then traveled to Italy twice in the next two years. He was careful at first to stay in Padua where he could conveniently correspond with the Ro-

---

Ambassadors at Queen Mary's Court, pp. 62ff; C.R.S. vol. ii, pp. 54–57.
[5] A.P.C. 1558–70, pp. 29, 47; J. Hurstfield, The Queen's Wards, pp. 244–45.
[6] C.S.P. Dom. 1547–80, p. 238; C.S.P. Rome 1558–71, p. 15.

man circle of his former friend, Cardinal Pole. It was not suit-able company for an Englishman of Englefield's status. By the spring of 1563, when the Queen's excommunication was be-ing debated within the Council of Trent, Englefield was rumored to be urging it and Queen Elizabeth summoned him home. He refused. Considering the Catholic circles he fre-quented on the continent he surely would have faced another sojourn in the Tower where his friend, Sir Edward Walde-grave, the former Chancellor of the Duchy of Lancaster, was already lodged. But Englefield could not escape the Queen's vengeance, and his goods and estates in England were at once sequestered to the Crown.

In August 1563 Englefield wrote from Termonde a brief and humble letter to the Queen in which he did not mention the charges against him but merely begged to be allowed to keep "the little estate left to me." [7] The Queen was unmoved.

The letter from Termonde was only the first of a long series that Englefield was to write to the Queen and his former friends at the English Court during the next fifteen years. Eight months later he tried again, this time to enlist the sup-port of the present Master of the Court of Wards, Sir William Cecil. He wrote at length insisting that the charges against him were groundless and that he was loyal to his sovereign. He concluded with his usual plea to enjoy his revenues undis-turbed. Yet nothing was done. How he supported himself during the next few years is largely a matter of conjecture. He was not destitute when he left England. He had departed with eight servants, six hundred ounces of plate and a hundred marks of money. [8] Possibly he managed somehow to secure the arrears of his former Spanish pension as a courtier of Queen Mary, for it had been unpaid for eighteen months when the Queen had died. In any case three years after the confiscation

[7] *C.S.P. For.* 1563, p. 463; B.M. Add. MS 33271 f. 10.
[8] J. Hurstfield, *The Queen's Wards*, p. 245.

of his estates he was virtually penniless. He was in the invidious position of submitting to the anger of Queen Elizabeth or
of entering the service of Philip II.

Late in the winter of 1566 Englefield journeyed for the
first time below the Pyrenees. He had not seen King Philip
in nine years; undoubtedly his reluctance to go to Spain had
been influenced by his earlier mistrust of the Anglo-Hapsburg
alliance. He apparently had decided to ask for help in getting
back his estates and nothing more for the present. Philip was
to prove sympathetic. He prepared a special letter to the
Queen which his ambassador, Guzman de Silva, duly passed
on to her. The Queen was cordial to the Spanish envoy but
she insisted that Englefield had violated her wishes by visiting
Rome and, what was more important, that he was still urging
Pope Paul IV to "declare her and her realm schismatic." King
Philip, after reflection, asked his envoy to make one last inquiry on Englefield's behalf with the remark that "the favor he
asks . . . is so reasonable." [9] The Queen remained ob-
durate.

Thus after nine years of absence from England and considerable efforts to remain free to enjoy his revenues, Englefield
entered Spanish service. In a letter of October 30, 1568 to the
Duke of Alba Philip II announced a pension for Englefield
of 1,000 florins a year. In his warrant for the Englishman's
employment Philip recalled that he had once served "myself
and the most serene Queen Mary, my deceased wife, being
one of our council of England." He briefly mentioned Englefield's previous trials because of his religious convictions and
then stipulated that the pension was granted only until he recovered "the estate which, as is known, the Queen has confiscated." [10] The pension was duly enrolled on the treasury

[9] *C.S.P. Spanish 1558–67*, pp. 615, 650; *C.S.P. Spanish
1568–79*, pp. 46, 62.
[10] S.A.C. Serie II legajo 6, original warrant.

accounts in Brussels and it would remain there until 1580 when again Englefield traveled southward to remain permanently at the Spanish court. However, the Englishman remained as determined as ever to regain his patrimony.

In the second letter to the Duke of Alba written on the following day the king explained that Englefield was being sent to the court at Brussels "for he desires to be engaged in matters pertaining to my service and, as there is no opportunity here, he has agreed to reside near you. I am of the opinion that with his warmth, fine manners and knowledge of England he can be of service to you in the States." [11] The duties of Englefield as an adviser to Alba were not onerous. Early in 1570 he was mentioned in a despatch of the Duke as planning the distribution of 4,000 escudos among other needy English exiles in Flanders. However, when Englefield asked that the restoration of his property be included among the articles of restitution negotiated with England in the spring of 1571 after the affair of the Spanish "treasure ships," Alba refused. He later explained to Philip that it was unwise to include such a "separate matter" in the treaty but that he would try and do what he could for Englefield "because he is a very fine man." [12] He did not succeed any more than the others.

Little more is known of Englefield's activities at this time. It is clear that his conservative outlook in religious matters had remained. For example, after the northern rising in England in 1569 a new stream of refugees had arrived in Flanders. As one contemporary described them: "Those who were at Louvain for religion before the rebels came used not to come in their company." The English colony in that town, "us Louvainists," as Englefield described them, were felt by the newcomers to be "too severe and scrupulous." They were even

[11] *Col. Doc. Ined.* vol. xxxvii, p. 495.

[12] Duque de Alba, ed., *Epistolario del III Duque de Alba* (Madrid, 1952), vol. ii, pp. 340, 441, 537.

being called "the Puritans of the Catholics."[13] Englefield's
circle included two devout priests, William Allen and Nicholas Sanders, who were intent on the foundation of a college for
Englishmen at the University of Douai. They were to become very closely associated during the coming six years even
while Englefield kept casting longing glances at his former
estates. When the Queen granted them to Leicester he wrote
to the Earl in November 1570, asking for justice but he met
the usual frigid reaction. Leicester retained the lands until at
least 1572 for in June of that year a client asked the Earl for
a lease of part of Englefield's lands as a reward. However,
they were placed under a Crown administrator after 1574.[14]

Englefield was not in want, his pension was paid in full in
1573 and it was to continue so for the next two years.[15] But
in 1575 the English colony at Louvain met a serious threat
from an unexpected source. Their safe refuge in the Spanish
Low Countries was denied them by the terms of a treaty which
Don Bernardino de Mendoza negotiated in England to ease
the mounting tensions between the two kingdoms. Each government promised to expel any refugees undesirable to the
other. While Englefield was fortunate enough to secure a
papal letter of recommendation to live in the nearby Bishopric
of Liège, the blow to his plans was obvious. During the past
year he had shared the common enthusiasm of the exiles over
a plan of having Don Juan, the popular hero of Lepanto, who
was to assume the duties of Governor of the Low Countries
late in 1576, lead a force against England. The expulsion
of the English from the Low Countries was, he confided to

[13] *C.S.P. Dom. Add. 1566–79*, pp. 284, 336, 352, 368.
[14] B. M. Cotton MS Caligula C II, f. 74–75; *C.S.P. Dom. 1547–80*, p. 447. H.M.C. *Salisbury MSS* vol. ii, pp. 58, 106; P.R.O. Land Revenues, Series I–98, f. 172.
[15] B. M., Vespasian CXIII f. 336; Lechat, *Les Refugiés An-glaises*, p. 233; T. F. Knox, *First and Second Douai Diaries*, pp. 298ff.

his friend, William Cotton, an action that "may deter many from lending assistance to the cause." [16]

There was in fact a sense of catastrophe among the exiles. Dr. William Allen confided at this time that "we shall suffer severely if God favour not these holy designs on behalf of our nation."

The "enterprise" as conceived by Englefield in a memorandum sent to the Cardinal of Como at this time insisted that "the state of confusion" in the Low Countries would be an opportune cover for any military preparations against England. The military plan was vague, the leadership of Don Juan very uncertain in view of the reverses of the Spanish hopes in Flanders, and Philip's finances were not sound. However, it was hoped that a conference in Rome would clarify matters. In September 1575 King Philip told Englefield that he could leave Liège and go to Rome "upon the English business." [17]

When Englefield reached Rome in February 1576 in company with Dr. William Allen he found enthusiasm for action among the English refugees at the Papal Court, but a notable lack of unanimity as to what to do. Moreover, the opportunities in Ireland were being considered by the Papal Court to be more promising, and had to be discussed alongside of the English Catholic problem. It was obvious that no one among the assembled Englishmen had the prestige and experience to resolve their differences. Robert Persons, who had come to Rome for the first time prior to his entrance into the Jesuit order, recalled that uncertain atmosphere in these terms: "Sir Francis Englefield, Dr. Saunders and Dr. Allen were commonly of one minde, but Sir Thomas Stukeley, Dr. Lewis and Dr. Morrice of another, and the Bishop (Goldwell) and the

---

[16] *C.S.P. Rome, 1572–78*, p. 202; *C.S.P. Dom. 1547–80*, p. 498.
[17] *C.R.S.*, vol. ix, pp. 44–47; *C.S.P. Rome, 1572–78*, p. 214.

Prior (Sir Richard Shelley) different from both as also the Lord Morley." [18]

Pope Gregory's Secretary of State, the Cardinal of Como, decided to advise Englefield and Allen to return to Flanders to await further events after Don Juan would assume his duties. Before he traveled northward Englefield prepared an unusual legal instrument to protect his estates in England. It was not until 1593 that the details of his scheme were revealed in an act of Parliament which nullified it. Apparently Sir Francis signed a document before witnesses in Rome which conveyed his estates to his nephew, "to the use of himself for life." By this conveyance the lands would revert to the original owner only after the tending of a gold ring to the nephew. [19] The idea was a striking example of the resourceful legal measures taken by English Catholics to protect their property from confiscation. The work of a lawyer and former Master of the Court of Wards, Englefield's conveyance was formidable enough to require a unique act of Parliament to become void.

In May 1576 Englefield left Rome in high hopes. He reported to a friend with obvious optimism that the "enterprise would probably begin within twelve months." [20] Meanwhile he decided to return to Flanders on the hope that the situation would become favorable under Don Juan of Austria's leadership. Events, however, were to prove a deep disappointment. The pacification of Ghent of 1576 and Don Juan's reluctant ratification of it in February of 1577 caused a sharp setback to Spanish prestige. Even the proud *Tercios* were being required to leave the Low Countries. Filled with bitterness towards the revived vigor of the Estates General, Don Juan was in no mood to receive favorably a petition to divert

[18] C.R.S., vol. ii, p. 64; See also P. O. de Törne, *Juan d'Autriche,* . . . , vol. ii, pp. 60–100, 180–98.

[19] *Statutes of the Realm,* 35 Eliz. cap. 5.

[20] *C.S.P. Dom. 1547–80,* p. 527.

his forces to assist a rumored English uprising in favor of Mary Queen of Scots. It was reported, however, that Englefield in February 1577 presented to Don Juan a list of names of English supporters of the imprisoned Queen. If true, it was at best a desperate measure, for the situation in Flanders was so tense that Sir Francis retired again, this time to Luxemburg. There was even worse to come. Queen Elizabeth's well-timed peace overtures were being willingly received within Rome and Spain. By May 1578 Englefield had reluctantly concluded that Pope Georgory XIII and Philip II were without any intention of rallying behind Don Juan as he had once expected.[21] The death of this popular, if overrated, hero in October 1578, and the novel threat of French intervention in the Low Countries once again made the "enterprise" on behalf of Mary Queen of Scots a political and military impossibility.

It was shortly after this that Englefield took a momentous step which, unknown to him, would be of considerable importance to many of his fellow exiles. It had become clear to him that some one should remain at the Spanish court to offer advice on English Catholic affairs. His former friend, Nicholas Sanders, had attempted to do this from 1573 to 1578 until Philip had reluctantly seen him go on the ill-fated and ill-planned papal expedition to Ireland in June 1579.[22] Accordingly, late in 1579 Englefield decided to visit below the Pyrenees. Despite their differences on the necessity of the "enterprise" at least he was more in Philip's favor than the volatile Sanders had been.

At the time of the Englishman's arrival Philip II and Cardinal Granvelle were deeply committed to their well-laid

[21] *C.S.P. Rome, 1572–78*, pp. 433–34, 560; The list of names is edited in C.R.S., vol. xiii, pp. 89ff., 486ff.

[22] T. Veech, *Dr. Nicholas Sanders and the English Reformation*, pp. 202, 228ff.

plans to claim the kingdom of Portugal. There was little to be done about England but he tried to console the Queen of Scots secretly with letters still promising help. Unfortunately for Englefield's purpose, these letters were carefully watched. His correspondence with Mary's unscrupulous agent in Paris, the Bishop of Ross, was also readily available to Sir Henry Cobham, the English envoy in France. He reported their contents to the English Privy Council on one occasion with a dry observation that Englefield had clearly become a "passionate Castilian." [23]

It would take more than Englefield's warm devotion to Spain to persuade Philip of the advantage of the "enterprise." The international tension over the Portuguese succession crisis, Parma's difficulties with Anjou's intervention in the Low Countries, and even the uncertainty of the political feuds in Scotland made Philip more reluctant than ever to damage his deteriorating relations with England. Cardinal Granvelle questioned Englefield closely, during King Philip's absence in Portugal, over the political and military opportunities in Scotland under the young James VI, but he was apparently more wary of the Guise policy there. [24] While Englefield's deepest convictions over the importance of assisting the imprisoned Queen were being slowly dulled by the hesitancy of the Spanish court he began to see a more useful purpose for his talents. His principal duty soon became something that he had not really foreseen. He turned to planning how the increasing number of English refugees could be assisted in the pension system of Spain.

In a lengthy letter to his closest friend, whom he would never see again, Dr. William Allen, he explained the situation in September 1581. He noted that his presence at the Court had prompted a flood of letters about the problem, "from

[23] *C.S.P. For. 1579–80*, pp. 163, 264.
[24] *C.S.P. Spanish 1580–86*, pp. 6, 7.

England, from Lovayne, from Namur, from Remes, from Roan, from Paris and from Rome." [25] Yet little could be done at first. In trying to assist his compatriots Englefield was hampered not so much by the indifference of court officials, as by the misunderstanding of the exiles of the actual method of the Spanish system of payments. Before seeing why Engle- field eventually played an important—if informal—role in increasing slowly the Spanish pensions for the exiles a survey of the entire system is in order.

The Elizabethan Catholic who had fled across the seas, usually with little funds and in secret, faced the immediate task of finding a livelihood. Occasionally a shrewd merchant could bring along a cargo to make a new start for his business. For example, in 1569 a Robert Hicks petitioned the Duke of Alba successfully to be allowed to remain in Flanders and to keep a license for the sale of his "100 lasts of herring and 200 lasts of cheese." He had been careful to present a testimonial signed by other *émigrés* who knew him earlier in England.[26] Other exiles of this period also managed to obtain letters of credit to bankers or friends on the continent. An English merchant named Raphael Letherbarrow lived in Rouen and Lille from 1564 to 1594 and eventually became a citizen of France. An English spy observing his activities in 1580, con- cluded that in effect he was the banker "to whom all the fugi- tives and papists make over all their money by exchaige and send cloth over to him under a collor as if it were his." [27]

In Spain, as Englefield had discovered, there were far less opportunities for new arrivals. The rare appointments at Court were only made available to those already well estab- lished in Spanish Hapsburg service. Still, a few found useful positions in the households of the Spanish nobility, such as

[25] T. F. Knox, *Allen*, pp. 105–6.
[26] A.G.R., P.E.A. 1687/2.
[27] A.G.R., P.E.A. 1869, n.f.; B.M., Yelverton xxxiii, f. 122.

John Pickford, who became the organist for the chapel of the Cardinal Regent of Portugal. By far the easier way to get a Spanish pension was to take military service. It was shortly after Englefield's residence at Court began that the Duke of Parma, the new Governor of the Low Countries, openly encouraged the policy of giving individual pensions from the funds of the Spanish military subsidy to designated English exiles.

From this period various classes of service by the English exile can be distinguished. The larger number fought in the army for the ordinary soldier's pay and were in effect mercenaries. Some of these earned a supplementary pay called a *ventaja* which could vary from 2 to 12 escudos a month, depending on the premium put on their performance. There was also a higher class of pensioners: the *entretenidos*, who were to serve at times with the army. However, there were many of these who were never expected to go near the armed forces. These included several women who were carried on the same Treasury accounts as the men. The present state of the records does not make terms of service of English *émigrés* easy to ascertain but this lack can be partially corrected by the very fortunate survival of certificates of residence in Brussels in 1597 [28] and various petitions for back pay that reached the Council of State through Englefield.

There is sufficient evidence at present to conclude that the actual number of English exiles living in Spain was always much smaller than in the Low Countries. The greater percentage of exiles below the Pyrenees were attending the two colleges founded in the last decade of the century. If one were to attempt to reconstruct the steps to secure a pension it would lead to the following pattern. Few Englishmen regularly attempted the difficult journey to the Spanish Court but were content to write to Sir Francis Englefield or, after his death,

[28] A.G.R., P.E.A., 1398/7.

Thomas Fitzherbert or Father Joseph Creswell to present a petition on their behalf. The petition had to be considered in the Council before the royal approval would be given. If a pension was not given, and this was frequent, an alms called an *ayuda de costa* could be ordered as a consolation. Once the *entretenimiento,* or "entertainment," was approved, the exile could be assured of a monthly allowance or salary. After 1587 it was customary to group all pensions under the accounts of the regiment of Sir William Stanley. An order for payment, known as a *libranca,*[29] was issued by the proper treasury official of the army in Flanders.

The system had all the defects inherent in a large bureaucracy, which can be seen, for example, in a review of English pensioners held in 1596. Then it was learned that *librancas* were being made out for several people who were dead and to three others who had returned to England over a year before. There was also the element of chance in the timing of the actual payments. As early as 1574 a list of payments made in Brussels shows some were in arrears for sixteen months and others for only seven.[30] Inevitably there were disputes between the exiles and the Spanish officials of the Hazienda on the wording of the royal "entertainment." On one occasion Englefield complained to Dr. Allen that the "Prynce" was "wresting the words of the kyngs letter to the worst sens for them that possybly the words can be drawen unto." It was a

[29] "A libranca is a bill of assignation for the recite of monie graunted to some one in particular or to two or three jointly or a hundred or more, as need shall require. It is first drawn and underneath signed by the chiefe secretary that attendeth on the generall. It is directed by the Duke unto the treasurer generall, commandinge him to paye the some of whatsoever monie hee shall haue within his charge, but first to see that the same be perused and registered in both the offices of the two *contados* of the armie and signed with their names and rubrikes . . ." Lewkenor (*The Estate of English Fugitives*), Sadler's Papers, vol. ii, p. 243.
[30] Lechat, *Les Refugiés*, pp. 233–36.

commonplace among the exiles to say that the wrangling and "courtly sewtes" about money divided them into factions more than any fervent political opinions. An English spy, Thomas Barnes, summed it up shrewdly with the remark: "The English pensioners are in bare estate and there are great divisions among them . . . those that are poorer envy those that have more." [31] Even a royal order to the Duke of Parma reminding him that the exiles had no other support did not improve the situation noticeably in 1592.[32] The English were not unique in this treatment, and the papers of the Council of State reveal the same complaints from Irish and Scottish pensioners. Even a small group of French exiles in Madrid in 1601 reported their extreme want after they had not been paid any grants for over six months.[33]

There were many reasons for this intolerable situation. The Spanish system of finances was cumbersome and wasteful, and court officials were preoccupied with other urgent affairs. The suggestions of the exiles for helping one another were few, their complaints were many. It is clear that they overburdened Sir Francis Englefield and a few other Englishmen at Court, irrespective of whether the Crown was asking them to perform other duties. It was the same elsewhere. Alphonso Agazzari, the Rector of the English College in Rome, was very generous in trying to expedite payments promised by the papal treasury, yet he became the object of considerable suspicion among the exiles.[34] Yet the serious situation had one significant danger. As William Allen remarked to Alphonso Agazzari: "If we cannot support them in exile, many will be forced to leave." [35]

[31] Knox, *Allen*, p. 105; *C.S.P. Dom. Add. 1580–1625*, p. 346.
[32] A.H.N. Estado lib. 251 n.f. letter of 15 Aug. 1592.
[33] E 2764 n.f. consulta of 20 Sept. 1601.
[34] C.R.S., vol. iv, pp. 130–35.
[35] Knox, *Allen*, pp. 111, 133.

In a private petition to Philip II Robert Persons was explicit on the resulting misfortune. He informed the king that, while he hesitated to touch on the matter because of the king's many favors to Englishmen in the past, the situation forbade silence.

Eminent persons have written from there saying that some have died from hunger . . . others are on the verge of doing so, and others under pressure of the same privations have decided to return to England and even throw themselves on the mercy of the heretics.[36]

The Spanish court was sympathetic but in the outcome nothing was to be done. The exiles would have to try the task of reforming the situation themselves.

One of the earliest plans to solve the problem can be seen in a letter of December 1589 from a Charles Browne [37] to King Philip. He had been refused a permit to travel to Spain by the Duke of Parma and he had decided to write his suggestions directly to the court. To his thinking, his fellow exiles were mainly responsible for the unrest over the entire question. His letter begins *in medias res:*

Your Majesty. Seeing the great affection that you have always held for those of my nation by doing for them many unusual favours, it grieves me to see the ingratitude of so many. By experience this was seen in the time of the Catholic Armada in contriving and circulating malicious reports of conquest and of becoming slaves to strangers. All this was a disgrace to those devoted to your Majesty . . .

[36] Stonyhurst MS Collectanea P f. 500.
[37] The natural brother of the first Viscount Montague, he entered Spanish military service in 1583 at 40 escudos a month. In 1597 he reported that he was living in Brussels with his wife and seven children; a private despatch from there once described him as "a restless spirit and not one of the best informed of his nation" (E 617/24; A.G.R., P.E.A. 1398/7).

To put an end to this, Browne advised that William Allen should be brought from Rome to Flanders, while all pensions were to be placed completely in his hands. They were then to be redistributed "to honest and honorable Catholics." He felt that the "bad" would then have no further chance to come and go to England "as they do at present every day." His letter concluded with the remark that every English Catholic would consider their Cardinal honored in such a post.[38]

Browne's letter was not even discussed in the Council of State yet it is important for the problem it raises in its own clumsy fashion. For this was an early description of the move-ment to remove a small clique of agitators against Spain who managed to stay on the pension lists during the 1590's and add to the tensions in an already difficult situation. Spain oc-casionally conducted a review of the personnel of its own armies and fleets but never according to the norm proposed by Browne. When a company of soldiers became too small through desertions or losses in battle, the remainder were either dismissed or reassigned to new companies. For example, En-glefield informed an English sailor named John Whitfield in 1591 that all those who were "not of good account" had been discharged from the Lisbon fleet and would have to find em-ployment in Flanders.[39]

The fundamental difficulty, of which Browne's letter was only a symptom, was that the English Catholics abroad did not have a recognized authority among themselves who could moderate complaints and inspire a plan of common action. While the pension system, if skillfully used, might well have become the means of molding the English *émigrés* into a faction with its own means of support and commonly shared ideals, it never did develop in that direction. Efforts to revise and reform the defects of the system met regularly with offi-

[38] E 596 n.f. letter of 19 Dec. 1589.
[39] B. M. Harleian 7042 f. 233ᵛ.

cial inaction. As far as can be seen Englefield could do little about it during his lifetime. It was only a few months before Englefield's last illness that his close friends, Sir William Stanley, Hugh Owen and Father William Holt prepared a complete survey of the English pensioners and their contribution to Spanish interests. It was a major attack on a problem that had annoyed everyone for a generation, but this time the clamor was sufficient to have the paper considered in detail by Philip II and his Council of State.

In March 1596 their report of twenty folios, which had clearly been preceded by several weeks of discussion with the new Governor, the Archduke Albert, was forwarded to the Spanish Court. It was an invaluable profile of the entire Spanish pension system among the English exiles during the closing years of the reign of Philip II. The credentials of the authors of the report could be supported by Englefield with ease as all three of the authors were known to both Courts. Stanley was the leading military figure among the exiles and had been in command of a regiment for Spain for nine years. Father William Holt had worked as a Jesuit in Flanders for eight years and Hugh Owen had been high in the administration of the court at Brussels for his espionage work for over a decade. They felt bound to state their intention of being objective in a judicious note at the end:

> This is a summary . . . of their judgement of each of these English pensioners. They are under the belief that all are Catholics, and that the greater part of them have lost country and property for that reason. The misery which they have endured and are enduring for some years in these regions has caused great unrest among them. Since this is the case it will be very much to the purpose and service of your Majesty that some of them either be accommodated elsewhere or be given greater satisfaction here . . .[40]

[40] E 612 / 125–127.

The writers carefully explained that some names on their lists had a letter "B"—for *bulliciosos,* or "troublesome"— placed next to them. These, it was suggested, should be transferred to some other part of the Spanish realms. The committee then suggested that it would be more fitting not to give pensions at all than to have the present state of neglect continue: "For many people are changing in their devotion, and serve France or return to England so that they go with our enemy." As a remedy they advised that only those English pensioners be sent in the future to Flanders who would be useful to Spanish service.

In keeping with their norm the committee then divided their report into categories according to the value of the pensioners' activities. They began with a group of eleven names which they advised should be removed from the list at once. Two had returned to England, three others had become students in the colleges for priests and could be supported by the funds for those foundations. Another had become a canon at Tournai and another was a pensioner of the house of Guise. Two others had private means and did not need a pension, and one had died. Clearly a reform was easy in these cases.

The next group was devoted to ten people who were described as retired but they did not have at present any other way to support themselves. They were elderly and most had been abroad for more than thirty years, in fact two were already dead. The committee only requested that some other means be found to help the remaining eight. At this point the Archduke added the impractical comment that they should all be transferred to Naples or Sicily. Then followed a category of six names of priests who were already employed elsewhere and did not require pensions annexed to the Spanish army. None of them were chaplains to the army and two of them were bluntly characterized as do-nothings. Thus far the suggestions were in fact reasonable adjustments, but thereafter thorny problems began.

A fourth category contained ten married men who had their families in Flanders and were not doing service in the regiment yet could hardly go elsewhere. They included Charles Browne, who had first brought up the question of reform seven years before; George Persons, the brother of the English Jesuit and Richard Versteghen, the author and printer. The opinion of the committee was that they were being overpaid as far as the regiment's finances were concerned, and they implied that they should be paid directly by the officials who were actually using them. A clear case was Richard Bayley who was serving with Juan de Ribas, the Spanish commander at the Ecluse. Here again the Archduke penned his marginal comment to have them transferred to Italy. It was as impractical here as before.

After this came a group of eight styled "married men, who have served in the wars and can return. They are not serving at present." No general excuse is given for their absence. The one exception was the obvious one of a Richard Zouche who had fled to a sanctuary in Mons after a murder.[41] The committee had no recommendation about them; apparently there would be no trouble with them if they were paid promptly.

A final category is, by far, the most interesting. It was labeled "various persons who are not married and can leave the Low Countries and be employed elsewhere." It was in this class that several of the "troublesome" were to be numbered. There were also some supernumeraries. For example, there was Gabriel Allen, the younger brother of the deceased Cardinal, who was living contentedly in Rome, and George Somerset who resided in Lorraine. Two others were dead. Another,

[41] The pension was canceled and he took refuge in France. E 617/24.

a colorful and trouble-prone character named George Herbert was temporarily in prison in England.[42]

The leaders among the "troublesome" Spanish pensioners were revealed to be the Earl of Westmorland, Sir William Tresham, Charles Paget, Oliver Eustace, Ralph Ligons, John Stonor, James Chambers and John Petit.

Charles Lord Neville, the sixth Earl of Westmorland, had fled across the channel after the uprising of 1569 and, despite a cold reception by the "Louvainists," had managed to secure from Alva the generous pension of 200 escudos a month. Of him the Archduke noted in the margin of the committee's report:

He is a man of very little substance as far as his judgement and manner of life, for there is no rule or order in his affairs. Nevertheless all rightminded people of his nation agree that he should remain pensioned because of his high birth which could be of advantage if he is present in an invasion of that kingdom.

Charles Paget was the third son of William Lord Paget, who had been a leader of the faction at Mary Tudor's Court opposed to Paulet and Englefield. After coming abroad, Charles Paget had conceived a violent dislike of William Allen and Robert Persons as far back as 1583. He had been given the high pension of 70 escudos a month. The committee described him severely as a man of

vague projects, very interested in novelties, every one believes him to be a Catholic, yet he is very troublesome. He is a man who has many affairs in motion, he would like to appear intelligent but . . . in effect he is a person to whom it is best to listen but then to proceed cautiously on his suggestions.

[42] A Spanish pensioner from at least 1586 to 1592 he attempted to return to England but was captured in Middleburg and accused of treason by the Dutch and sent to England. (*H.M.C. Salisbury MS*, vol. v, pp. 226, 279, 515.) He managed to explain away the charges and returned to Brussels in 1597 but failed to regain his pension.

Sir William Tresham was a soldier of good family who had first served as a captain in the long disbanded regiment of the Earl of Westmorland. Since then he had apparently done nothing. Ralph Ligons, John Stonor and the others were described as "idle, restless people" who never went near the regiment.

If the scrutiny of the committee in Brussels and the Archduke's comments had any immediate value, it was to clarify the sources of the deep unrest among the exiles. Ordinarily some action should have followed, but the spring and summer of 1596 were a period of great military activity both in Spanish ports and in the Low Countries. There was no opportunity for the Spanish Court to consider what it obviously viewed as family quarrels among the *émigrés*. There was an armada planned for the Irish coast and the Archduke Albert was to earn respect for his quick penetration into the defenses of Calais. Its capture from the French was as startling as its loss nearly forty years before to the Duke of Guise. The pension system revision could wait, and the suggestions of the committee were effectively shelved for several months.

In the meanwhile the "troublesome" pensioners were vigilant. Even though it was not planned by the committee to remove them totally from the lists but rather to transfer them elsewhere, they drew up a counter petition of their own against Stanley, Owen and Holt.[43] The Duke of Feria, who was well acquainted with the tensions among the exiles described the incident in a special letter of January, 1597 to King Philip.

> I recently saw a memorial from the discontented, signed by eight or nine of them . . . against Hugh Owen and others who think with him on the affairs of England . . . It will be well to take care of the heads of this party, particularly Charles

[43] Westminster Cathedral Archive (Hereafter, W.C.A.) Series A, vol. v, f. 179, petition of 28 May 1596.

Paget, William Tresham and Ralph Ligons, by sending them to Sicily . . . but I would not deprive them or the others . . . the Earl of Westmorland, Timothy Mocquet, Charles Brown, Richard Gage and John Stonor of their pensions . . ."[44]

His reason was that this would only make them more dangerous to their fellow exiles if they returned to England.

The Court at Madrid still did not display any serious concern for the problem. It was nearly a year later that the Archduke wrote to King Philip asking his decision on the report of the pension system's merits and defects. He explained: "It is imperative that I know the will of your Majesty so that I may decide together with those of that nation what is suitable for the royal service." He commented that he had been deferring any new requests for aid as he needed fresh advice, even though the treasury was still obliged to make payments to everyone on the list.[45] Philip replied on April 5th by sending the copy of Feria's letter of January advising him to "read and ponder well everything the Duke says." The king wanted his opinion over the suggested transferral of the discontented to Sicily or another part of Italy, but he was to act cautiously so that "neither one nor the other could see the reason why it was being done."[46]

In effect neither Court troubled to take the initiative. While everyone advised caution another summer campaign was soon opening. Thus nothing was done, and the tensions remained to fester for three years more when the matter was to be reopened completely. In March 1600 King Philip III sent a special request to the Archduke to report on all the English pensioners in his armies. On April 9, 1600 another complete survey was prepared by Stanley, Owen, and a new member to the committee Father William Baldwin. The Archduke

---

[44] W.C.A. Series E, vol. ii, f. 6; also E 2224 (1) f. 243.
[45] E 613/47 letter of 14 March 1597.
[46] E 2224 (1)/245.

had hardened his attitude somewhat against the "troublesome," advising that "some or most of them are suspect and of slight credit," and should be sent elsewhere.[47] However he had done nothing more.

It was not surprising that nearly all of the "troublesome" leaders were still on the lists. Only two had left of their own accord for France. Of Charles Paget they reported: "He writes letters to the Queen of England and some of her Council . . . it appears from these letters that he is trying to obtain a pardon. He is completely dedicated to the Scottish party . . ." Sir William Tresham had also left for France, where he was corresponding further with the Privy Council about his offer to spy on his fellow émigrés.[48] As before, the Earl of Westmorland continued to be a problem: "To everyone he appears a man of high birth but little use, for nothing of great moment can be entrusted to him." The others were said to be wavering in their partisanship for Scotland but were still not of any great devotion to Spain. Would anything be done this time? There was, but it was of almost comic proportions. In May 1601 Don Baltazar de Zúñiga wrote hurriedly to Philip III that the English exiles in Brussels were disturbed that some of the most deserving had been stricken from the lists. Apparently one of the first victims of the pressure for revision had turned out to be a new convent of English Benedictine nuns. The Council of State had to order that an alms be given to the nuns at once.[49]

It was not until July 23, 1601 that Philip III finally announced his decision, but it was maddeningly unprecise. He simply intimated to the Archduke that he should proceed against "those who have done nothing deserving our support.

[47] E 617/23.
[48] E 617/24; See also C.S.P. Dom. 1598–1601, pp. 221, 312, 328.
[49] E 618 n.f. letters of 1 and 5 May 1601.

Your Highness is to command that they be excluded." It was
an order that did not answer the basic question of where they
were to be sent or to what new services they were to be attached. Thus after five years of waiting the suspicions of the
exiles went unchecked.

Finally, on learning of the news of the death of Queen
Elizabeth the *Veedor General* of the *Hazienda* in Brussels,
Don Hieronimo Zapata, inquired of King Philip whether he
did not believe all the pensions for the exiles were now a
needless expense. It was, he wrote, costing the crown a total
of 13,688 escudos a month.[50] The demand was official in
character and could hardly be met with a typically vague statement of policy. The Council of State after a lengthy debate
voted that the advantages of the pension system should be retained.

The payments to the pensioners are not much. The army is
the foundation where these people from all nations are supported, some out of obligation and particular reasons which cannot be ignored, and others, especially in their service with the
troops of Spain, are trained to be soldiers of quality. Of these
there is great need . . . and so nothing is to be changed in
this affair.[51]

The Council bypassed its previous recommendations that
the undeserving should be struck off the lists. They clearly
felt that the work of the two committees in 1596 and 1600
had not produced any significant reasons for reform. The policy of giving pensions was sound and as such it was not to be
altered.

The reasons for this attitude can only be partially understood at the moment. The Courts at Brussels and Madrid were
preoccupied with weighty and urgent problems and would
not touch the nettle, which clearly required great discretion to

[50] E 2224 (2)/202 letter of 30 March 1603.
[51] E, K 1606/60 consulta of 26 July 1603.

explain even in the documents reaching to them. They apparently expected the exiles to work out their differences among themselves, especially when all were agreed on the need for supporting the "troublesome" somehow. However while the Council never dreamed of giving the committee the authority to render an ultimate decision, it avoided taking the initiative on its own.

Within this system of pensions, as understood by contemporaries, the place of Sir Francis Englefield can now be fixed more readily. He had a key role but a small one. After he had taken up residence at the Spanish Court a large portion of his time was devoted to pursuing William Allen's pleas for manifold help for the exiles. For the last sixteen years of his life Englefield was to become the spokesman for the needs of his countrymen, presenting petitions from those who wrote to him or arranging an introduction for those who would plead in person. In his task of propagandizing a complex human problem he faced insuperable indifference in many places, nor were many of his compatriots aware of his difficulties. Without him undoubtedly the problem would have become far worse, yet with him, and even with his friends on the committee in Flanders, there was not the cogent eloquence to persuade the Spanish Crown of the lost opportunities and the weaknesses inherent in its haphazard and divisive policy.

The basic reason for the failure of pension reform is that the need of it was seen only if Spain's larger objectives in the north of Europe were to be reappraised and realigned. Apparently the Hapsburgs were not anxious that their pensioners speak with solidarity. This can be seen in surveying Englefield's other activities at this time, for their results are similar to his trials with the pensioners. Two years after Englefield arrived in Spain his eyesight failed him and he was forced to dictate his many letters to trusted secretaries. He kept a rather narrow circle of friends—Juan de Idiaquez in Spain, the

Cardinals Allen and Aldobrandino in Rome, and Robert Heighington in Paris. In his letters to them can be traced his preoccupation with the political problems implicit in the prolonged difficulties of the English recusants. For example, in 1583 he was deeply concerned over the future of the Queen of Scots. When his friend, Hugh Owen, came to Spain to make a last urgent appeal for help it was Englefield who secured the Welshman's interview with the King. Yet Owen was not successful, for King Philip was far more concerned over the turn of events in France and possibly another entente with the Guise faction. By July 1584 Robert Persons had decided from his observations in France that even the Guise interest in "our affayre" was aimed at securing the favor of the young King James, "without moch mention of respect as it seemeth of the Queen of Scots." Philip in line with this attitude preferred not to think of action on behalf of the imprisoned Queen, so that finally Englefield had to report "nothing in dede is meant from Spayne." [52]

However, in the spring of 1584 when the possibility of Spanish intervention on the behalf of the Queen of Scots was actually so remote, there was discovered in London a conspiracy known as the "Throckmorton Plot." Englefield's name figured prominently in two ways. During the trial of the most prominent conspirator, Francis Throckmorton, the Attorney General, Sir John Popham, announced that "about four years" previously Englefield had advised King Philip to invade England, and later, in November 1583 that Throckmorton had been corresponding with Englefield about the certainty that the forces of Spain would be ready for an uprising. [53] These disclosures were a significant factor in the breakdown of the

[52] C.R.S. vol. xxxix, pp. 224, 246, 249.
[53] *H.M.C. Salisbury MSS* vol. xiii, pp. 273–74. The conspiracy is described in J. B. Black, *The Reign of Elizabeth* (2nd ed.), pp. 360–64.

Anglo-Spanish amity which had been faltering during the last two years of Mendoza's embassy in England. There is sufficient indication that Popham was confusing Englefield's high hopes with actual events. Four years previously there was no plan for military action against England since the Portuguese succession crisis had demanded all of Philip's interest.

This had been well known to Englefield. Yet an accurate report of the trial stated that "the most important thing" charged against Throckmorton was a supposed letter from Englefield in which King Philip was announced to have readied his troops for an invasion.[54] Throckmorton and Englefield were both attainted for high treason. In June 1584 Throckmorton was executed despite his appeal to the Queen's clemency and a brave insistence on the scaffold that he was innocent.[55] By the same judicial sentence all of Englefield's lands—the object of such determined pleading over the years —were confiscated. Over a year later in August 1585 Thomas Rogers, one of Walsingham's more reliable agents in the Low Countries, pointed out to him that the information about the conspiracy had been distorted through the activity of Charles Paget.[56] Undoubtedly, as Englefield realized that his manors had been permanently lost to his family, he could also feel the need for some defense among the exiles against the bitter intrigues of "a troublesome" pensioner of the calibre of Charles Paget. Yet he could do nothing for the Court considered the "troublesome" pensioners a small matter.

Because of his rising prominence among the exiles Englefield was kept under the close scrutiny of the resident ambassadors at the Spanish Court. In February 1587 the Venetian envoy related that Englefield was "in long and secret

[54] *C.S.P. For. 1583–84*, p. 501.
[55] *C.S.P. Dom. 1581–90*, p. 179; C.R.S. vol. xxix, p. 227.
[56] *C.S.P. For. 1584–85*, p. 717.

conference" with Don Juan de Idiaquez, and he decided that Spain was at last moving towards an *empresa* "in many ways and from many sides." [57] However, Englefield continued to be excluded from any useful role in the affair. At best he was advising on the genealogies of the various claimants to the throne of England and he was corresponding with Rome. This hitherto unknown aspect of his career will be seen to form a part of his contribution to the *Conference About the Next Succession*.

At the same time Englefield assisted in the scrutiny of dubious characters mingling among the exiles visiting the Spanish Court. Two cases were of special interest, but from his occasional allusions to this problem he must have assisted in others. For example, there was Anthony Poyntz, the younger brother of Sir Nicholas Poyntz, a recusant in England. Anthony had arrived in Spain with a valid recommendation from Don Bernardino de Mendoza in Paris. Poyntz had received this useful support because he had shown Mendoza a warrant from the Queen for his expenses and had confessed that he was under orders to spy in Spain. After a short visit to Madrid he returned to Paris and was then allowed to go to Flanders in January 1587.[58] It was Sir Edward Stafford who revealed to Walsingham what had happened to Poyntz after he had met Englefield in Spain.

Writing from Paris he warned Walsingham that Poyntz "sent by you into Spain," had there announced that he could either through his own efforts or his sister's, secure the death of Queen Elizabeth for the price of 4,000 crowns. After Englefield's scrutiny it was decided that Poyntz was "either sent as a spy, or at least unfit to do what he offered." The Spanish Court had allowed him to leave unmolested since he was being watched all the way in hopes of learning of any

[57] *C.S.P. Venetian 1581–91*, p. 465.
[58] *C.S.P. Spanish, 1580–86*, pp. 570, 574, 662, 689.

friends or correspondence. Philip II also warned Mendoza that he was to be wary of Poyntz since "a very bad opinion was held of him here by all the trustworthy English Catholics." [59]

A short time later an even more bizarre figure was examined by Englefield. Arthur Dudley was an adventurer who had been traveling about Flanders for over a year spreading the report that he was the natural son of Elizabeth and Leicester. It was a silly credential but capable of becoming for the naive an intrigue as dangerous as that of the days of Perkin Warbeck. Englefield's examination of the glib adventurer lasted five days. He then dictated a long report to his secretary. He had concluded that the young man was encouraged by "the Queen and her Council" to claim that he was a Catholic in order to spy out "the intentions of other princes to his claims." He noted shrewdly that he was put in mind of Don Antonio, the natural son of the Duke of Bejar, who was by then a feeble if noisy claimant to the throne of Portugal. He was careful to add in Dudley's case: "It cannot be denied that France and the English heretics, or some other party, might turn it to their own use or at least use it as an excuse to prevent the reform of England." Englefield recommended that Dudley be kept in close custody, and there he was to remain in fact for over a year, [60] after which nothing further was heard of him.

Meanwhile back in England the new incumbents of Englefield's lands were facing litigation over their titles to retain them. On December 6, 1589 Francis Englefield, the nephew and namesake of the exile, was examined by Sir John Perrot about the famous conveyance made in Rome over

[59] *C.S.P. For., June 1586–88,* pp. 181–82; *C.S.P. Spanish 1580–87,* p. 11.
[60] *C.S.P. Spanish 1587–1603,* pp. 101ff.; B. M. Harleian 295, f. 190.

thirteen years before. Francis did not reveal anything, in fact he was reported to have said: "The truth is not to be told at all times." [61] The uncertainty over the lands was to continue for nearly four years longer until the act was passed in parliament in 1593. In a unique preamble parliament declared that Englefield had been "the chiefest mover and setter on of the late intended Spanyshe Invasion" and had illegally conveyed his lands in violation of the law restraining the enrollment of conveyances by "traitors." [62] It therefore annulled the conveyance of 1576 in Rome and thus quashed probably the most indefatigable effort to preserve an inheritance ever undertaken among the Elizabethan exiles.

During these years as he observed in Spain the reversal of his hopes for the immediate benefit of the English Catholics Englefield turned optimistically to the consideration of a Catholic successor to Elizabeth. The train of thought was understandable: so much could be changed under a new monarch. In company with his close circle of friends he began to contribute to the theoretical basis needed to prepare the thinking of his compatriots. *The Conference About the Next Succession* which was published in Latin and English in 1595 was to become the classic expression of this political theory of the English Catholic exiles. [63] The book was to be supplemented by one of the last acts of Englefield's career at Court. He joined the Duchess of Feria and two English secular priests in signing a petition to King Philip II asking for a declaration of the candidacy of the Infanta for the throne of England. [64]

What was of special interest was that Sir Francis Engle-

[61] *C.S.P. Dom. 1580–90*, p. 632.
[62] *Statutes of the Realm*, 36 Eliz. cap. 5; 28–29 Eliz. cap. 3; 13 Eliz. cap. 3. Cf. n. 19, *supra*.
[63] See L. Hicks, "Robert Persons and the Book of Succession," *Recusant History*, vol. iv (1957), pp. 104ff.
[64] *C.S.P. Spanish 1587–1603*, pp. 636–37.

field had a definite role in the composition of the famous *Conference*. When the book was being secretly prepared rumors of its purpose and content were already circulating in Rome. Even though Cardinal Allen was still alive and ready to explain its intent, the General of the Jesuits, Claudio Aquaviva wrote to Robert Persons in Spain inquiring into the purpose of a book which might be harmful to the Catholics of England. Persons replied that the difficulty was: "The affair does not depend entirely on me, but on three or four others at least who have their share and opinions in it as well." The only name in this context that he gave was Englefield's whom he described as one of those residing in Spain who had done considerable work on it.[65] Later after the Englishman had died, Robert Persons felt it safe to publish Englefield's name, when explaining for the first time in print, the book's multiple authorship. In his famous *Brief Apologie* he commented that charging him with the authorship of the *Conference* was a "presumption." He noted that "the late Cardinal Allen, Sir Francis Englefield and other principal men of our nation . . . concurred in the laying together of the book."[66]

What then was Englefield's contribution? The one part of the Conference which reflected his interests at this time was the lengthy discussion of the genealogies of the possible contenders to the throne. There was already an undated memorial in Spanish in the file of the Council of State bearing his name entitled "A Relation of the claimants for the crown of England."[67] He was, moreover, corresponding regularly with another exile, Robert Heighington, who had already prepared, at the urging of Don Bernardino de Men-

[65] A.R.S.J. Hispania 136 f. 362.
[66] *A Brief Apologie or Defense of the Catholike Ecclesiasticall Hierarchie*, p. 187ᵛ (Antwerp, 1602).
[67] E 838/122, 123.

doza, a tract on the genealogies of the various pretenders. This had a significant dedication to Philip II. After Heigh-ington's death, Englefield was in correspondence with his son and heir "about some things of mine he had in charge." What these "things" were cannot be learned, but their cor-respondence was significant enough for the "troublesome" Earl of Westmorland to offer to send reports on it to Lord Burghley.[68] It was highly probable that Englefield's interest in genealogy, which he had in common with Heighington, had found expression where it was important for the theory of the *Conference* on a Catholic claimant.

During the final year of Englefield's life there occurred an incident which was to bring considerable bitterness to his de-clining days. It was well known that, despite his age and blindness, Englefield still kept in regular correspondence with his circle of friends in Flanders and Rome as well as with many officials at Court. John Whitfield described him later as the "principal man who gives intelligences unto the king of Spain, for every post that goeth between Spain and Flanders he writeth by them . . ." [69] Allowing for the ex-aggeration in such a statement it is still clear that Englefield's secretaries had to be reliable and that his correspondence would be of great interest not merely to the English Court but even more to his enemies among the exiles.

In 1595 there was consternation when John Slade, his secretary, suddenly fled from Madrid with all of Englefield's ciphers and papers and prepared to hand them over to Owen Lewis, the ambitious bishop of Cassano, and an open enemy of Allen and Englefield since 1583. However Slade died suddenly while en route to Rome and all of his papers were recovered and sent to Rome to Roger Baynes, the former

[68] *C.S.P. Dom. Add. 1580–1625*, p. 296; *C.S.P. For. 1586–88*, p. 672; *C.S.P. Spanish 1587–1603*, p. 171.
[69] B. M. Harleian 7042 f. 233.

secretary of Allen, with whom Englefield still corresponded. Unfortunately the old man refused to believe in Slade's treachery and to take steps to prevent its recurrence. He revealed to Baynes his pain that anyone should question "my judgement and choice of those to whom I commit the reading and writing of my letters and affairs." Since the trusting Englefield persisted in this attitude his correspondents began to avoid writing to him any news of significance. He was deeply affronted at this treatment although his complaint to Baynes was quite restrained. He admitted that he could not "but feale a little" this distrust "for it was more than 24 yeares that myself could write or read" and in all that time he had dealt with "many great personages and matters of import" without trouble. He admitted "John Slade his treacherye" but asked that similar cases elsewhere be recalled, and observed that the treason of Antonio Perez had not destroyed the faith of Philip in those about him.[70] Although the matter was eventually smoothed over it was a harsh ending to his career to find that he was considered unreliable by his oldest friends.

The successor to Slade was a Cornish merchant named Nicholas Baldwin, who gave every evidence of being reliable in the short time his help was needed. Another important figure in Englefield's household was a resourceful merchant named John Reve. He had once been in business in Barnstable, but had fled England and begun to serve in the Spanish navy in 1583. Early in the 1590's Reve had been allowed to fit out a ship at the cost of 4,000 escudos with artillery and supplies. It served for a time as both an armed merchantman and a privateer before he was asked to help Englefield. In 1603 the Council of State was to grant Reve a pension of fifteen escudos a month to live in Lisbon. The Council then noted that "the intelligence that this man re-

[70] W.C.A. Series A, vol. v, ff. 115, 125, 159.

ceives from England" would be best collected in that port, which indicated that, after Englefield's death, Reve remained as part of the network of correspondents on English Catholic affairs.[71]

In September 1596 the aged and sickly Englefield felt that his end was close. He decided to travel northward in his coach to St. Alban's College in Valladolid to pass his last days with the young English students. He was seventy-four years old and he wanted quietly to arrange his affairs, and make his will. He also prepared a final letter to his long time friend, King Philip, to be opened after his death. His message was a reaffirmation of all the principles that had guided his service to Spain since 1568. As Englefield wrote he knew that an armada was in the planning and it was a plea that it be sent directly against England. The high enthusiasm of the "enterprise" of the 1570's was alight once again. He pleaded that "even the seminaries, powerful as they are in preparing men's minds for a change must fail to complete their purpose without the aid of temporal force." He admitted that a Spanish victory "may excite the jealousies of other states" but he saw the conflict as ultimately vital to Spain's survival. "Either these arms must redeem England . . . or England will become a source of ruin to this country." He had never abandoned his narrow viewpoint that the motives for the Anglo-Spanish discord were solely religious. He was wise however in reminding Philip that, should his fleets be at last successful, the crown of England should never come to him. He believed that in the vital question of the succession their only hope was that the candidacy of the Infanta or "some third person" would end Europe's suspicions of Spanish aggrandizement. He concluded his letter with a few lines which were really "business as usual." He asked that the pensions due to the regiment of Sir William

[71] E 2741 n.f. consulta of 31 July 1603.

Stanley be paid and that Philip would be gracious to whoever was Englefield's successor at court.[72]

In his last will he asked that he be buried in the chapel of the College of St. Alban's and that after all his debts were paid that any residue of his estate be divided between the English colleges at Valladolid and Seville. He gave legacies to John Reve, Nicholas Baldwin, and three Spanish servants, nor was he unmindful of his nephew in England. He asked that from a sealed chest which had been left at Douai many years before, "the finest piece of plate and the finest jewel" be sent to England to his nephew "the heir of my house." [73]

In London six months later a legal inquiry was conducted in the court of the Exchequer to establish "whether is the sayd Sir Francis Englefield dead, yea or no." From this document many authentic details can be learned of his final days. One of the witnesses in court, a Thomas Thorpe, "stationer," testified that five months before he had been in Spain where "by the meanes of Father Persons he did ly in the said Sir Francis Englefield's house at Madrid . . . by the space of three weeks after the death of the sayd Sir Francis." He related that John Reve had hurried back to Madrid and "gatheringe all the keyes of his sayd late maister's lodginges and chestes did lock up everythinge in the sayme rooms." Reve had hoped to conceal the news of Englefield's death until all of his pensions were paid. Later, Thorpe testified, Robert Persons had gathered up all of Englefield's papers and correspondence and brought them to his room in the Jesuit residence.[74]

With these slight ripples in Spain and the Court of the Ex-

[72] *C.S.P. Spanish 1587–1603*, pp. 633–34; W.C.A. Series E, vol. ii, f. 1.
[73] W.C.A. Series A, vol. v, f. 219 copy.
[74] Oxford, Bodley Library, English Hist. B. 172f. 1–2, copy of the I.P.M., dated 27 May 1597.

chequer in England there passed from the midst of the exiles a man who had been, even with his handicaps, truly one of their most respected personalities. There is little doubt that he had never altered his devotion to his country's ancient faith, and with William Allen he had retained a conviction that "the reform" of England required a military victory as prelude. Yet his respected position at the Spanish Court did not come from such notions as these, for Spain shared them only when the hard realities of its policy in the north found them convenient.

How successful was he? In his primary concerns which were centered about the retention of his lands and the dream of the reversal of the policy of the Queen in religion, he had nothing to show. It was rather in the undoubted fact of his personal acceptance by Philip II that his success was to lie. This enabled the problem of the exiles' survival to receive an attention which would not have been otherwise granted. His integrity and skill contributed much to salvaging the most from a difficult situation. His hundreds of letters of recommendation, his personal interviews with the courtiers of King Philip kept some assurance of the payments of pensions or the distribution of alms. Whatever the many vagaries and limitations of the pension system, the resourceful Englefield was the vigilant agent, keeping open a place in it for his needy compatriots in exile.

CHAPTER THREE

An "Intelligencer" : *Hugh Owen*
1538–1618

"*Thou secret keep'st the Kingdoms Secrets, even
so secret that Faith to thy faith is given.*"

The Latin Epigrams of John Owen,
Lib. II, no. 17
trans. by T. Harvey, 1677.

SECURITY IS A TASK for the sharp-witted. Hugh Owen,
who rose to the official duty of gathering intelligence on England at the Court of the Archdukes in Brussels, was also
responsible for spotting the bogus petitioner, or the paid informer, who might mingle with the exiles. It was an unavoidable duty in which, if the animosity of some of the English Privy Council could serve as a rough criterion, he was a
conspicuous success. Any one who enters the perilous profession of espionage must suffer the burden of rumors and
misinformation which inevitably grow attached to his name.
At times Owen was thought to be a "Jesuit," then, a leading

soldier, and finally even a dominant councilor to the Archduke Albert who ruled "all courses for England"—as one
spy's florid despatch put it. It will be useful therefore to reconstruct the authentic details of his career and then attempt
to establish his place in the cold war of 16th century espionage.

Hugh Owen was born at Plas Du on the Lleyn peninsula
in Caernarvonshire in 1538. During the reign of Elizabeth
the family properties were in the control of his older brother
Thomas, while Hugh, and a younger brother Robert, lived
abroad after 1570. There was never any doubt of the Catholic sentiments of this branch of the Owen family. In July
1578 Thomas Owen was arrested and tried before the Council in the Marches of Wales, and he was indicted again for
recusancy a year later in the Caernarvonshire quarter sessions. Plas Du was known to have harbored six priests during
this period for it was considered to be a "Mass center" for
the area.[1] Although Robert Owen was not ordained a priest
until after his studies later on the continent, as early as 1560
he had the revenues of a living at West Felton near Oswestry,
but he was later deprived. After living in Rome and Paris,
Robert resided for most of his life at Le Mans where he
eventually secured a canonry.[2]

A controversial figure for most of his life, even the accounts
of Hugh Owen's activities before his departure from England
excited a debate among his contemporaries. This was largely
due to the fact that up to 1571 he had been the secretary of
Henry Fitzallan, twelfth and last of his house to possess the

---

[1] P. Williams, *The Council in the Marches of Wales under
Elizabeth I*, pp. 87, 92; M. Cleary "The Catholic Resistance in
Wales, 1568–1678," *Blackfriars* (1957) xxxviii, pp. 112–13;
Dictionary of Welsh Biography, pp. 697–98.

[2] T. F. Knox, First and Second Douai Diaries, p. 5; A. H.
Dodd, "Two Welsh Catholic *Emigrés*," *Bulletin of Celtic Studies*
(1937) viii, pp. 346ff.

Earldom of Arundel.[3] When Owen reached the Low Countries he was publicly denounced for his involvement in the Ridolfi plot and it was charged that he had fled to escape capture. However, Lord Lumley who had been acquainted with him, asserted quite definitely that he did not believe Owen had been "in any wise privy to any matter concerning the Queen of Scots."[4]

It is far more likely that Owen went abroad for two simple reasons: Henry Fitzallan's fortunes were clearly on the decline, and, with Hugh's brother, Robert, already expelled from his living, there was obviously no future in England for a Welsh Catholic. At the age of thirty-three he had decided to seek a patron abroad. It was to be nearly eight years before he was to have a new one in Alessandro Farnese, the Duke of Parma and Governor of the Low Countries. Owen's first years in Flanders remain difficult to trace. According to a reliable spy's report Owen was at the Court of Philip II from November 26, 1572 to February 10, 1573 after which time he returned to Brussels with only the meagre pension of 20 escudos a month.[5] It was minimal support for services considered of little significance. There was as yet no evidence that Owen moved in Englefield's circle.

It was apparently around 1580 that he succeeded in securing Parma's full confidence. The special talent that he had to offer was his ability to organize a correspondents' network extending gradually into England and having many links with the Low Countries and France. The need for it

[3] P.R.O., S.P. 12/105/10.

[4] H.M.C. Salisbury MSS, vol. i, p. 540; the principal witness against Owen was a hearsay report from the suspect Bishop of Ross, on whom see D. Lockie, "The Political Career of the Bishop of Ross, 1568–80," University of Birmingham History Journal, vol. iv (1953), pp. 98ff.

[5] B. M., Lansdowne, vol. xviii, f. 174; Lechat, Les Refugiés, pp. 233–36.

] 54 [

had become more urgent as the pressure of the English Privy Council began to increase sharply against Catholics at that time. Their concern about the English living abroad was both natural and evident. For example, a John Sledd had come to the continent in 1580 and had lived for several months in Rome and then, after journeying back with a small party of itinerant English priests, he left them in Paris to hurry to denounce them all in London. The notes of his observations, entitled bombastically "The General Discourse of the Popes Holyness Devices"—were in effect an accurate dossier of 285 Englishmen, students, priests, soldiers and merchants whom he had noticed in the preceding months. He frequently gave their family connections and in certain in-stances a physical description to assist in their identification on their return.[6] Not every informer was this successful or painstaking but the need for security among the Catholics in both England and on the continent was quite evident. The embassies of the Catholic powers at the English Court had been of some importance in sending news of events in Lon-don but their value had proved uneven. After Mendoza's expulsion from London early in 1584, Spain was to be without even this rudimentary listening post.

Obviously the secret contacts of the exiles with England can only be seen through the occasional signs of their ex-istence. For example, in September 1584 Robert Persons reported to a friend that he had set up a small "establishment" at Rouen where "some can make trips to the coast to arrange for boats to convey people across," and others "take charge of the preparation and introduction of books into the coun-try" and others send vestments to England and do "many other services" for the priests working there in secret.[7] At this time Hugh Owen had journeyed to Spain again in his fruit-

[6] C.R.S. vol. lii (1961) pp. 193–214.
[7] C.R.S., vol. xxxix, p. 236.

less effort to rally support for a plan to rescue the imprisoned Queen of Scots. Robert Persons informed Queen Mary that he had given "the sayd Mr. Owen" a copy of the cipher used in her correspondence on the chance there would be good news from Spain. He pointedly assured her that Owen was "a very active, diligent, faythfull and secret Sollicitor." [8]

Thus it is clear that Owen had become a reliable correspondent in the opinion of the Duke of Parma and at least one of the leading English priests. He still had further to climb, however, for his salary was only 25 escudos a month in 1584. [8a]

The opening of the Anglo-Spanish War in 1586 was to give him his chance. Information about English affairs had become of premium value and interest while Owen's evident talent for languages was contributed as well. Sir Roger Williams recalled a few years later that his despatches to Leicester during the Sluys campaign were intercepted and "Owen a Welsh gentleman had much ado to put my foul hand in Italian to the Duke." Shortly after this Owen was assisting Sir William Stanley with the screening of Welsh volunteers for an attack on Ostend. [9] Little else of his work has survived.

It was not until two years after the defeat of the Armada of 1588 that three circumstances gave convincing proof that Owen's role as intelligencer had been at last completely accepted. The first was his journey to Spain with Sir William Stanley early in 1590. After this visit—his third to Spain—his salary was more than doubled to 60 escudos a month. [10]

---

[8] C.R.S., vol. xxxix, p. 248.
[8a] E 2851 n.f. Pension list of exiles.
[9] *A Brief Discourse of Warre*, p. 61; *C.S.P. For.*, *Jan.–June 1588*, pp. 81–82.
[10] A.H.N. Estado, lib. 251 n.f., cedula of 3 April 1590.

Moreover, from about this time the number of *avisos* from England that survive in the files of the Council of State increased noticeably. Lastly, there is the contemporary description by Lewis Lewknor who had observed some of his network in action. Lewknor reported that many English letters were being received by Hugh Owen, or his friend Versteghen, in Flanders and that the reports were then sent to Spain. Lewknor named a Richard Hopkins as "their ligger in Paris for intelligence," a Humphrey Shelton was "their intelligencer from Roan," Edward Barlow and Francis Ridgeley were in Bruges and "inform from thence" and that Anthony Rolston was their "intelligencer from Spain." [11] The last named agent was, unknown to Lewknor, really a correspondent for the Earl of Essex.

Father Henry Walpole, in his declaration in London in 1593, also gave some further details of the network as he knew of it. He reported that regular despatches from Versteghen's house in Antwerp went to Cardinal Allen and others. He said that he believed that news was received from England through Father Henry Garnet.[12] It is surprising that Garnet's name occurred in this context since he was complaining at this time that the sending and receiving of letters was a long and uncertain affair. Persons informed the General of the Jesuits that "up until now, these people over there never had a satisfactory way of conducting their affairs . . ." and he noted that Garnet's letters were so cautiously worded as to verge on the obscure.[13] Garnet was constantly on the move and in hiding so that his letters could never be regular. It was more likely that the friends of the Jesuit were in a more secure position to help. For example Don Esteban Ybarra reported to the Council of State in

[11] P.R.O., S.P. 12/233/32.
[12] C.R.S., vol. v, p. 262.
[13] A.R.S.J. Hispania vol. 139, f. 136, letter of spring 1593.

September 1594 that "in London two people directed by the Jesuits offer to hold regular correspondence should it be useful."[14]

These anonymous correspondents at the London base of the network did not merely send out reports, but occasionally even original copies of statements made by Catholics in the courtroom and even some letters of the Privy Council. Versteghen once reported to Persons about a packet that reached Antwerp in which were found: "A discourse in writing conteyning 50 sheets of pages, being the confession of Mr. Anthony Tirrell written by himself, before his later fall . . . sundry copies of the treasurer's letters, and others in authority unto him, besydes divers articles, interrogations, practices of Walsingham . . ."[15] This was not a unique incident. For example, in August 1598, when Robert Persons learned of the letters of his enemy, Charles Paget, to the Privy Council, he secured full copies of them. He implied that this had happened on other occasions: "They have already sent us previously other letters of much the same content . . ."[16]

The ways of getting the news out of England were novel and ingenious. A likely means, of course, was through the students of the various colleges on the continent. A student arrived in Valladolid in the spring of 1595 with a number of notes from different prisons "concealed in buttons, shoes and other more secret places."[17] The ships of friendly merchants were also a safe conveyance to and from England for people and messages. Occasionally these couriers were foreigners. In 1602 Joseph Creswell described to the Secretary, Andres de Prada, the work of a Jacques Ghibles of Antwerp who had served "many years in carrying letters and people

[14] E 608 n.f. despatch of 27 Sept. 1594.
[15] Stonyhurst MS Collectanea B f. 103.
[16] A.S.V. Nunziature Diverse vol. 265, f. 224.
[17] S.A.C. Serie II, legajo 1 n.f. letter to Creswell.

to England and sending reports on all the secret activities of the enemy."[18]

All of these sources contributed to Owen's *avisos*. The Archduke Albert shared Parma's good opinion of Owen for at times he would remark in his private letters to the Spanish Court "the reports which I have from England I new send to you . . . the correspondents of Hugh Owen I hold to be the more reliable."[19] On another occasion he was more expansive:

> Hugh Owen is a man of great intelligence whom the king has used and is using in many affairs. He is diligent, very discreet and suitable for any business. The Duke of Parma made use of him and always put in writing his great satisfaction in him to the king. When I was leaving Spain I was told to profit from his services and I have found them good.[20]

There was no reason to deny either Owen's industry or his discretion, but there is a contemporary aura to his work that must be appraised more carefully. To some observers he appeared to be "ruling all courses for England."[21] On this point the evidence is not convincing. The Archduke and the Council of State in Spain were very much masters of their own policies, and they placed English—and Catholic—affairs within the overall pattern of their aims in the Low Countries, France and the Mediterranean. When it was a question of policy, the *consultas* of the Council of State rarely mention his name and then only for certifying reports. Hence while Owen was to be the most prominent figure among the English pensioners at the Brussels Court he suffered from the same restraints that Englefield had experienced in Spain. For example, when he tried to win the approval of the Archduke

[18] E 1744 n.f. memorial of 7 Jan. 1602.
[19] E 613/120 letter of 3 April 1597.
[20] E 613/125, 7 March 1596.
[21] *H.M.C. Salisbury MSS*, vol. v, pp. 34–35.

for the candidacy of his wife for the succession to England, he had to inform the sceptical Duke of Sessa and Baltazar de Zúñiga that every appeal was being received coldly and he concluded that "the Archduke is making small account of that kingdom." [22]

It would be impossible to appraise Owen's achievement without a consideration of the problem of espionage as prac-ticed by Spain and England during his career. Then the con-ditions under which he worked, the objectives he sought and his constant fear of English espionage in Spain and the Low Countries can be more readily grasped.

A reading of the reports of agents and foreign travelers available in the Salisbury Manuscripts and the State Papers needs to be balanced by their counterpart in the *avisos* in the files of the Council of State. From these it becomes evident that the major concern of both Courts at this time was for military information. Eacn was particularly anxious to know of the concentrations of ships in ports, whether in northern Spain, Lisbon and Cadiz for action against England, or at Plymouth for expeditions against Portugal, Andalucia and the West Indies. Owen's reports on the sailings of English ships for the Indies were always given the highest consideration in the Councils of State and of the Indies.

It was inevitable that, in the quest for information about Spain, some of the English agents abroad would choose the convenient disguise of a Catholic exile. During the war some agents were discovered to be acting as "pilgrims for Com-postella" or even as itinerant friars. Understandably, this dis-guise was particularly alarming to Hugh Owen for it would put the rest of the exiles under suspicion. This fear was quickened by the fact that the Spanish Hapsburgs, in their concern for internal security, had already ordered elaborate countermeasures during the Anglo-Spanish War.

[22] E 619 n.f. letter of 5 May 1601.

The Inquisition was in all the principal ports with authority to scrutinize suspicious foreigners, but its prime concern was still heresy. However there were also three supplementary forms of inquiry into suspicious foreigners. In 1596, for example, the Count of Puñonrostro conducted a lengthy search for English merchants who pretended to be Scottish or French neutrals while engaging in contraband trade in Andalucia. This activity, while ostensibly to enforce the embargo, was also motivated by the fear that English spies were pretending to be traders. There was also the Governor of Guipuzcoa, Don Juan de Velasquez, who patroled the northern frontiers in matters of security. There were, lastly, the *ad hoc* orders that constantly came from the Spanish Court to investigate a new report. For example, in May 1590, Philip II wrote to Hernando de Mendoza, the Governor of Navarre, that he was sending the description of an English agent who had penetrated Spain. The king added: "If he has not passed through, you are especially warned to detain him, or if he has passed through, send someone after him." [23]

There was not however a coordinated effort to acquire information about other foreign powers. Much was usually left to the ingenuity of each resident ambassador. For example, the Council of State informed Don Baltazar de Zúñiga, who was at that time in Paris, that in the event that he employed English, Flemings, or Italians as informants in Paris and Flanders he must do so without any public connection with his embassy and handle the whole matter in complete secrecy.[24] The order implied that Zúñiga was developing his own coterie of agents afresh.

Although it was not until 1613 that the office of *Espia Mayor* was officially created at the Spanish Court and con-

[23] E 167/130.
[24] E, K 1426/28 consulta 1 Jun. 1604.

ferred upon Andres de Velasquez, Philip III took the occasion to recall, in the wording of his patent, the previous services of his father as the Governor of Guipuzcoa. He gave generous praise to Juan de Velasquez for his services "in the duties and correspondence dealing with intelligence and secret affairs," which he had rendered in the north and then "by my command in residing at Court." [25] Apparently Juan de Velasquez began this work at about the same time that Hugh Owen was given his large increase in pension. There is a long report from Velasquez written in Fuentarabia on April 19, 1591, summarizing his work during the previous past year. He did not as yet consider English espionage a serious problem in his area at that time. He only noted:

> In St. Jean de Luz there is an Englishman, who wears the habit of cleric who has written to get permission to enter here. He reports that there is another Englishman also in St. Jean who wears the same habit and has arrived from England with four others. The man is not a cleric but a spy, and I am making every effort to arrest him. [26]

Significantly, Velasquez had been particularly interested in France where he was in contact with that capable double agent, Chateau Martin, who was also sending reports to Sir Robert Cecil. Philip II valued the services of this Frenchman so highly that for a time he was paying him 100 escudos a month. [27] Chateau Martin's correspondence with England was known in Spain, but he had little news of England to offer, and instead his reports concentrated on Henry IV's activities. Philip demanded good service for these high wages. At one time, when Chateau Martin had failed to gain some needed information, the king angrily told Velasquez to deal

[25] M. G. del Campilla, "El Espia Mayor," *Bolletin de la Real Academia de Historia*, vol. cxix, pp. 317ff.
[26] E 168/44.
[27] E 168/50.

with him "whatever way he wishes." [28] Soon after the resourceful agent had returned to Spain's favor, for the Governor of Guipuzcoa was very pleased with a long report on
Antonio Perez' dealings with Henry IV and on Venetian
contacts with the Turk.[29] Gradually, however, English affairs began to occupy more of Velasquez' attention. By 1596
there had even been sent a memorandum to him on "the disguises used by the English who come to spy on events
here." [30]

The disguise of a pretended Catholic continued to worry
the English *émigrés*. An exchange of letters in March 1602
over this was very illuminating. On March 7th Father Joseph Creswell reported to Andres de Prada that two young
Englishmen, who had been servants to the household of a
Court official, had fled recently towards the Biscayan ports.
He asked Prada to send letters to Irun and Fuentarabia to
have them detained and their papers examined. "I insist in
this case that there is no demand for their punishment," he
wrote, "if only to avoid the public damage to religion that
will come if they are found to be bringing letters or notes
from some enemy spy." The Council of State issued orders
at once." [31] But there were immediate repercussions, for a
week later Philip III sent to the Governor of Fuentarabia a
very stern order:

I have decided that no Englishman of any sort is to be allowed to come from France into these kingdoms without having
first registered and the cause of his coming scrutinized. It is well
known that, aside from certain Catholics who come to live in
our holy faith, there are others who come with bad intentions

[28] E 169/185.
[29] E 170/62.
[30] E 176 n.f. letter of 15 Nov. 1596.
[31] E 188 n.f. letter of 7 March 1602; E 191 n.f. letter of 8
March 1602.

and are not Catholics. They come to spy here. For this reason I have decided to order you to show particular care, for there must not be a failure. With the assistance of the *Licenciado* Puerta, commissary of the Holy Office, and Martin Errasquins, you are to compile the register of the English and grant no exceptions . . .[32]

The response of the Governor and the two officials to the royal order was notably honest on the problem.

For many days past, they can not recall any Englishman coming through here. Whoever arrives usually goes to the house of Errasquins, as the seminary priests do, when going to or returning from England. Those who might excite suspicion arrive in ships from La Rochelle, or from Ireland and Scotland which usually trade in Santander.[33]

An unhelpful, if polite, reply which pointed out the difficulties inherent in the simple solution proposed by King Philip. There were too many subterfuges in entering Spain to be handled adequately in that way. Philip III had probably received the idea from Father Creswell for he had suggested it nearly five years before to Cardinal Aldobrandino to solve the same problem in Rome. At that time he had urged that no Englishman should reside there "without knowing whence he comes, what his purpose was, and what was his occupation" after which he could be given a license to remain."[34] The suggestion had not been adopted in Rome either.

The most significant discoveries of English agents in Spain were usually made through the betrayals of their compatriots. For example, in 1597 Juan de Velasquez received word from an Englishman whom he bluntly called "an out-

[32] E 191 n.f., letter of 16 March.
[33] E 1744 n.f. letter of 27 March.
[34] A.S.V. Fondo Borghese, III, 124 g2, f. 74. Sir Thomas Mildmay had a similar plan for England. See Strype, *Annals*, vol. iv, p. 296.

right knave named Monpalmer" who offered to reveal "all the secrets of England, as well as the many spies there are in Spain and their plans." [35] Velasquez was referring to the notorious Edmond Palmer, who on this occasion demanded 500 escudos for his information. It was well worth it. Through him Velasquez learned of an English agent of the Earl of Essex named Thomas Marchant who had been staying in San Sebastian. Marchant was usually in correspondence with another agent using the name Le Blanc living in Seville. Moreover there was another agent appropriately named Philip Scamps who was described as traveling about in northern Spain en route to Lisbon, Seville and San Lucar. "Scamps carries a great sum of money by letters to Iturbide who lives in Lisbon."

At once the hunt was on, but it took a month to capture Marchant and Le Blanc, who soon admitted that they were in fact agents of Essex. Marchant, who was a cousin of Le Blanc, made a full statement on his career. He was an Englishman, born in the Channel Isles, who had been told to send his reports to an Alonso Faribaoult in Rouen. Marchant had left London in 1595 with a cargo of merchandise and had been trading in the northern ports of Spain since then for two years. Nicholas Le Blanc had followed the same instructions after beginning to trade in merchandise in Bilbao.[36]

Velasquez continued to use Palmer, for his name was soon rumored to be linked with a bigger scandal. Apparently his betrayal had become known to two other agents from England. One of them, a Thomas Bradshaw, complained to another, named Philip Honyman, in July 1599 that Palmer was empowered to search the ports for English shipping engaged in contraband in Portugal and Andalucia.

---

[35] E 180 n.f. letter of 8 March 1597; See also T. Birch, *Memoirs*, vol. 1, pp. 94–95.
[36] E 180 n.f. letters of 22 May, 3 June, 10 July 1597.

Bradshaw thought that English commerce to the value of 300,000 escudos had been seized. In fact, however, Bradshaw was deceived, for the confiscations of this time were largely the work of others. It is very likely that the rumors connected with all investigations were easily attached to a discreditable man like Palmer.[37] The truth of the matter was that for his work as informer Palmer received the usual percentage of goods confiscated from merchants such as Marchant and Le Blanc. Ironically Palmer never lost his favor completely in England for he was also sending reports there again prior to 1604.

There was another Englishman, who, while serving in the Spanish navy for several years, was to gather accurate information on English ports. This was Richard Burley of Malcombe Regis who had lived in San Sebastian, as a merchants' factor, since 1580. At that time he had earned the approval of the local authorities for denouncing another merchant, John Donne, as a spy. The accusation was well founded for, after Donne's release from prison and return to England, he gave a complete report on Spanish shipping in the northern ports. After the war began Burley entered the Spanish navy, together with his brother.[38] Shortly after the defeat of the Armada, Burley submitted a memorandum to King Philip II urging the recruitment of sailors and pilots among the English for service in Spain. The king was sceptical of the idea since he thought it would only be opening the door to persons of doubtful loyalty.[39] However Burley received encouragement from Don Bernardino de Mendoza who invited him to Paris to explain his idea in more detail.

[37] C.S.P. Dom. 1598–1601, pp. 242–43; L. Stone, Sir Horatio Palavacino, pp. 249–50, note 5.
[38] C.S.P. Dom. Add. 1580–1625, pp. 36–38, 255.
[39] E, K 1449/28, 29.

Late in August 1589 Mendoza reported to Martin de Idiaquez that, while the plan had many difficulties, he was still confident that Burley could lure a number of English volunteers into Spanish service by using the ships of Breton captains as a cover. Mendoza indicated these ships to be "the boats that carry the priests" and the plan implied virtually a ferry service of clergy in one direction and mariners in the other. It was a naive scheme which would have been all too easily uncovered. Undaunted, Burley on one occasion wanted to use the ship of Don Pedro de Zubiaur, who was in England on a negotiation for the exchange of prisoners, to bring out fourteen pilots whom he declared ready to serve Spain.[40] This dubious suggestion was also abandoned, but Burley was to be heard of again.

Over a year later he appeared in Spain with letters from the Governor of Le Havre calling for a large squadron of twenty ships to patrol the coasts of Brittany at the cost of 25,000 escudos a month. Burley's papers gave details of provisions, powder supply, and even the names of various captains of the Spanish fleet who were to be moved into the new assignment. Brittany was, of course, a vital and sensitive area in the English campaign assisting King Henry IV, but Philip could hardly risk such an enterprise in the hands of a foreigner. However he did send the powder requested to the Governor of Le Havre and left the memorandum with the Council of War and Don Diego de Ybarra.[41]

It was at this time that the first rumors reflecting on Burley's loyalty to Spain began to be circulated. Father Henry Walpole, who had first met him when the Brittany plan was under consideration,[42] later reported in 1593 to Anthony

[40] E, K 1569 n.f. letters of 27 August, 4 September, 31 December 1589.

[41] E, K 1575/88, 92–97.

[42] Stonyhurst MS, Anglia AI n. 61, letter of July 25, 1591.

Bacon that Burley was "discovered to be a spy employed from hence." [43] This contradicted the earlier disclosure of John Whitfield in December 1592 that Burley was still high in the confidence of the Spanish and that he was a "spy of the king at 40 crowns a month." [44] In Spain, however, nothing was done against Burley for some time. He continued to serve in the galleys off Brittany until the summer of 1595 when he was one of the captains in the squadrons of four ships that raided the coast of Cornwall. [45]

Shortly after this, however, he was arrested and imprisoned on charges of spying for England and remained in prison until the end of the war. Then in December 1603 the Council of War reversed the conviction and advised the Council of State that the evidence against Burley was not sufficient. The Council reinstated him with back pay since the date of his arrest and recommended that he serve in the fleet near Naples and Sicily, "although it sees no objection to his serving in the galleys near Spain." [46]

Why the reversal of Burley's conviction? There is sufficient evidence that he had been the victim of a clever trick of Sir Robert Cecil. In the memoirs of Sir William Monson, who had commanded English fleets in the narrow seas for many years, it was later revealed that Cecil was angered at Burley's role in the raid on Cornwall:

> To be even with him for so foull a fact, Sir Robert Cecyll, the Principal Secretary, writ a letter to him residing in Lisbon, pretending that he was employed as a spy, and gave him thanks for particular service he named he had done, when in deed there was no such cause for the man was ever too honest to that side. [47]

[43] C.R.S. vol. v, p. 269.
[44] B. M. Harleian, 7042 f.233.
[45] T. Birch, *Memoirs*, vol. i, p. 270.
[46] E 2741 n.f. consulta of 11 Dec. 1603.
[47] *Monson's Naval Tracts*, vol. ii, p. 262 (Naval Records Society, 1902).

As the war between England and Spain dragged on, the English espionage penetration of the Iberian peninsula increased in effectiveness and coverage.[48] Various observers were sent to watch the ports of the Biscayan provinces or Galicia or Lisbon where the squadrons for the northern seas were fitted out. The instructions prepared in London in November 1591 for an agent named Austin Halfacre illustrate this pattern very clearly. He was ordered to confine his work to northern Spain but to return at once when he had finished. He was directed to concentrate on Corunna and Ferrol and the strength and fortification of the areas thereabout and also to observe as many warships as possible in the Biscayan ports.[49]

In a later series of instructions endorsed: "Things fitt to be advertized hither, with such other additions as wether the times of occasion shall bring forth," an agent destined for Spain was told to notice all military preparations and also to find out "what hopes they have of parties or favorers to come with them being landed, or to give them easy landing at first."[50] Despite Palmer's betrayal of the agents of Essex, Sir Robert Cecil was able to place eight observers in Spain in 1598. In the north there was Paul Theobast at Corunna and Ferrol, Hans Owter at Compostella, and an unnamed "maryner" who was in partnership with Cecil in a cargo of merchandise for the Biscayan ports. In Lisbon there were also three agents, William Resold, Peter Gerard and Baltasar Peterson. In Seville there were two agents using the aliases of "Massentio Verdioni" and "Andover."[51]

The work, for obvious reasons, was hazardous and ex-

[48] See C. Read, *Mr. Secretary Walsingham*, vol. ii, pp. 318–38; L. Stone, *Sir Horatio Palavicino*, pp. 230–66.
[49] *H.M.C. Salisbury MSS*, vol. iv, p. 158; see also vol. v, pp. 481–82.
[50] P.R.O., S.P. 94/5/166.
[51] See L. Stone, *op. cit.*, pp. 325–30.

pensive, yet it is very difficult to gain a very detailed picture of its financing. The payments varied according to the agent, and probably the expenses of the correspondence as well. In one accounting of "money for Intelligence into Spain" covering July 14, 1599 to October 9, 1600, a Thomas Wilson received £150, while a Francis Lambert received £109 for the same period.[52] The Queen demanded good results for her expenditure. An *avisos* prepared by Hugh Owen in May 1599 pointed out that there was dissatisfaction with "the present intelligence from Spain" in the English Court. He noted "they are attempting to send new correspondents there by using persons with French names." He had learned of this from "a friend of ours" who was offered 1500 felipes a year but had refused because "he thought it too dangerous."[53]

The method of relaying reports to England became, by the end of the century, extremely complex. One plan for an agent of Sir Robert Cecil who was to live in Lisbon listed the following routes:

He is directed to write overland, and to direct his letters to Samuel Robinson, merchant in London, with a cover directed in Spanish to Diego Gardía de Paredes, mercador en Roan, or Juan Donayre, Correo Mayor en Paris or to Alonso Faribaoult, mercader en Roan. By Calais he is directed to send his letters to Jean Van Dale and to superscribe them to Giles Snode. By Scotland, to direct his letters to Andrew Hart, bookseller at Edinburgh, to be delivered to Mr. Alexander Johnson, that is Mr. Nicolson, the Queen's agent. By Ireland to Robert Meagh, priest, and to cover them to William Meagh, or to Robert Coppinger at the Starr in Cheapside.[54]

There is little difference worth noting in the English and Spanish methods of espionage. Cecil's policy of leaving an

[52] P.R.O., S.P., 94/7/124 and 222.
[53] E 616/171 avisos of 26 May 1599.
[54] P.R.O., S.P. 94/7/232–33.

agent in an important location, such as Lisbon or Corunna or even the Spanish Court was matched by Owen's network of correspondents in London and on the continent. Occasionally Spain would send a supplementary agent to travel through England who would report on his return. For example, there is the final statement of an agent who left San Lucar in January 1601 and traveled to Waterford, Bristol, London, Calais and Flushing, then back to London, then over to Barnstable, then to Bristol where he secured a passage for Spain in November of the same year. His principal observations had been made on the English fleet and its preparation for Ireland.[55]

Another noticeable difference between the rival espionage networks was that England had a larger number of merchants, formerly resident in Spain, who could supply information and advice when needed. For example, Roger Bodenham had lived with his family in Seville from at least 1579 to 1585. There are extant his letters to Leicester, Walsingham and Lord Burghley which are accurate descriptions of Spanish strength from his own observations. His knowledge of Spanish made him suitable to meet with the agents of the Duke of Parma in the unsuccessful peace overtures of 1586,[56] but he did not try to return to Spain.

Thomas Honyman was another merchant whose services were more valuable to Cecil as the war progressed. There is extant a copy of a letter of December 1595 from Honyman to Velasquez, the shrewd governor of Guipuzcoa, in which discussions on trade were suggested. Since Honyman wrote that he had not written before "to preserve my credit with my Prince and country and to remedy a certain jealousy in the head of a Lord of the Council" it is obvious they had been in communication before. Yet this time Honyman was

[55] E 840/167.
[56] E 590/68, 123, 141.

really looking for information for shortly after this there was issued a "note of money delivered to Mr. Honyman, im-ployed into Spain" for £50.[57] Later, in Sir Robert Cecil's memorandum on his agents composed in October 1598, he described Honyman's activities:

> I have freighted a shippe with prohibited goodes . . . to colore a voyage to Ferroll, and in this Honiman, a merchant, beareth the venture of 500 ducats and I as much. This shippe is appointed to return with all speed, allsoe, after having tarried 20 daies in the Spanishe portes to discover them better . . .

There is also evidence of Honyman acting as paymaster for two other agents in Spain. A friend of Sir Walter Raleigh named Suedall was given £30 by Honyman "by warrant out of the chequer" and he also arranged a similar amount for a "Dutch shipper taken prisoner in Spaine being im-ployed." [58]

But the greatest confrontation of the two networks from Owen's viewpoint was the activity of the Privy Council to learn more about the identities of the English Catholics abroad. Opportunities to observe them in Flanders were far more numerous, but south of the Pyrenees were two colleges and a small but diligent group near the Spanish Court. In-formation about them was eagerly sought.

As early as 1586 a memorandum was prepared at the English Court for the selection of agents for this special work in Spain. The author, who cannot as yet be identified, first discussed the qualities of the agent to be chosen and he elimi-nated three different types at once. The agent was not to be a "foreigner," nor "an Inglishman joyned in consanguinity with Spanish blood," nor was he to be a "well meaning sub-ject that is greatlie known by frequenting that country." These were too much of a risk to be reliable. The only way to

[57] P.R.O., S.P. 94/5/65 and 142.
[58] P.R.O., S.P. 12/265/133; S.P. 94/7/236.

gain "creditt and safetie there in Spaine" was to secure a recommendation from some Catholic in England. To secure
this, the agent was to pretend to be a Catholic and visit the
prisons and there seek out the friendship of a priest or "some
Papist that hath werked some disgrace and lyeth emprysoned
there." He suggested that the agent was to speak along these
lines:

> He is to yeilde himself, as it were, under shyfte to have
> advice and goastlie counsell, alleginge a malcontendedness in
> hym with repyninge at his present fate: being desyrous, if it
> might please sweet *Jesu*, for his deare mother's sake, to gain
> some friends for his better access into foreign parts and Catholike
> countries, there to pass the tyme with the quiet and comfort of
> his conscience and in the causes of his poor distressed country-
> men . . .

The author then stated his conviction that any agent would
be given considerable "lewd counsell, egginge forwards and
other assurances of well entertaynment." [59]
The significance of this suggestion is not so much its shock-
ing cynicism, but rather in its awareness of the fact that only
by penetrating the exiles' confidence could very accurate observations be made. Moreover, just as England was far more
vulnerable to those who sent information abroad while keeping their position unnoticed in England, so also would Catholics and pseudo-Catholics among the exiles provide the
greatest amount of news about Spain.
In the spring of 1591 occurred an incident which made
these fears of the English Catholics in Spanish Hapsburg
territories come true. In November of the preceding year
two English priests, John Cecil and John Fixer, left Saint
Alban's College in Valladolid to go to work secretly in England.[60] Both were soon captured and questioned extensively

[59] B. M., Harleian 295 f. 195.
[60] *C.S.P. Dom.* *1591–94*, pp. 40–42; C.R.S. vol. xxx, p. 7.

on the new college in Spain and other matters concerning the
exiled Catholics. For example, in answer to "Interrogatories"
on May 22, 1591, Fixer said that he had only come to England "to obtain license to live according to his conscience
. . . or to go to Germany." He also begged "not to be
urged on the point of assisting to apprehend the Catholics
from Spain" but he finally offered to go to some prison and
be directed by a prisoner to a Catholic, "from whom he will
get to know more." John Cecil offered some facts but he also
apparently added distortions which were as dangerous to his
fellow Catholics as they were misleading to Lord Burghley.

The news of the betrayal by the two priests gradually came
back across the channel and Cardinal Allen informed Robert
Persons finally in January 1592 that he had warning, "two
or three months ago . . . how the two companions,
N. & N., were with the treasurer and were suspected to have
discovered all they knew, and perhaps added somewhat of
theire own more than they knew." [61] The misleading statements of Cecil and Fixer undoubtedly contributed to the famous proclamation of October 1591 against the exiles and
their colleges in Spanish Hapsburg lands. [62]

Allen, however, also saw the whole position of the exiles
endangered. For the scandal in Spain and its court would
damage the hard-won confidence that could so easily be denied to them in the future. It was very much to the credit
of Allen that he saw the folly of publicly denouncing Cecil
and Fixer, out of fear that it might make them do something
worse. Instead he tried to get word to them that they should
leave England at once. This became known in the English
Court through the statements of another captured priest,
James Yonger, who had been a student with the two trouble-

[61] Knox, *Allen*, p. 339.
[62] *Tudor and Stuart Proclamations*, vol. i, nos. 837, 839, text
in Strype, *Annals*, vol. iv, pp. 78ff.

makers at the college in Valladolid. When he was questioned in August 1592, Yonger admitted that he was "also willed to make means for Fixer, a priest who had dealings with the Lord Treasurer about Spain" to return to the continent.[63] He was empowered to offer him a post as chaplain to Cardinal Allen, where the prelate could obviously keep an eye on this unreliable man.[64]

This was not the worst case that the exiles endured during this period, even if their vigilance had increased in the interim. For, early in August 1600 two other former students of St. Alban's, Roger Filcock and Mark Barkworth were arrested in London. Their trial revealed that there had been among their fellow scholars three informants, who were present in court, ready to identify them for the crown's evidence. The first informant was named John Ingleby who lived in Valladolid from January 1596 to July 1598 without becoming a priest.[65] During this trial Henry Garnet reported to Rome that "Ingleby . . . proveth a spy as it is feared to be too true he hath betrayed and now seeketh to undermine Fil-

---

[63] *C.S.P. Dom. 1591–94*, p. 255.

[64] John Cecil also became a chaplain to Allen for a short time. Fixer, however, was appointed a chaplain at the priest's residence in Lisbon where he remained until he came under Spanish suspicion again. An agent of Essex related that in September 1594 he was "recalled from Lisbon" as a man who was "too great a friend to his countrymen" (Birch, *Memoirs*, vol. i, p. 127). He was rusticated to the diocese of Siguenza for several years, and was forgotten until the Appellant clergy in Rome asked for a trial for a "captive" named John Fisher [*sic*] who "dare not go out of the limits of Castile, who now for seven years with great patience has endured the heavy yoke." Since Fixer did not enter their faction, they spread a report that he was dead. (W. Clarke, *A Replie Unto a certaine libell* . . . [1603], p. 70 and T. G. Law, *Archpriest Controversy*, Camden Society, 1898, vol. ii, pp. 190–91). In 1607 Sir Charles Cornwallis saw Fixer in Madrid and noted that he was still corresponding with John Cecil (Winwood, *Memorials*, vol. ii, p. 337).

[65] *C.R.S.*, vol. xxx, pp. 35–36.

cock and Barkworth."[66] But Ingleby's evidence was supported by two others: Stephen Parrot and Thomas Singleton, who also had left the college without becoming priests.[67] On his return to England Parrot became a gaoler at Bridewell where he had Father Barkworth as his prisoner. The young priest protested to Sir Robert Cecil at the exorbitant charges exacted by Parrot for "the liberty" of the prison.[68]

The dramatic scene of the trial on February 23, 1601 was summarized very simply in Henry Garnet's report: "Barkworth declined to leave his cause to the jury. He said that he knew that Parrot, Ingleby and Singleton were ready to give evidence that he was a priest and so he wished the whole guilt of his death should rest upon the judge."[69] It was of no avail, as both Barkworth and Filcock were sentenced to death. Parrot and the others continued to act as informants and their notorious profession was shared by the renegade priest William Atkinson and a William Wilson who had also studied in Spain.[70]

Such was the world of espionage as understood by Hugh Owen and the English exiles. Military information, news of politics, dangers to individuals, all became the object of his secret appraisal and investigation. What was Hugh Owen's

[66] Stonyhurst MS collectanea P f. 552, letter of 16 Aug. 1600.

[67] Parrot had also played the spy in Rome, Douai, and the Benedictine monastery of San Martin at Compostella. There he was discovered to be intercepting the correspondence of the monks, and before his expulsion he had the effrontery to offer to "send them novices from Douai who would enter religion" (Letter of Creswell to the General of the Benedictines, E 1857/419, 20 Oct. 1603).

[68] C.S.P. Dom. 1598–1601, pp. 140–41 (letter misdated by the editor).

[69] A.R.S.J. Anglia, 31(1) ff. 172–183, letter of 17 March 1601.

[70] C.R.S., vol. xxx, p. 20, 15; J. Foley, Records of the English Province, vol. vi, p. 160, vol. i, pp. 505ff.

AN "INTELLIGENCER" : Hugh Owen

role within this vital problem of security? There is no room here to examine his *avisos* in detail. It would be more suit-able to estimate the quality of his work by analyzing some of his activities in detecting a famous conspiracy.

In the spring of 1598, as France and Spain were negotiat-ing for the peace that would be concluded at Vervins, many of the principal advisers of the Archduke in Brussels felt that a similar accord might be attempted with the Estates General of Holland. Friendship with England was also considered possible. Three wealthy and influential Walloon nobles, Jean Richardot, the President of the Council of State, Charles-Philippe de Croy, the Marquis of Havré, and his nephew Charles de Croy, Prince of Chimay and Duke of Aerschot, began informal discussions with the leaders of the Estates to that end.[71] The house of Croy shared the typical Burgundian sentiments of the Walloon aristocracy which favored a re-newal of their ancient bonds with England. These overtures were not a well-kept secret; even the Venetian ambassador learned of them at the Court in Madrid. Late in July 1598 he reported that Havré was optimistic that the Estates would "lend an ear to the terms of an accord," although they were without sufficient support from England. Thus everything would remain uncertain until it was known "what course the Queen of England will adopt." [72] As the Estates hesitated, the temporary Governor of the Low Countries, Cardinal Andrew, sent a member of his Council of State, Andrew Coemans, to England late in December 1598 to sound out and even encourage English sentiments to a peace in the Low Countries.

The Queen was interested but noncommittal, and after a month Coemans returned to Brussels to receive further in-

[71] P. Geyl, *Revolt in the Netherlands*, pp. 240–41.
[72] *C.S.P. Venetian*, vol. ix, pp. 332–33; J. B. Black, *The Reign of Elizabeth* (2nd ed.), p. 343.

] 77 [

structions. In March 1599 Coemans came back to England while in the meantime the Estates General had announced their rejection of the "accord" offered by Havré. On this second visit Coemans was accompanied by a Carlo Lanfranchi,[73] an Italian informer who occasionally corresponded with Sir Robert Cecil from Antwerp, offering news and doing minor services.[74]

Unknown to Coemans, Lanfranchi carried special letters to the English Court purporting to be on behalf of the nobility of Flanders and Brabant. They offered a general pacification in the Low Countries by a league of the Walloon nobles, the Dutch Estates and England, towards reuniting the provinces and excluding Spain. Hardly had the letters been delivered at the English Court when they were summarized and reported to Hugh Owen.[75] Havré and his nephew, Aerschot, were mentioned, but Owen reported to Spain that Cardinal Andrew was still unaware of the intrigue. At frequent intervals his *avisos* on English affairs gave new details of the secret discussions. In April Owen learned that the Walloon nobles were demanding that Queen Elizabeth should guarantee their security without having any authority over them, and moreover, they wished the speedy reunion of all the provinces of the Low Countries "without any further quarrels over religion." In his report Owen noted a "double treachery" was involved. One against Cardinal Andrew, "under whose shadow they play this comedy" and the other against the Spanish control of the Low Countries. He warned that a conference on peace between Spain and England could become a "trick" to deceive King Philip into a false security.[76]

[73] T. Birch, *An Historical View*, p. 191.
[74] *H.M.C. Salisbury MSS*, vol. ix, pp. 83, 159; vol. xi, p. 142.
[75] E 616/160 despatch of 27 March 1599.
[76] *Ibid.*, despatch of 2 April 1599.

While in England Lanfranchi revealed that the nobles were also negotiating with some "Princes of the Empire" who would join a league "without any question of religion." The gesture was optimistic since the Germans were reported to be outraged by the recent Spanish atrocities in the Duchy of Cleves.[77] A week later the visit of Coemans ended and, according to Owen's informants, the secret envoys left England in his party. Two weeks passed before Lanfranchi finally wrote from Antwerp to Cecil offering an excuse why there had been no further word from the others. He pleaded guardedly that there was much traveling to do: "Those to whom he must refer the matter are some way off from this place." Later he was still giving vague assurances that "the friends are where one cannot go and return as one would," but that Coemans would come to England soon "and finish off the matter."[78] To keep a personal control of the development of the crisis Owen moved to Antwerp, from where he informed Don Martin de Idiaquez at the Spanish Court that he was sending all news concerning England directly and in a new cipher.[79]

By May 23rd, Hugh Owen had returned to Brussels. He was satisfied apparently that he could report that there had not been a return messenger from the "discontented nobles," he reported a growing belief at the English Court that it had all been a snare.[80] At the end of the month he composed a brief history of the original conspiracy. He related that the intrigue had been first broached to Sir Robert Cecil through one of his agents in the Low Countries. This would explain the presence in London of Carlo Lanfranchi. Owen's informants told him that the Queen had never been enthusiastic

[77] *Ibid.*, despatch of 8 April 1599.
[78] *H.M.C. Salisbury MSS*, vol. ix, pp. 138, 148.
[79] E 616/163.
[80] E 616/157.

about the plan since there were too many vague details, and the attitude of France had never been carefully sounded. She had consulted Buckhurst and Effingham and they were also sceptical of the solid basis of the intrigue.[81] It may also be noted that Noel Caron, the envoy of the Estates in England, had recently informed Cecil that the German princes had become cool to the idea of sending an army to help the Dutch provinces.[82] Shortly after, Owen learned that a certain embarrassment in Cecil was observed over the "lack of substance" in the conspiracy, for the current explanation was that Havré and Aerschot had only meant to offer a league to restore a general peace.[83]

The coup of Hugh Owen in penetrating the intrigue so rapidly should not be underestimated, even if Queen Elizabeth's reservations about the usefulness of the intrigue had doomed it from the start. His unmasking of the activities of nobles still prominent at the Court in Brussels was of great importance to the Archduke Albert. It was to reward such a performance as this, that the Archduke was to write personally to King Philip asking that Owen's "great and special services in the affairs of England" be honored.[84] The Spanish Council of State voted a supplementary pension of 500 escudos a year for life to the loyal Welshman.[85]

Three years later the Archduke wrote again in praise of Hugh Owen, this time citing the testmony of the Constable of Castile, who had just returned from England and the signing of a peace in London in the preceding August. He noted that the special pension of Owen had been attached to the Spanish taxes in Sicily and it was difficult to collect as his

[81] E 616/171 despatch of 26 May 1599.
[82] *H.M.C. Salisbury MSS*, vol. ix, pp. 169–70.
[83] E 616/173, avisos of 6 June 1599.
[84] E 2288 n.f. letter of 13 Jan. 1601.
[85] E 187 n.f. Orders to the Constable of Castile, 28 May 1601.

"advancing years"—Owen was sixty-six—had prevented him from going to Spain to have the affair arranged properly. The archduke asked that the revenues of some place nearer Brussels be tapped for the pension.[86] The eagerness of the Archduke to praise the Welshman's services was understandable. Owen was loyal, and he had been flatteringly partisan in the unwanted candidacy of Albert's wife, the Infanta Isabella, for the throne of England.[87]

Although the Archduke had never encouraged the candidacy of Isabella, and the idea had been virtually abandoned in 1602, Owen's prominent role in the affair had prompted Villeroy, the secretary of Henry IV of France, to approach Robert Owen, the canon at Le Mans, to ask him to probe the substance of Spain's intention in this matter. Villeroy sent Robert Owen to Brussels to interview his brother. As Robert revealed the mission in a secret despatch prepared by his brother, Villeroy had given instructions in these words:

We are informed that you have a brother in Flanders who is a man of affairs and in control of the disbursements for all the intelligence about England. He will be more versed in these matters than you, and so the king desires you to go to Flanders to take up the subject with him. Find out as much as you can concerning the succession and in particular you must return with information as to whether the Catholics will receive the Scot if they are assured of their religion.[88]

Robert's visit to Brussels was only a part of the complex diplomatic intrigues of the autumn of 1602 in which France, Spain and the Low Countries tried to appraise the other's intentions. Hugh Owen had remained suspicious of any French concern in the matter, even if the respect of Henry IV for his own views was a subtle flattery. Nor did Owen's

[86] E 623/72 letter of 27 Dec. 1604.
[87] E 2288 n.f. memorandum of 3 May 1598.
[88] E 620 n.f. endorsed "Relacion que hizo un canoniga de Mans en Francia, hermano de Ugo Oen."

personal dislike for King James alter after hearing of Henry's suggestion that James might offer the Catholics more freedom.

The peaceful accession of King James to the throne did not at first change Hugh Owen's commission to arrange reports of events in England. He took special care to advise the new envoy of Spain to the English Court, Juan de Tassis, on the condition of the English Catholic affairs. In this matter Philip III was most anxious to gain a mitigation of the recusancy laws before a treaty with England was concluded.[89] Hugh Owen had only a minority of support at the Court of Brussels for the notion that the Archduke should energetically assist Spain in its desire to improve the lot of the English Catholics. Jean Richardot had coolly informed Juan de Tassis when he visited Brussels that "the matter of religion was completely unnegotiable and without any hope of success, even if there are negotiations."[90] The decision of the Archduke to leave the whole matter to Spain showed his greater concern over a possible English withdrawal from the Dutch alliance.

Owen had never believed in King James' secret protestations of tolerance. Six months after the reign began Hugh wrote to his brother at Le Mans: "I perceave there is no hope at all of amendment in this stinking king of ours. An ill quarter to look for righteousness: at the hands of a miserable Scot." He saw, in another note, no reason for optimism in James' enmity for the Puritans for he suspected that it was only "to get opinion amongste us and Catholicks generally, and bring us asleepe."[91] Owen's cynical suspicions of James were typical of many of the exiles' disappointment with the turn of events.

[89] E 840/118 despatch of Tassis, 4 July 1603.
[90] E 840/109.
[91] *Bulletin of Celtic Studies*, vol. viii (1937), pp. 357–58, note 3.

It was only after the treaty of peace between England and Spain and the Low Countries had been concluded in August 1604 that the need of Owen's reports on England began to decrease. There was only one negotiation on which his advice still figured as important in Brussels. For the Archduke still hoped to buy from the impecunious James the cautionary towns in the territory of the Estates General. The negotiation failed but it was under lengthy discussion for several weeks in London in February and March 1605. While the Baron de Hoboken and the Count of Villa Mediana probed the issue in London, Owen advised the Archduke on the method of approaching the English Court. When Villa Mediana wrote to Philip, he expressed his alarm over the English attitude to Owen's role with the sentence: "The name of Hugh is more hateful here than that of the devil." [92] At once King Philip commented: "If the scandal of Owen's activity close to the Archduke is so great . . . it will be better to have him stay in another place where he can do the same service by maintaining his intelligences." [93]

The complaints of the English Court were only the beginning of Owen's troubles, within six months he was to be in danger of his life. In November 1605 the Court at Brussels rang with the denunciations of Owen by King James and the Earl of Salisbury. Their charges were apparently based on the confessions of Guy Fawkes and the surviving Gunpowder Plot conspirators. [94] By order of a court official in Brussels Owen was immediately imprisoned while Sir William Stanley and Father William Baldwin were also arrested for com-

[92] E 2584/17 letter of 17 March 1605.
[93] E 2225 n.f. letter of 7 May 1605.
[94] Jardine, *Criminal Trials*, vol. ii, pp. 138–40, 273–74; J. Gerard, *What was the Gunpowder Plot?* (London, 1897), pp. 173–74, 185–95, unravels the inconsistencies of the evidence against Owen; S. R. Gardiner, *What the Gunpowder Plot Was* (London, 1897), did not discuss it.

plicity. However, after a month it became clear that the charges against them would not be pressed by James at that time and they were released. They were not included in the Parliamentary act of attainder as Hugh Owen was eventually to be.

In Owen's case, however, it was evident from the beginning that King James, out of deference for Owen's friendship for the Archduke, would deny that Albert had any knowledge of "the horrible conspiracy." Owen was involved "directly of himself." Yet the King would not offer any form of documentary proof to either the Baron de Hoboken in London, or to Sir Thomas Edmondes his envoy at Brussels. There were only assurances that proof would soon be forthcoming.[95]

Owen was quite energetic in taking steps for his own defense. To his consternation all of his correspondence had been seized, and there was an immediate danger that his whole network would be exposed. In a personal letter to the Duke of Lerma, Owen begged that his friends, the Constable of Castile, Don Juan de Idiaquez, Don Andres de Prada and Esteban de Ybarra, all of whom had been receiving his reports for years, should be informed of his personal danger. He quietly reminded the duke that his present predicament came "solely from my services to Spain. "[96] He had appraised the Spanish Council well, for these were powerful personages indeed. Their strong reaction to his letter was to be the principal excuse for the Archduke's tenacious protection of Owen as a crisis over his extradition rapidly developed.

Owen did not merely plead for help to Lerma, he enclosed a memorandum of his defense which he intended to be

[95] H.M.C. Salisbury MSS, vol. xvii, pp. 497, 508–09, 533–37, 646.
[96] E 624 n.f. letter of December 14, 1605.

] 84 [

immediately circulated in the Spanish Council of State. It was in fact the most complete survey of his career that he ever allowed to be made.

He began by noting that his arrest was unlawful since no one had first placed charges against him nor had there even been an interrogation. He asked why a devoted servant of Spain should be given a treatment reserved for known public thieves and traitors. His greatest anxiety, he explained, was over his papers which covered his service during close to twenty-five years.

There are the reports and plans for the reform of England, and the activities on behalf of the rights of the Most Serene Infanta. There are some letters, over the names of various English lords and many leading personages, which undertake by pledges of their persons and fortunes to assist his Majesty and his Highness whenever an opportunity came. Furthermore there are the original *avisos* for many years past and the ciphers by which they can be read with the names of the correspondents as well as the manner used to forward their letters during the war and after. Among the above mentioned *avisos* are the ones which reveal a certain recent uprising which the late Queen tried to foster in these provinces when his Highness had left for his wedding in Spain. In them various great personages of these provinces are named as having intrigued in company with the Queen.[97]

An incredible file to fall into the hands of anyone outside of the Archduke's confidence and clearly it would have been of paramount interest to the Earl of Salisbury. Owen warned that if anyone hostile should see the file, "it will do great injury to his Majesty and be a betrayal of many English Catholics who are his devoted followers."

He then turned to the charges of the Gunpowder Conspiracy with short blunt phrases:

[97] *Ibid.,* enclosure, "Tocante la prision de Ugo Oen."

In the above papers not a word will be found which touches the said conspiracy, for I take my oath that no human being ever wrote to me about it, nor did I write to anyone about it, nor did any other person do so by my order.

He recalled that the animosity of the English Court to him was not a new thing. "They acted the same way in the days of the late Queen, with a thousand false tales of my sending people to kill her, although I never dealt with such people nor have I ever known them." He then appealed for the protection of his private secretary, Richard Bayley who had worked with him since 1596.[98] Owen reported that Bayley had gone to England on a perilous mission during the reign of Elizabeth at the Archduke's request "to discuss with various people secret matters of great importance." Owen revealed nothing more. This simple but dramatic report of his career ended only with a request that "those who consider themselves hurt by my profession should not be both my accusers and my judges."

Because of the slow communications with Spain in the winter, the Council of State was not alert to Owen's predicament until after the first week of January. In Brussels in the meanwhile Edmondes, King James' envoy, had, not unexpectedly, demanded Owen's file of correspondence. The Archduke refused with the remark that they could not be seen "without prejudice to others," but he suavely promised that "should anything be found in them concerning the late practice he would faithfully impart the same."[99] In London

---

[98] In one spy's report Bayley is listed as receiving 30 escudos a month in 1593 (Lambeth Palace MS, vol. 649, f. 41). His certificate of residence in Brussels of August 6, 1597 said he was 43 years old and residing there 8 months (A.G.R., P.E.A. 1398/7). In 1605 Salisbury urged his arrest, although he admitted "hitherto we have not heard his name mentioned." *H.M.C. Salisbury MSS*, vol. xvii, p. 536.

[99] *H.M.C. Salisbury MSS*, vol. xvii, p. 557.

the envoys of Brussels and Spain, Hoboken and Pedro de Zúñiga, were getting the full brunt of the royal fury against Owen. In some amazement Hoboken reported "the Council is obsessed with obtaining Owen," and then, after subsequent interviews with Salisbury, he made the curious conclusion that Owen, whom he described as "so dear to us," was the victim of a special hatred by the two Howards, Northampton and Effingham.[100] Zúñiga was very poised in the midst of the furor. He first mollified King James by giving solemn assurances that the case was being thoroughly investigated. When the council warned him that Owen's delivery to English hands as a prisoner would "surely improve the peace," he observed coolly that England had never troubled to hand over rebels requested by Spain in the past.[101]

In Spain there was by mid-January an unaccustomed urgency over the tensions provoked by Owen's arrest. Prada wrote to the Duke of Lerma that the retention of Owen's papers in Spanish hands was mandatory, for he had learned that they were at present in the custody of Louis Vereyken, the Audiencier of the Brussels Court, whom he sarcastically dismissed as "a Flemish lackey, a creature of Richardot."[102]

On January 16, 1606 the Council of State convened to discuss Hugh Owen. Juan de Idiaquez spoke first and he used such incisive words that Philip III merely repeated them almost *verbatim* in an executive order issued shortly after. Idiaquez asserted that he was so convinced of the importance

---

[100] A.G.R., P.E.A., liv.365, f. 70, 73, letters of 22 Dec. 1605; and 12 Jan. 1606.

[101] E 2585/2 y3, letter of 17 Jan. 1606. He also noted a disappointment among the Councilors that there was not enough evidence against the Earl of Northumberland because of the death of his cousin, Thomas Percy. He suggested that Thomas Percy had been the chief plotter, for he believed Percy to be a "heretic," anti-Spanish and too friendly with the French.

[102] E 624 n.f. letter of 5 Jan. 1606.

of Owen's position that he wanted a "flying courier" to be sent to take charge of his files. He was adamant on the point of Owen's delivery to the English for as a prisoner he would be tortured into compromising the trust of "those who have pledged their lives and fortunes." He was cynical at the thought of improving the relations with England by handing him over, for he feared there would be so much trouble that the peace would be endangered.

The Constable of Castile agreed and then turned to the legality of the extradition by noting that the wording of the treaty required that after indictment each king's subjects should be tried by the laws of the country where he resided. Therefore, he argued, if the matter ever came to a trial Owen had to be tried in Brussels.[103] The Count of Olivares, the Count of Chinchon and the Duke of Infantado each insisted vigorously that Owen and his papers must be kept in the hands of the Archduke.[104] King Philip agreed and issued orders that Don Juan de Mançiçidor, the secretary of Spanish affairs in the Archduke's Council of State, should take Hugh Owen and his papers into his own custody. He was long known to the English as a close friend of the Welshman,[105] and his protection at this time was vital to Owen's security.

Meanwhile the English envoy in Spain, Sir Charles Cornwallis, was trying feebly to divert Philip's resolution by reminding him that it was the duty of kings "to punish the wicked." This was brushed aside by a curt denial of any wrongdoing on Owen's part. As time passed with both sides unyielding in their positions, Salisbury reported to Cornwallis

[103] See also *H.M.C. Salisbury MSS*, vol. xvii, p. 508, for the Archduke's opinion as expressed to Edmondes.

[104] E 2024/25 consulta 16 Jan. 1606.

[105] *H.M.C. Salisbury MSS*, vol. xvii, p. 497; Winwood, *Memorials*, vol. ii, p. 190.

that King James was growing less interested in Owen's papers "which he persuaded himself had been well visited before this." [106]

In effect the stalemate was resolved by Owen's trial *in absentia* in England while the Hapsburgs never wavered from their determination to protect him. His name was to figure darkly in the coming trials in London early in the spring of 1606 where Sir Edward Coke followed Salisbury's instructions: "You must remember to lay Owen as foul in this as you can." [107] However, no satisfactory evidence was produced which invalidated Owen's oath asserting his ignorance of the conspiracy.

As the weeks passed it became evident that the only decision left to the Archduke was the timing of Owen's release from the mild house arrest in which Mançiçidor had placed him. In an unusually cold letter King Philip reminded the Archduke Albert that the arrest of Owen had been "inconvenient" in the first place and had surely not been well considered before hand.[108] However, since the damage had been done he advised that any evidence available should be presented in a trial in Flanders and thus King James could be satisfied.[109]

Although King James had the opportunity, he steadfastly refused to send over any new evidence against Owen. Finally the Archduke decided to release the Welshman from all official restraints. Edmondes noted rather gloomily to Cornwallis that the sufferings of the former prisoners "serveth only to make them more recommendable, for their opinions

[106] B.M., Harleian 1875, f. 322–324ᵛ; Winwood, *Memorials*, vol. ii, p. 191.

[107] P.R.O., S.P. 14/19/94, letter of 27 Jan. 1606.

[108] Edmondes admitted that were it not for his "sudden surprising of the Archduke" Owen would not have been arrested. (*H.M.C. Salisbury MSS*, vol. xvii, p. 546).

[109] E 2226/179 letter of 19 Feb. 1606.

sway as effectuative as ever they did touching our nation here." [110]

The following summer Hugh Owen decided to leave Brussels and travel to Madrid. He was 68 years old and he had not seen his friends on the Council of State for sixteen years. Undoubtedly the alarm caused by the seizure of his papers and ciphers—which he never mentioned again—had damaged his network considerably. It was evident that both Philip and the Archduke would have to rely heavily on their resident ambassadors for information about England. Hugh Owen's arrival at the Spanish Court in September 1606 was a singularly quiet event. Even Sir Charles Cornwallis imagined that the famous Welshman was afraid to go out of doors out of chagrin over what was supposedly "the cold countenance" of the Court. However, after two months had passed he had changed his mind and discovered Owen was still in "theyr secret favour." [111] It is difficult to learn what Owen had discussed with his friends at Court after his visit ended in March 1607. It is certain that Owen was granted another increase in his pension which was now at the high rate of 80 escudos a month where it was to remain even after his retirement. [112] The principal point under discussion at this time at the Spanish Court was the first stage of negotiations with the Dutch provinces for a truce. It is probable that as a confidant of the Archduke he was asked to give his views, but this can hardly be considered a decisive voice. The fact was that there was less need for his professional services than before.

Owen was still the object of the vengeance of the Earl of Salisbury. In August 1608 Thomas Wylfourd, to the scandal of the Court at Brussels, admitted attempting to kidnap

[110] B.M., Harleian 1875 f. 510 letter of 22 June 1606.
[111] Winwood, *Memorials*, vol. ii, pp. 259, 269.
[112] E 626/89 pension survey of 1609.

the seventy-year old Welshman to bring him to England on
the orders of the Earl of Salisbury. The foolhardy plan had
been discovered by Owen himself in intercepted despatches
to England. However, the Court was soon believing that
Wylfourd had been intending to murder Owen. In England
Salisbury denied heatedly any murderous intentions, although he admitted freely that he knew Wylfourd and had
talked about his "liking that by some stratagem, he [Owen]
might have been stolen into a ship and brought to England." [113] The plan was reminiscent of the fate of Dr. Storey.

Sir William Stanley, who was in Madrid when the incident occurred, at once brought it to the attention of the Council of State. Again a special meeting was held to discuss the
safety of Hugh Owen. [114] Spain was not anxious to create a
furor over the affair since it was wooing English favor for
the truce negotiations with the Dutch which had been pros-
pering for eight months. However Philip III felt obliged to
write to the Archduke that he should at least investigate Wylfourd thoroughly and punish the guilty. [115]

Even if the Wylfourd plot had been foiled it had high-
lighted a problem which the Archduke was reluctant to face.
If the long sought truce was to succeed the Court at Brussels
could not remain a shelter for those whom the English ambassador still obstinately called "the powder men." At this
very time King James was hinting broadly to the Archduke's
new envoy in London, Louis de Groote, that he would be
pleased if Owen would be removed from "the face and protection" of his master. [116]

The tide of events was too strong for the retention of the
services of one individual, but a satisfactory plan was hit upon.

[113] T. Birch, *An Historical View* . . . pp. 291–92.
[114] E 2025/145, consulta 18 Sept. 1608.
[115] E 2226/154 letter of 1 Nov. 1608.
[116] T. Birch, *An Historical View*, p. 305.

Spain offered to move Owen to the staff of its embassy in Rome, where even his supplementary pension of 500 escudos from Sicily was to be guaranteed *"por via de gastos secretos."* The Archduke eagerly agreed to this solution and replied to Philip that it was the most suitable idea considering the animosity of King James.[117] Shortly after this, Owen left Flanders for good to travel by a safe route to Rome where he was determined to live quietly in retirement. He had many friends there including Father Thomas Fitzherbert, and even for a short time Father Robert Persons. It was probably the most pleasant period of his life, living in honored retirement and security amid the baroque elegance of the Spanish embassy. He was to die there in 1618 at the age of eighty.

Hugh Owen's position among the Catholic exiles was surely unique. That he should eventually be pursued so implacably after the peace with Spain was concluded was understandable. A brilliant, gifted man whose various despatches show him at home in Latin, Spanish, Italian, English, Welsh and French, he took upon himself the incredible task of organizing and bringing to a high rate of effectiveness the network of correspondents who strove to protect both Spanish and Catholic interests. His anonymous friends in England, who related to him countless small details and items of news, were successfully protected in turn by their leader in Brussels. From the attitude of the Duke of Parma, the Archduke Albert and the elder members of the Spanish Council of State he evidently performed many services whose real importance at that time they alone fully appreciated. They risked a diplomatic crisis from 1605 to 1609 to protect him. The Hapsburg attitude to Owen's achievement was echoed by the exiles as well. For to him they entrusted the task of penetrating the disguises and intrigues of those who menaced them; not the least of Owen's talents was that he never underestimated

[117] E 626/89.

the skill of the Earl of Salisbury and others who countered his objectives. In the cold war of the sixteenth century Owen emerged as a man to whom desperate exiles looked to make their residence in Hapsburg territories the safe haven it was meant to be.

CHAPTER FOUR

"A Leader" : *Lady Jane Dormer*

1538–1612

"Who shall find a valiant woman? . . .
She is like the marchant's ship
She bringeth her bread from afar . . .
She hath put out her hand to strong things
And her fingers have taken hold of the spindle . . ."

The Douai version of *The Book of Proverbs*
Chapter XXXI, vv. 10, 14, 19

THE EARLY Tudor monarchs were proud of their achievement in stifling the frequent feuds and political intrigues that
had formerly centered in the English aristocracy. They appreciated, however, that any successful resistance to their increasing demands for absolute obedience would still involve
those who by tradition had always borne the sword. In a
despatch of the Venetian envoy at the Court of Henry VIII
there appears an illustrative anecdote. When an Italian visitor
asked an English acquaintance whether any of his family had
suffered death for treason and was told "No," another Eng-

lishman took the Italian aside to whisper: "Do not be sur-prised, he is not a gentleman."[1]

Since many aristocratic customs and attitudes from the old regime lingered throughout the century, the Spanish Eliza-bethans were not immune from this disruptive pattern. On the contrary, the English nobility's capacity for intrigue, as well as the vigorous ambitions of some of the Catholic landed gentry were not abandoned when they crossed to the conti-nent. *Coelum non animam mutant.* At various times, for ex-ample, an Earl of Westmorland, the wife of Northumber-land, a Lord Dacres, Lord Paget, a Lord Morley mingled with the exiles. Each of them was far more preoccupied with politics than with recusancy. They were usually well pen-sioned by Spain,[2] yet they remained impatient to recoup their fortunes in England. They needed and ambitioned to acquire a large clientèle among the *émigrés*. The position of an ac-knowledged leader or spokesman would go far to satisfying losses in prestige, lands and influence. Did they exercise a leadership to which their social and political advantages en-titled them? It is important to probe the reasons why they failed to rally any noticeable influence among their com-patriots abroad.

There were, of course, particular reasons in individual cases. For one thing, the conservative "Louvainists" under Englefield's leadership, had little sympathy with those who after 1569 were preoccupied with personal ambitions. For another, the pattern of the Spanish pension system and its army's deployment dominated the lives of a large number of exiles by setting them under the direction of the Governor

[1] H. F. M. Prescott, *Mary Tudor*, p. 19.
[2] Westmorland for several years received 200 escudos a month; Northumberland received 2,000 florins a year from the Governor of the Low Countries in 1573; Dacres was given 100 escudos a month; Paget 70 escudos a month, Morley was listed as receiving 800 florins a year in 1573.

of the Low Countries. Yet this did not remove the fond ambition to rally the exiles under the banner of some prominent
English personage, who would not be a figurehead but rather
their spokesman and the arbiter of their dissensions.

In the dossier of Jane Dormer, the Duchess of Feria, the
proper qualifications for this role of "A Leader" were plenti-
ful. She had been a close friend of Sir Francis Englefield,
and her grandmother, the dowager Lady Dormer had lived
among the "Louvainists" for ten years prior to her death in
1570. She possessed relatives and influential friends among
the powerful at the Courts of both Queen Elizabeth and
King Philip and yet her name was never clearly linked with
conspiracy. In the history of her failure to acquire leadership
among the exiles, a peculiar problem of their age can be explored.

Jane Dormer was born in January 1538 in Heythrop,
Oxfordshire, to a wealthy landed family which was related
to the Sydneys and the Howards. Her maternal grandfather,
Sir William Sydney, a courtier of cultivated taste, was se-
lected by Henry VIII as one of the tutors of Prince Edward.
As a child Jane played and danced with the young boy who,
as she recalled later, liked to greet her with a happy "My
Jane." A few years later Jane had entered the household of
Princess Mary and she was to remain her devoted companion
until as a luckless Queen she died in November 1558.
Shortly after this Lady Jane married Don Gomez Suarez de
Figueroa de Cordoba, the Count of Feria, who had been
Philip's envoy since the King's departure from England in
July 1557.

The first months of the reign of Elizabeth made clear to
Jane the new strain on her accustomed loyalties. Her husband, in company with the large majority of the Marian
episcopate, had pointedly absented himself from the young
Queen's coronation. It was a harsh gesture that was hardly

likely to enhance the success of Feria's prime diplomatic objective, the renewal of the Hapsburg alliance. Apparently Henry II of France estimated the possibility of Feria succeeding far higher than did Elizabeth, for he insisted that Feria be made one of the diplomatic hostages—along with the Flemish nobles Egmont and Horn—for the treaty of Cateau Cambresis.[3] It was the unnecessary suspicions of France, and not his own intransigence, that prompted the removal of one of Philip's most trusted favorites from the English Court. Ironically, Feria never had much chance of securing his alliance; Henry II's insistence had let the Spaniard retreat with honor.

In May 1559 the Count of Feria left England while Lady Jane Dormer remained for two months longer making arrangements for the exodus of her large household. Her relations with the new queen had been far more cordial than her husband's, aside from some shortlived suspicions over the inventory of the crown jewels which had been entrusted to her for safe keeping by the dying Queen Mary.[4] On July 30, 1559, the young Countess left England for good, but she left many friends at Court. Her husband's name would excite the rancor that follows the hostile critic, a fact which would be recalled for the next two decades.

In Malines in September Jane's son, Don Lorenzo was born. In the following months the Count of Feria was one of the most prominent members of the dwindling Spanish faction at the Court of Marguerite of Parma, the regent of the Low Countries. Since Ruy Gomez and the Duke of Alba had already left for Spain with King Philip, Feria's opinion assumed a greater authority in Brussels. Queen Elizabeth

---

[3] A. Teulet, *Papiers d'État* (Paris, 1852–60), vol. i, p. 475, 508, 114; vol. ii, p. 54.
[4] *C.S.P. Dom. 1547–80*, pp. 146, 147; *C.S.P. For. 1583, Add.* p. 438.

soon detected a new coolness in the leadership in the Low
Countries and warned Bishop Alvaro de Quadra, the new
Spanish envoy, of her displeasure at remarks she ascribed to
Jane Dormer. The Count hastily explained to Quadra that
whatever statements were current in Brussels came from him.
He assured the English Court that his wife had been "really
most reticent, and has never said a word." [5]

In March of 1560 the Feria household left Malines to
begin a slow and expensively ostentatious journey through
France to Spain. The Count's ascendancy in the confidence
of Marguerite is striking in two of her later letters to King
Philip wherein she begged the king to give special weight
to the advice on England of his former envoy. [6] However,
when they reached the Spanish Court at Toledo, although
Philip gave them a splendid reception, he refused to adopt
Feria's critical and suspicious attitude of Elizabeth. Even
a year later, although he was celebrating with great so-
lemnity the feast of St. George, and reserving a place of
honor for the Count of Feria, [7] Philip was still protecting
Elizabeth from reprisals after she refused to receive a papal
envoy.

In the two years since his departure from England Feria's
name had become identified with the hard line against the
Queen. It was only natural that the English Court reacted
with a suspicious curiosity about any of the Count's activities.
For example, shortly after Lady Jane had arrived in Spain
and set up her household at Zafra in Estremadura, George
Chamberlain attempted to write to her. Although his family
had had estates in Oxfordshire where Jane Dormer had lived

[5] C.S.P. Spanish 1558–67, p. 117.
[6] L. P. Gachard, Correspondance de Marguerite de Parme,
vol. i, pp. 50, 151.
[7] C.S.P. For. 1561–62, p. 117.

as a child, still he was closely questioned over his reasons for writing.[8] Nothing came of it at that time, but Chamberlain was eventually to leave England permanently in December 1571 and travel to Spain where he received a large grant of 300 ducats and a pension in the Low Countries.[9] Similarly in May 1562, when Lady Margaret Douglass, the Countess of Lennox and a possible pretender to the throne through her mother, Margaret Tudor, was suspected of rallying supporters in England, one of the strongest charges against her was a secret correspondence with Feria.[10] Inevitably reports of this mounting official hostility reached Spain and Sir Thomas Challoner, the English ambassador, attempted to moderate the Queen's anger by sending a letter in praise of the Count and Countess of Feria in which he pleaded that they "both show great frankness with the English." [11] There was obviously a pleasant relationship between the English colony and the Feria household during these early years of the reign of Elizabeth. English merchants were sending the Countess occasional gifts: "two barrels of herring," "an English cheese," and even "raisins of Corinth." [12] When Elizabeth was seriously ill with the smallpox late in 1562 Challoner again made a special point of informing the queen that Jane Dormer was "most joyful" at her recovery. Clearly the English envoy found the Feria hospitality very congenial, for, when he could not visit their Zafra estate as often as he wished because of the critical situation in France in March 1563, he made his excuses gracefully to the Countess with the remark: "Your honor may esteem that both of you are my

8 *C.S.P. Dom. 1547–80*, p. 163.
9 B.M., Lansdowne 18, f. 174–75; Lechat, *Les Refugiés*, p. 233.
10 *C.S.P. For. 1562*, p. 12.
11 *Ibid.*, p. 201.
12 *C.S.P. For. 1561–62*, pp. 337, 568, 615, 633.

avowed Spanish saints whom I will in my stations, make my first devotions unto." [13]

Despite the happy exchanges of the Feria household with those who knew them personally, the early years of Jane Dormer's residence in Spain continued to be overshadowed by hostile rumors in England. Yet Philip's favor was secure. In October 1567 the house of Feria was raised to the rank of a dukedom as mark of his king's gratitude. In the following spring when the first serious crisis in Anglo-Spanish relations erupted with the troubles over the Sea Beggars, and the mounting piracy in the Indies the English accusations against the Count were equally grave. Queen Elizabeth, ever mindful of Feria's criticisms in 1560, was convinced that Philip's policy was being guided solely by the Duke's opinion. In May 1568 in a bitter tirade to the Spanish envoy in England, Guerau Despes, she singled Feria out for biting sarcasm. She announced that she would never believe he had been kind to any of her subjects in Spain and declared that anything creditable to their name "was owing to the Duchess." [14] Things only went from bad to worse in the furor aroused by the expulsion of John Man, the last resident envoy of Elizabeth to Spain. He had been an unsuitable choice as ambassador to any country and in the tensions of that year he earned enemies rapidly. Although he was denounced by the Inquisition for proselytising, it was not unexpected that when he reached England he charged his disgrace was due entirely to the animosity of the relatives of the Duchess of Feria. King Philip in some exasperation ordered Despes to explain in London that they had nothing to do with the case. [15]

Meanwhile, the Duke was accused afresh by no less a per-

[13] *C.S.P. For. 1562*, pp. 89, 236.
[14] *C.S.P. Spanish, 1568–79*, p. 35.
[15] *Ibid.*, pp. 46, 67, 105.

56068

son than Sir John Hawkins who implicated him in his plot of
revenge on Spain for his losses sustained during his famous
third voyage to the Caribbean in 1567. In 1569 Hawkins
had pretended, in an unfamiliar role as *agent provocateur*, to
be willing to enter Spanish service. He later declared that
the Duke had attempted to persuade him to assist in the northern uprising in England.[16] The charge was not substantiated
but it kept alive the suspicions against the Feria name.

After a decade of such incidents the attitude of the Duke
in his meeting at the Escorial with Henry Lord Cobham was
understandably severe. Cobham had come to Spain in June
1571 to convey Queen Elizabeth's request that Guerau
Despes be removed from his embassy in London because of
certain papers in the Crown's possession after the "Ridolfi
conspiracy." Moreover there was hope that the trade griev-
ances on both sides could be negotiated and possibly the
whole situation in the Low Countries could be discussed.[17]
Little came from the meeting, but it was significant that
Philip placed the presentation of the Spanish position in Feria's
hands. The confidence of the king in his ability was so high
at this time that he had kept him at Court during the summer
of 1571 to discuss all the aspects of his appointment as Governor of the Low Countries. However, it was not to take
place. The sudden death of the Duke of Feria on September
7, 1571 changed the fortunes of Jane Dormer over night.
It would be only speculation to imagine her position in
Brussels as the wife of the Governor, but clearly there would
have been significant and obvious differences in the history
of Spain's troubles in the north if Philip had removed the iron-
handed Duke of Alba two years earlier.

In the autumn of 1571 the Duchess of Feria, as she

[16] *C.S.P. For. 1586–88*, p. 177; Froude, *History of England*, vol. ix, pp. 510–20.
[17] *C.S.P. Spanish, 1568–79*, pp. 313ff.

mourned the death of her husband, obviously realized that a position of power and influence had almost been hers. It would have been an easy step for Jane Dormer to assume the leadership of her Catholic countrymen who needed financial help and advice in the Low Countries or even in England.

At the time of her husband's death the house of Feria was heavily in debt. This was partly the result of the habitual slowness of Philip to repay his servants and partly the result of the outlandish expenditures needed to maintain their position at Court. The four months' progress from Malines to Toledo in 1560 was reported to have required 50,000 escudos. Yet with reasonable caution much could be done to restore the Feria fortunes. At that time the English patrimony of Jane Dormer and of her grandmother had been expressly declared exempt from the rigorous law enacted in Parliament in April and May 1571 against those living abroad without a licence.[18] Moreover, her Spanish estates were estimated reliably to have revenues of 100,000 escudos a year.[19] Even Philip II was mindful of his former friend. On November 3, 1571 he granted to her son, Don Lorenzo, shortly after his twelfth birthday, a membership and revenues in the order of Santiago.[20]

The next decade was a period of relative retirement from the Court for Jane Dormer. She raised her son, Don Lorenzo, and managed to free the house from the debts incurred. Occasionally she seized an opportunity to help those exiles

---

[18] *Statutes of the Realm,* 13 Eliz. cap. 3. It is noteworthy that this was the only parliament which her father Sir William Dormer attended (*Commons Journal,* vol. i, p. 83). It is possible that her relatives in the Lords also assisted; on May 19, 1571 the Act was passed in the Lords, but "with a new proviso and certain amendments to it" (*Lords Journal,* vol. i, p. 690).

[19] M. Fernandez Alvarez, *Tres Ambassadores de Felipe II en Inglaterra* (Madrid, 1951), p. 53.

[20] A.H.N. Ordenes Militares, Santiago, Expediente 7933.

who sought a pension.²¹ When Sir Francis Englefield came to live at the Spanish Court in 1580 she found an old friend who had served with her in England in the household of the Princess Mary. Moreover, her grandmother, prior to her death in Louvain in 1571, had been associated with Engle-field in distributing alms among the refugees.²²

The young Duke of Feria was on the point of beginning his career in the service of the Crown. In the spring of 1580 Don Lorenzo was ordered to serve under the Duke of Alba with a command of 5,000 troops which were ready for the campaign in Portugal.²³ In the following years the second Duke was to rise rapidly in Philip's confidence. By 1585 Don Lorenzo was made Governor of Naples and in the fol-lowing year he offered the homage of Philip II to Pope Sixtus V on his election.²⁴ Since the name of Feria was once again becoming prominent in Spanish court politics, the dow-ager Duchess, Jane Dormer, soon became the subject of the schemes of a number of adventurers.

Typical of this sort of boondoggling intriguer was Nicho-las Sedgrave. This Irish adventurer had been born in Dublin in 1548 and at the age of twenty-one had entered the Jesuit novitiate in Rome but left after a year. He had then become a member of the reckless expedition of Thomas Stuckely sup-posedly to free Ireland under a papal banner from English rule. He had a bitter argument with that highhanded leader and wound up condemned to the galleys from which he was released later by Cardinal Henry, the king of Portugal, late in 1578. After this Sedgrave decided to become a priest and eventually he secured a benefice through the Guise family. His restless spirit was not satisfied in France and through a

²¹ *C.S.P. Dom.* 1547–80, p. 500.
²² B.M., Cotton Vespasian CXIII, f. 336–37.
²³ *C.S.P. For.* 1583 Add. p. 542.
²⁴ *C.S.P. For.* 1585–86, p. 520.

recommendation of the Duke of Lorraine he secured an army chaplaincy from the Duke of Parma.[25]

On January 17, 1589 Sedgrave approached the Duke of Parma with a scheme to negotiate secretly with Sir Robert Sydney, the English Governor of Flushing, for the fort's surrender. "He is an uncle of the Duchess of Feria," he wrote, "and he is not as heretical, or as pleased with the Queen's role, as may appear."[26] Sydney was not unfriendly to his niece, for as far back as 1561 he had openly expressed the hope of visiting her.[27] However Sedgrave's clumsy intrigue was based entirely on a misestimation of the family ties of two people he had never met. With nothing to lose, Parma allowed Sedgrave to begin writing to Sydney "according to his position and the matter's requirements."[28] For a few weeks the Duke received occasional reports from the optimistic Irishman which led him to inform Philip II that there were some hopes of success in that quarter.[29]

Sedgrave was actually in correspondence with the rather surprised Governor of Flushing but at that time his letters were concerned with his safe conduct out of Flushing if Sydney granted permission to see him. As yet he was not mentioning a surrender at all but simply his eagerness to report to Sydney about "things of the utmost importance." These eventually turned out to be vague but ominous warnings to the effect that England was "most certainly to be invaded and the chief instruments of the present government destroyed . . ."[30] Shrewdly Sydney decided to report this incredible correspondence to the Privy Council in England

[25] C.R.S., vol. xxxix, p. 1; E 612/125–27.
[26] E 598/13.
[27] C.S.P. Spanish 1558–67, p. 179.
[28] E 598/57 letter of 20 May 1589.
[29] E 598/92.
[30] Lambeth Palace MSS, vol. 652, ff. 114, 116; See also T. Birch, Memoirs, vol. i, pp. 303–06.

with a comment that Sedgrave's gambit was intended to frighten him into a surrender of his post for money. The whole silly intrigue ended there.

However, the indefatigable Sedgrave was soon in communication with Count Mansfeldt, the Governor of the Low Countries during Parma's absence in France, offering to provide details about the surrender of Ostend.[31] The Duchess of Feria was probably unaware that her name had figured so prominently in Sedgrave's suggested negotiation. However, three years later, when her son tried to meet Sir Robert Sydney, while both were attending the Estates General in 1593, Sydney would not even answer his letter.[32] Sedgrave's posturings as a man of intrigue had made the Duchess look ridiculous, but there were other trials before her.

In 1592 Francis Dacres, the brother of Leonard Lord Dacres, the prominent leader in the northern rising of 1569, arrived at the Spanish Court in Valladolid. The Council of State had first heard of him in an *avisos* from Hugh Owen in October 1587 which reported that Francis Dacres had fled from London to Scotland, with the note: "They fear that if he finds favor there he will be able to cause trouble."[33] Six years later, one of Dacres' servants, a John Whitfield, was captured on his return to England carrying letters to Dacres' friends.[34] Whitfield's examination disclosed his master's activities until that point. He revealed that Dacres had stayed at the Court of King James VI and, after "long continuance," was given a license to travel to Spain. After first journeying to Rome, where he secured a letter of commendation from Cardinal Allen, he had gone to San Sebastian where his behavior caused his arrest as a spy. Only when Anthony Rolston

[31] A.G.R., P.E.A. 1830/3 letter of 6 Sept. 1590.
[32] E, K 1590 f. 76 punto 5.
[33] E 597/70.
[34] H.M.C. *Salisbury MS*, vol. iv, p. 333.

wrote to the Duchess of Feria and Sir Francis Englefield had he been given his release.[35]

On reaching the Court in 1592, Dacres was offered the hospitality of the Duchess for over a year. He had been preparing notes for a military campaign which would require Spanish forces to land in western Scotland and proceed to invade England from there. The only merit of the enterprise would appear to have been the use of the memory of the Dacres name in the north, and it was obviously aimed at regaining his properties.[36] There was little interest in the Spanish Court in such a plan, and Dacres was gradually judged by the Duchess and Englefield to be a restless, ambitious character who would easily endanger the other exiles. They recommended to the Council that he be placed in safety on the pension lists of the Roman embassy. This would keep Dacres from the sensitive areas of Flanders and Spain. Dacres chafed under the restraints imposed on him for three years until he finally succeeded in getting his pension transferred to the treasury of the Archduke in Brussels. There his compatriots reported soon that "he is angry at the small account in which he is held."[37] Dacres became the center of wild rumors after this. Robert Persons once noted that Dacres was thought to have been "dryven out of Spayne and all other Spanish dominions, being slaundered to be a spy for England and would burn the Kinges fleet."[38]

Dacres had been another warning to Jane Dormer of the dangers of helping those who were ambitious. Through her advisers in Spain she was saved from the worst effects of giving her confidence or hospitality to adventurers. Yet some damage was done. Anthony Rolston later reported that the

[35] B.M., Harleian 7042, ff. 222v–33.
[36] *Ibid.*, f. 231.
[37] E. 613/125–27.
[38] R. Persons, *A Manifestation of the great folly and bad spirit of certayne in England* . . . (Antwerp, 1602), pp. 47v, 50v.

Feria family was declining in prominence and that "the Duchess . . . had no credit, and did not meddle in English matters," but he noted that Jane Dormer was not "so ill affected, as times ran, to England as most supposed." [39]

Yet the future for Jane Dormer was by no means as cheerless as Rolston implied. She had turned increasingly to her circle of Catholic compatriots whose long residence in Spain had made them all especially valued friends. Her cousin, Margaret Harrington, who had come from England in her suite in July 1559, remained near her in Madrid and the Duchess had given her a dowry on the occasion of her marriage to Don Benito de Cisneros. There were also Sir Francis Englefield and the two English Jesuits, Robert Persons and Joseph Creswell, through whose persuasion she became a benefactor to the two English colleges.

There is a charming picture of Jane Dormer's deep interest in the affairs of her circle in a brief letter she wrote in Madrid to Englefield in the summer of 1593. It contains the trivial but newsworthy items that she felt confident would interest her friend:

Good Ser Francis. Yesternight your servant, Pullen, delivered me your letter wrytten last wednesday which I thanke you hertly for, and for that sent me with all from my Lord Cardinall [Allen] from whom I have fresher newes than this bringes. Yet it is most welcome to me. I pray you commend me to good Father Persones who, I know, lakith no business to occupy him. God geve him helth that he may be the better able to travel in so many matters of importance as he hath of his charge. When he hath any occasion to wryght to me I know he wyll find time for it, how occupied so ever he be. My cosen Margret Harrington hath her lyttel daughter syke with a falle so great and perilous. And her hedd hath bene opened! And she out of her wyttes all these daies with greve. The phisicians and sorgeans saye it is now out of perel. So dere cost childrene. When she is come to her selfe, I shall see that she wryght and answere.

[39] T. Birch, *Memoirs*, vol. i, p. 203.

Your louing friend, the Duches of Feria, I dare say Father Creswell is no better fried in Seville than we be here sins the caniculares came in.[40]

It was not until 1596 that the most valuable confidant within Jane Dormer's circle of English friends arrived at the Spanish Court. Thomas Fitzherbert was already well known to Englefield from four years of official correspondence.[41] However, it was largely the admiration of her son, Don Lorenzo, that recommended Fitzherbert to the Feria household. This bond was to last through a great family crisis and continue for several years after Fitzherbert had left Spain in 1602. For example, in October 1606 when Jane's nephew, Sir William Dormer, was to visit Rome and hoped to journey to Messina to see his cousin Don Lorenzo who was then Viceroy of Sicily, she asked Fitzherbert to take the young Englishman into his house for a time "and to favor him with your advice and to make perfect what yet is rawe." [42]

Born in Staffordshire in 1552, Thomas Fitzherbert came from a family which had been prominent in the legal profession. For a time, he later admitted, he too had hoped to follow in the footsteps of his grandfather, Sir Anthony, who rose to the post of a Justice of Common Pleas, by visiting the assizes and the sessions of the Queen's Bench. However, his Catholic leanings soon brought him under suspicion for recusancy and he was even imprisoned for a short time at the age of twenty. Eight years later he became one of the group of young Catholic laymen who assisted Edmund Campion and Robert Persons in the first year of the Jesuit mission in England in 1580. Shortly after Campion's execution Thomas Fitzherbert was imprisoned again, this time in the Marshalsea in London. After two years he was released, possibly with

[40] S.A.C. Serie II/6 letter of 24 July 1593.
[41] P.R.O., S.P. 94/4/143, 272.
[42] W.C.A. Series E vol. ii, f. 244.

the understanding that he should live in France. In March 1586 he wrote to Sir Francis Walsingham, in rather friendly terms, thanking him "for his favorable dealing in my behalf with her majesty." [43]

For nearly three years Fitzherbert lived in Paris, where for a time he served as secretary for English letters to Catherine de Medici. He was also in touch once again with his friends among the circle of Robert Persons and one spy even went so far as to name him the "secretary to the Jesuits' party." [44] When the political chaos of 1589 engulfed Paris, Fitzherbert fled late in the year, together with Anthony Standen and Anthony Rolston, to the Spanish Court. There all three were given pensions as "intelligencers" to report from different cities in France. On April 26, 1590 Philip II informed Don Bernardino de Mendoza that Fitzherbert was being assigned to Rouen at a salary of 30 escudos a month. The King ordered Mendoza to expedite the Englishman's dispatches to Spain.[45] This arrangement was not very successful. Over a year later Fitzherbert complained to Juan de Idiaquez that he had been trying to send reports to Mendoza and "serving his majesty as best I can." Yet he could not as yet establish his connections with England "where before now there would have been set up a fine system of corresponding if the lack of money and my referring the plan to Don Bernardino . . . had not prevented the execution of my hopes." [46]

Who precisely his friends in England were, he never revealed. However, in 1592 Fitzherbert began his mysterious correspondence with William Sterrill, a close friend of Thomas Phelippes, the decipherer for the English Court. Each

[43] C.R.S. vol. xli, introd.; *C.S.P. For. 1585–6*, pp. 503, 716.
[44] *Ibid.*, p. 717.
[45] E, K 1449 f. 116; T. Birch, *Memoirs*, vol. i, pp. 85–86.
[46] E, K 1576 f. 27.

party apparently tried to ensnare the other. Sterrill once re-marked to Phelippes in 1593 that "wonderful circumspection must be used in writing to Fitzherbert; only to answer his (letters) and not to offer any service, but readiness in general, otherwise he will be jealous." This correspondence continued for nearly seven years under close secrecy on both sides. In April 1603 Sir Ralph Winwood finally discovered that it had been going on, through his agent Colville in Paris, but by that time it was ended and Fitzherbert was living as a priest in Rome.[47]

It was the arrival in Paris of the second Duke of Feria that was to secure for Thomas Fitzherbert his most powerful patron in Spain. The duke, at 34 years of age, was only seven years younger than the Englishman yet he soon made him his ad-viser and confidant. Fitzherbert in effect became a member of his household and they were together in France and Flan-ders until late in 1595. The young grandee's protection was to be invaluable for Fitzherbert in Flanders when two Eng-lish prisoners declared falsely after torture that he had been an agent of Sir Robert Cecil. Feria at once insisted on a new trial for his friend where he forced the judge, in Fitzherbert's words, "to restore my honor and to do me such reparation of the wrong that I rested satisfied." [48]

Early in 1596, when the Duke of Feria returned to Spain, Fitzherbert was quickly introduced to Jane Dormer's circle. It was but a brief step for him to assume most of Englefield's duties as a secretary at Court later in the year. His pension was now 40 escudos a month. From the fortunate survival of a volume of letters from the personal files of Fitzherbert covering

[47] P.R.O., S.P. 12/244/15; S.P. 12 255/51; Winwood, *Memorials*, vol. i, p. 404.
[48] W.C.A. Series A. Vol. vii, p. 489; T. Fitzherbert, *An Apology of T.F. . . .* p. 3.

the years 1597 to 1612 an interesting profile of his work can be obtained. He had begun almost at once to send advice and "intelligence" on English affairs to many influential courtiers. These included, of course, the Duke of Feria, who had by then become the Viceroy of Catalonia, but also Don Esteban Ybarra, a member of the Council of War; the Duke of Medina Sidonia, the commander of the Spanish fleets; Don Juan de Idiaquez, the influential adviser on English affairs in the Council of State; Don Pedro de Franqueza, the Secretary of the Council; the Duke of Sessa, the Spanish envoy at the Papal Court from 1591 to 1603; and the Duke of Infantado, also of the Council of State, who was the father-in-law of the Duke of Feria.[49]

The letters from the Duke of Feria to Thomas Fitzherbert show Jane Dormer's son continuing to seek his advice on a wide range of topics, from trivial family matters to some of his most difficult official decisions as Viceroy. In his personal outlook Don Lorenzo is revealed to be a blunt man, as his father had been before him, rather cynical, if not fashionably stoical, yet still possessing high principles and devotion to his service to the crown. For two years the Duke was strongly tempted to resign his offices and retire to his estate at Zafra while Fitzherbert, playing his role of confidant with excellent discretion, warned the restless grandee against acting in extreme moods.

Meanwhile Fitzherbert had to perform his secretarial duties inherited from Englefield. The Council of State had designated him officially as an "interpreter of the English language and collector of reports on events in England."[50] Through the commendations of his friends at Court Fitzherbert was to rise higher in the confidence of Philip III for he raised his pension

[49] W.C.A. Series E vol. ii passim.
[50] E 2741 n.f. consulta 14 Nov. 1599.

to 50 escudos a month, and gave him lodgings at the royal expense "so that he could be maintained in keeping with his quality." [51] When Fitzherbert left the Spanish Court to become a priest in Rome he carried an unusual commendation from Philip to the Duke of Sessa at the embassy there. His pension was transferred to Rome and the envoy was asked to value Fitzherbert's advice "in English affairs and any other opportunities for my service." [52]

Thomas Fitzherbert's accepted status both within the Feria circle and the Spanish Court was to assume its greatest significance in a crisis that developed between Jane Dormer and her son Don Lorenzo in the decade after 1592. At stake was the question of leadership among the English exiles in Spanish Hapsburg lands which had never been adequately discussed for many years. The crisis began when Jane Dormer began to consider seriously the advantage of leaving her quiet life in Spain to go to Flanders and publicly assume the leadership of the English community.

The first contemporary reference to the plan appeared in a garbled statement made by the English priest, James Yonger, after his capture in England late in the summer of 1592. At that time he informed the Privy Council that the Duchess of Feria had recently made "importunate suit" to Philip II to be made regent of the Low Countries with her son, the second Duke, as commander of the armies which Parma was soon to relinquish. Yonger believed that King Philip had even consulted Cardinal Allen, "who seemed to like it." He also believed that the Duchess of Feria might well have succeeded except that letters were intercepted in Flanders, which indicated that the whole plan was a "covert plot devised by Morgan and his adherents." The person who had approached the

---

[51] E 185 n.f. consultas of 3 Oct. and 9 Nov. 1600.
[52] E 1595 n.f. ayuda de costa of 31 Dec. 1602; W.C.A. Series A vol. vii, f. 35.

Duchess was revealed to have been a lapsed Carthusian monk still known to his compatriots as "Friar Arnold." [53]

Unknown to Yonger, Thomas Morgan, the declared enemy, with Charles Paget, of William Allen and Robert Persons since 1583, had been trying to gain the confidence of the Duchess, since as early as 1571. Significantly, his first efforts had coincided with the expectation that her husband would be appointed the Governor of the Low Countries. At that time Morgan had sent letters from England to Jane Dormer begging her assistance. When these papers were intercepted in London, they were described as "supposed to be from the Queen of Scots." [54] In the belief that she was helping the imprisoned Queen the Duchess had pleaded for Morgan's request. She was favorably received by Philip II who was under the similar impression. At the same time that this rather presumptuous intrigue was going on, the sister of the Duchess, Anne Dormer Hungerford, had fled England in disgrace to live in the Low Countries. Anne had figured during the three preceding years in a notorious divorce case in which her adulterous love affair with a William Darrell had been paraded openly in court. [55] When her husband refused to give her maintenance she had fled penniless to Flanders where, with her sister's influence she secured an excellent pension. [56] However, it was to be nearly twenty years before Morgan began in earnest, together with Anne Hungerford, to influence again the Duchess of Feria.

[53] *C.S.P. Dom. 1591–94* p. 267. (Yonger's *alias* was George Dingley). For Arnold see C.R.S., vol. ii, p. 205 and *C.S.P. Spanish, 1587–1603*, p. 543. Two original letters of Arnold urging a bishopric for Owen Lewis are in E 839/22 and 31.

[54] *C.S.P. Dom. 1547–80*, p. 427.

[55] H. Hall, *Society in the Elizabethan Age* (5th ed.), pp. 11–12, 240–47, 260–63.

[56] She received 1,100 livres a year in 1573 (Lechat, *Les Refugiés*, p. 236). Later, in 1583 Philip II ordered a pension of 50 escudos a month.

Since 1583, when he had been deliberately excluded by the English exiles from their consultations on ways to assist the imprisoned Mary Queen of Scots, Morgan had remained ostracized. There was good reason for the decision of the English *émigrés* for the treacherous Welshman had been on the fringe of several well publicized conspiracies. From 1583 to 1585 Morgan had been imprisoned in France by King Henry III after Queen Elizabeth's accusations resulting from the "Parry Plot," and again for a year in England in 1587 for his mysterious connection with the "Babington Plot." On returning to the continent he was arrested again in Brussels in January 1589. At this time a long dossier was prepared against him under the personal supervision of the Duke of Parma, who was frankly amazed by the incredible labyrinth of the intrigues which English *émigrés* charged against Morgan. For example, one witness before the court in Brussels, Charles Browne, who had written to Spain about the "malcontents" of the pension lists the year before, asked the Duke to transfer Morgan to Spain for trial by the Inquisition. Parma reported that there were depositions by ten English laymen and five English priests describing Morgan's activities.[57]

It was proved before the Brussels court that Morgan possessed a chest containing the incredible sum of 8,000 escudos, roughly the equivalent of £2,000 in Elizabethan money. Moreover, his private papers contained elaborate ciphers whose purpose Morgan refused to disclose. It was charged that Morgan had bribed the Master of the Post in Antwerp so as to intercept the correspondence of the Duke of Parma, and report on it to England. Other witnesses charged that he had formerly been a "creature" of the Earl of Leicester and Sir Francis Walsingham.[58] Most significantly of all it was charged

[57] E 599/87 letter of Parma, 22 Feb. 1590.
[58] E 598/72, also E 839/21, partial summary in *C.S.P. Spanish 1587–1603*, pp. 565–69.

] 114 [

that Morgan, while acting as the agent for Mary Queen of Scots, had regularly betrayed many of her followers, which would explain the suspicions of William Allen as far back as 1583.

The Duke of Parma informed King Philip that he was sending the entire dossier on Morgan to Spain and added his own advice that as far as could be seen Morgan "attempts to sew cockle and intrigues and to undo everything that Cardinal Allen and Father Persons and other good Catholics are doing . . . both within and without the kingdom." [59]

The charges were serious, the reasons for suspicion ample, yet Philip hesitated, with typical caution, to prosecute Morgan more fully. Father Henry Walpole, the chaplain of Colonel Stanley's regiment in Parma's army, reported from Brussels: "They that handle it say there is very much information against him, but he avoideth, without full proof, in great matters." [60] Eventually it was decided to banish Morgan from all Spanish territories. He then proceeded to Rome and later to Savoy where he began his correspondence with the Duchess of Feria. Years later Morgan was to be imprisoned for a fourth time. Henry IV of France would suspect the Welshman's connection with the Biron sedition and would send him for two years to gaol after which he would expel him from French soil. [61]

It was this odious "confidence man," who, in the spring of 1593, began urging Anne Dormer Hungerford to agitate for her sister's coming to Brussels. In a lengthy memorandum sent to the Spanish Council of State Anne expatiated with a lavish

[59] E 598–23.
[60] Stonyhurst MS Anglia A I f. 52.
[61] A versatile liar to the end, Morgan at the age of 74 persuaded Don Inigo de Cardenas, a Spanish envoy in Brussels, to grant him a pension of 20 escudos a month, "for being a good Catholic and a servant of the Queen of Scots" (E. K 1427/1 consulta of 5 Jan. 1610).

imagination on "the great and particular services" that would soon come to the Spanish crown. She began with the advice that the Duchess of Feria should best make an ostentatious progress to the Low Countries as this would be Philip's recognition that she was of a noble family "superior in titles and dignity to all there are in England today." [62] She explained that it would be folly for Spain to do without the manifest advantages of having an "English Catholic duchess" in the Spanish domains nearest to England. She believed, fatuously, that should Philip II show this honor to Jane Dormer she could then cause "more pain and grief" to Queen Elizabeth than "any other person of any other nation." She imagined a virtual panic in the English Privy Council as it sought to learn why Philip showed favor to "a person so important." It was even promised, as Nicholas Sedgrave had pretended four years before, that Jane Dormer would be able to influence the surrender of northern garrisons in Holland through her uncle, Sir Robert Sydney.

While this petition was still en route to Spain, Anne Hungerford persuaded the aging Cardinal Allen to write to Philip II and urge that the Duchess of Feria should leave Spain. However, the reasons alleged by Allen were deceptively moderate, and it was clear that he was quite unaware of the far more flamboyant intrigue which Anne, in fact, was sponsoring. His letter merely advised that Jane Dormer would be in better health "because of the more salutary climate" of Flanders, and that she would then be able to "console and assist her relatives" and encourage many other exiled Catholics. The Cardinal explained that the Duchess had hitherto not gone to Flanders "because of the youth of her son." [63] Allen did not advert to the fact that Don Lorenzo was then thirty-four years of age and had been outside of Spain, serving

[62] E 962/117.
[63] *Ibid.*, enclosure, letter of June 1593.

in Portugal, Naples, Flanders and France for over thirteen years.

What then was at stake? What if Jane Dormer should travel publicly to Flanders and there submit to Anne's guid-ance, and indirectly to Thomas Morgan's faction? Implicit in Anne's letters was a clear ambition to have her sister assume a leadership that the declining health of Cardinal Allen had al-ready warned would soon be vacant. The sentiments of Anne Hungerford and Morgan had been already partially reflected in the restless complaints of another Welsh exile, Owen Lewis. In 1588 Lewis criticized the dominant role of Allen and his friend Robert Persons, in advising the policy of the exiles: "Truly this ambition of the monopolie of all busyness of our nation is a very dangerous thyng, and I know they can-not do yt, and are not so fit as they thinke to doo all alone . . ."[64]

In effect, the intrigue expected that Jane Dormer, as a long respected person at the Spanish Court, would become a domi-nant figure and an easy way of access in Brussels for Anne's circle. The wails of the ostracized were public knowledge everywhere, and even Lewis Lewknor reported their bitter sentiments to his English readers in his *Estate of English Fugi-tives.* He described the "one over ruling faction that hath drawn them [the exiles] into mightie partialities and strange

[64] Cited in R. Persons, *A Briefe Apologie, or Defence of the Catholicke ecclesiastical hierarchie* (Antwerp, 1601) p. 34ᵛ. A re-cent rehabilitation of this naive ecclesiastic is available in G. An-struther, "Owen Lewis," *The English Hospice in Rome (The Ven-erabile,* Sexcentenary Issue, Exeter, 1962) pp. 274ff., who notes however, that he had a "genius for befriending the wrong people." A contemporary opinion of Lewis' ambitions is recorded in Cardinal Sega's report on the troubles of the English college in Rome (Foley, *Records,* vol. vi, pp. 1–17). An objective description of the factions among the exiles which was prepared by the Papal Nuncio at the Spanish Court in September 1595, Camillo Caetani, is in A.S.V. Nunziatura di Spagna, tomo 46 ff. 789–95.

extremes of one against the other." He knew well the first open display of the rivalry in 1583 and even informed his readers that the anti-Allen faction was at present under the guidance of Thomas Morgan,

> a man not inferior to anie of them all in driftes of policie . . . The Jesuits have had many a plucke at him, but Morgan being wise, strengthened himself alwaies with such friends that they could never do him anie hurt, but rather every now and then he gave them a secret blow.[65]

It is certain that Morgan remained a friend and correspondent of the Duchess of Feria, to the obvious chagrin of her circle in Spain, until at least 1604. How much her protection was useful to him, however, is only matter of conjecture.

One of the principal causes of dissatisfaction which strengthened the case of the critics of Cardinal Allen had always been the slow payment of Spanish alms when promised to the exiles. Dr. Barrett, a former Rector of the English College at Douai, confided to his friend Robert Persons in 1596 that it was essential to satisfy the pensioners. "Our adversaries are well monied," he wrote, "and they maintaine their faction more by that meanes then anything els. Men follow such as are able to pleasure them."[66]

With the death of Cardinal Allen in 1594 the possibility of leadership by Jane Dormer was no longer remote. It was a delicate problem. An easy solution, which would have continued the idea of having an English Cardinal to represent "the nation," was soon found on closer examination to be fraught with difficulties. To this end Robert Persons was asked by his friends at the Spanish Court in 1594 and again early in 1597 whether he would consider accepting a Cardinal's hat. On both occasions he wisely refused. In the first approach,

[65] *Sadler Papers*, vol. ii, pp. 256–57.
[66] T. F. Knox, *The First and Second Douai Diaries*, p. 384.

Cardinal García de Loyasa had approached Father Creswell in Madrid inquiring into Person's attitude but the prelate was warned that Person's elevation to the purple would only place the Jesuits in England in an even more invidious position with the English Court.[67] Later, after he had left Spain in the spring of 1597 and arrived in Rome, Persons was asked directly by Pedro Ximenez de Murillo, the secretary of the embassy of the Duke of Sessa, to reconsider his objections. The Jesuit replied that the problem had never been whether an English Cardinal was needed since every one thought that there should be one. However, he could not see a clear choice of an individual who was competent and yet "had the consent and agreement of all."[68]

The question of leadership could not be left in such a stalemate. Fully aware of the gambit connected with the Jane Dormer candidacy, Persons suggested, without referring to it directly, that there be a meeting in Brussels to discuss the problem of the exiles with the young Archduke Albert. He had just arrived, early in 1596, to assume the duties of Governor. The Jesuit asked that the principal Spanish officials meet in a conference with various English exiles from all walks of life. Sir William Stanley for military problems; Hugh Owen for information on English affairs; Gabriel Traherne, a one-time merchant in Andalucia; Dr. Thomas Worthington, the Rector of the English College at Douai; Dr. William Pierse, an Englishman who had lectured in theology at the Sorbonne until 1595; and William Holt, the superior of the English Jesuits working in Flanders among the exiles. Father Persons suggested to the Council of State that this *junta* might review all the problems facing the exiles as a group. They were to try to

[67] A.R.S.J. Epist. Hispaniae, vol. 138, f. 10 letter of 3 Dec.
[68] T. F. Knox, *The First and Second Douai Diaries*, p. 393.

unite the nation in the service of your majesty and especially, in what touches the succession, remove the groups, factions and dissensions . . . allocate Englishmen who are now in your majesty's service in conformity with their talents . . . bring it about that more come over from England . . . look for an opportunity to go on the offensive, receive reports from England, apprehend the spies that are sent here, and finally give life and spirit to the cause of the Catholics.[69]

This was an agenda to challenge any leader or committee. The plan was passed on to the Archduke but its wide ranging topics and the urgent problems of the war apparently prevented its adoption. In effect there could not be either a committee nor a head "of the nation." Instead the criticism by the discontented followers of Morgan was to continue with mounting exasperation and frustration. The serious problems enumerated by Robert Persons were to be in effect left to the skill of interested individuals who had the confidence of Spain. Meanwhile the Feria family crisis remained to be pacified.

The dimensions of the ambitions of Anne Dormer Hungerford were not lost upon her nephew, Don Lorenzo, the second Duke of Feria. When he first had learned of his mother's plans he wrote from France to the Duke of Sessa asking why Cardinal Allen was involved in supporting such a notion. The ambassador replied that nothing could have surprised him more than the projected journey of the Duchess in pomp and circumstance to Brussels. It would contribute nothing to the king's service, he wrote caustically, and her age and health were against it in any case. He had inquired why Allen had written his letter, and had learned to his annoyance that the kindly English prelate had even asked Pope Clement VIII to write in favor of it but had, fortunately, been rebuffed. He wrote that Allen had admitted later that he had acted hastily and that he had not been "looking to the public affairs of Eng-

[69] E 839/129.

land." [70] Satisfied over this part of the intrigue, the Duke still kept silent for three months.

Finally on September 3, 1594 Don Lorenzo decided that the situation was sufficiently critical to require his direct appeal to the Council of State. His memorandum of 12 folios was clearly an embarrassing paper to compose since he had by now abundant proof that his mother enthusiastically agreed with her sister's pretensions. The tone of his paper reveals him to be conscious of the dilemma of the call of filial sentiment with the duty of protecting the honor of his family name.

The Duke began by flatly denying the possibility of a peaceful residence for his mother in Flanders. He predicted that she would in turn become the object of the same scurrilous invective that Cardinal Allen, Robert Persons and William Holt had been enduring. He scoffed at the notion that Queen Elizabeth would be alarmed, and foresaw that his mother's position in the Low Countries would only provide the grounds for greater antipathy to the unfortunate Catholics at home. He observed that all the English relatives of the Duchess were prominent Protestants and he was noticeably cynical over any influence that could be exerted by Jane Dormer over her uncle, Sir Robert Sydney. From his own experience, he recalled, he had tried to see him at the opening of the Estates General in the preceding year "to set out some doubts about Bearne" but Sydney had not even answered his letter.

The Duke then turned to studying the faction which supported the idea of bringing Jane Dormer northward. He called them a dubious group at best. He openly charged his aunt with wanting more authority through the prestige of the Duchess. He dismissed the rest of her supporters as people "who nourish differences and factions within that same nation against Cardinal Allen." He was equally disturbed over the fact that

[70] E, K 1590 f. 75 letter of 15 May 1594.

rumors that Spain was about to mount an *empresa* would cer-tainly circulate when in fact there were neither the intention nor the resources to undertake one.

After Anne Hungerford the Duke singled out as another baneful influence on his mother a former servant of his family named Ralph Parsley.[71] Don Lorenzo recalled that this man had visited him when he was stopping in Rome for a brief visit a year before. There the English servant had spoken of the plan concerning his mother and urged the subterfuge that the Duchess would "take the waters at Spa" as a public ex-planation for her departure from Spain. The Duke observed dryly that lying about the reason for his mother's journey would only make her activities more suspect. He concluded his lengthy paper with a final cynical observation that all those in favor of her departure would say anything at all as long as they achieved their goal.[72]

It was a devastating commentary on the whole shoddy intrigue and all the more embarrassing to everyone, since in-evitably it admitted a deep family quarrel and a division among the friends of the Duchess. Fearing the reversal of his plans, Morgan actually tried to visit Spain at the end of the same year but he was soon expelled and took refuge again in Savoy. The likelihood of the Duchess being allowed to go to Flanders had diminished considerably.

Yet Anne Hungerford would not admit defeat. In May 1595 she confided in her friend, Owen Lewis, that she was amazed "that any of the nation should hinder the success of

[71] A former servant of Anne Hungerford's at a salary of 15 es-cudos a month for nine years, in June 1589 he became a member of the household of the Duchess at 20 escudos (A.H.N. Estado lib. 251d, n.f., *cedulas* of 19 April and 31 June 1589). Robert Per-sons later described him as "deeply infected" by the Morgan circle, and that "he endeavored by all meanes to draw unto the same the young Duke" (C.R.S., vol. ii, p. 207).

[72] E, K 1590 f. 76.

the matter in question . . ." She admitted that the number of those objecting to it at present was great, although at first the opposition had been confined to a few whom she styled "the ambitious to retain in their own hands the handling of English matters." She had also discovered that "little can be done with her son." [73] The following year, after the appointment of the Archduke Albert as Governor she opened up her campaign again. She was, apparently, quite a persuasive speaker for on September 17, 1596 the Archduke wrote to Philip II approving the desire of Anne that her sister should come north "to live in her company, and for the other reasons for which she requests it." [74] It is highly probable that carried away by the news of the preparation of an Armada for the autumn of 1596, Anne Hungerford envisioned some nebulous role of importance for her sister in English affairs. Once again the Duke of Feria quietly intervened to prevent her departure.

Yet the worry nagged his thoughts for at least two more years. In his letters to Thomas Fitzherbert discussing his cares of office in Catalonia he would break off with an admonition to the Englishman to inform him at once if his mother went to Flanders, and with what authority, and who were her companions. He was particularly disturbed by the rumor that the Duchess might go there in the suite of the Infanta and the Archduke when they traveled northward after their marriage.[75]

Even after Anne Hungerford had reluctantly given up the struggle, Thomas Morgan continued to send letters to the Duchess of Feria. In February 1599 Don Lorenzo reported to Fitzherbert that the Welsh adventurer was telling Jane Dormer that Queen Elizabeth was contemplating a change in her religious outlook.[76] This outrageous misinformation might

[73] *C.S.P. Dom. 1595–97*, p. 41.
[74] E 611/136.
[75] W.C.A. Series 1 vol. ii, ff. 13, 14, 44, 53, 59, 62.
[76] *Ibid.*, f. 99ᵛ, letter of 4 Feb. 1599.

have easily stimulated some indiscretion from the Duchess which could be misinterpreted in the English Court. In any case the Duke was eventually satisfied that the far more dangerous intrigue of having his mother set up a household in Brussels as head of the English refugees in Flanders was at an end.

From subsequent letters in the file of Fitzherbert it appeared that everyone in Jane Dormer's circle was anxious to forget the quarrel. However, there was an obvious trace of bitterness in a letter of Jane Dormer to Fitzherbert after he had traveled to Rome in 1602. After giving some typical family news she asked to be commended to Sir William Stanley who was stopping in the eternal city and especially that she wished him to have "a good jornay to that godly land of Flanders, where I wold I were, that shall never go out of mi house." [77]

Although the quietly effective opposition of her son and many of her circle had prevented Jane Dormer from assuming a position she was incapable of managing, there were further attempts to prod the house of Feria to mingle in English affairs. These moves occurred shortly after the accession of King James. Once again the plan apparently originated in Flanders. In August 1603 the Papal Nuncio in Brussels, Ottavio Frangipani, recommended to the Papal secretary of State a plan concerning the Duchess that had been suggested to him. It required the moving of the sixty-five year old Duchess of Feria to England to serve as a lady-in-waiting to Queen Anne. The Nuncio commented that the Queen was known to be a Catholic and he expected that she would find congenial the advice of the Duchess. However, the reception in Rome of such a naive idea was notably chilly. After a delay of three months, the Papal secretary, Cardinal Aldobrandino, vetoed the idea. He wrote that Pope Clement had decided that the plan required "great consideration and maturity and it could not be

[77] W.C.A. Series 1 vol. ii, f. 180 letter of 21 Feb. 1602.

decided at present whether it was good or not" since it would easily allow suspicions to rise in the mind of the new king.[78]

While Rome had debated the plan, and it was likely that the Duke of Feria as Viceroy of Sicily was consulted, Thomas Morgan began a new invasion of the Dormer family's affairs. On September 28, 1603 he wrote a letter to King James begging that Jane's nephew Robert should be made an Earl. He brazenly presented the argument that the friendship of the Duchess must be secured "for the house of Feria will be a strong house in Spain." In addition he reminded the king that Jane Dormer had done many "good offices" for him and his mother in the past.[79] There is little doubt that Sir Robert Dormer would have been pleased with the honor since he was to pay £10,000 for the title when it was actually granted to him twelve years later.[80]

It was little to James' liking that a man who had been in prison in France for a role in the Biron conspiracy should enter so boldly into the affairs of one of his courtiers. It was clear that Morgan was still blindly trusted by the Duchess. In October 1603 Jane Dormer wrote a warm letter to King James expressing her loyalty to the new sovereign. She excused her tardiness with the remark that her previous letters to the King, which had all been sent through Thomas Morgan, might have been lost. She then informed the King that

albeit plesed Almighty God to order me to lyve in thease partes severed from mi contre . . . I shall deseir your Majestie to have that good conceite of me, as no alteracion of contres could ever in the lest jott alter me towards thous of the blood rial of mi contre.[81]

[78] A. Louant & L. van der Essen, *Correspondance d' Ottavio Miro Frangipani*, vol. iii, part 2, pp. 424–25, 714.
[79] *C.S.P. Dom. Add 1580–1625*, p. 429.
[80] See *Journal of Modern History* (1961), vol. xxxiii, p. 143, and D.N.B. *sub* Robert Dormer, Earl of Caernarvon.
[81] P.R.O., S.P. 94/9/81.

The letter was a more impressive gesture than any of the exaggerated pretences of Thomas Morgan, yet there is no evidence that King James replied.

At this time the house of Feria's association with English affairs was encouraging new speculations at the Spanish Court. In April 1604 Thomas Wilson, Robert Cecil's secret agent at the Spanish Court, reported that the Duchess of Feria was planning to have her son become Philip III's envoy to England. Obviously the appointment would be only another gambit for Jane Dormer to return to the English Court and still become a lady-in-waiting as rumored in the preceding summer. At the time of Wilson's despatch the negotiations in London for a treaty between James and Philip were being debated in the Council of State. The Count of Villa Mediana, the first Spanish envoy to King James to greet him on his accession to the throne, was expected to be replaced after the English ratification in the coming summer. In fact a new envoy was not appointed for another year. Wilson gave another reason for the speculation which would be equally interesting. He noted the ambition of the rising *valido* of Philip III, the Duke of Lerma against Feria. "I believe," he wrote, "that he who rules the rost here would gladly send him away into some coyne or crude corner for the disparence there is betwixt them is as much as betwixt any." [82]

The Duke of Feria, however, was well aware of what the plan really involved. It would have been quickly remembered in England among the Puritans that his father had been a critic of the religious changes of the first months of Elizabeth's reign. The old charges of the house of Feria's ill will could be easily dusted off. From the Duke's letters to Thomas Fitzherbert it was clear that he viewed the condition of the Jacobean Catholics with his father's partisan distaste. For example, he was extremely proud to learn of the resistance of the Viscount

[82] P.R.O., S.P. 94/10/1.

Montague in the House of Lords to the ratification of the penal laws against Catholics. On learning that Montague had been sent to the Tower he noted "I am very honored to have such a man as my relative," and then warned that no change in the lot of the Catholics could be expected.[83] Since he was as blunt as his father had been before him, his usefulness as an envoy was not high in England.

The visit to Spain in May of 1605 of Jane Dormer's cousin, Charles Lord Howard of Effingham, to secure Philip III's solemn oath to ratify the recent treaty [84] once again fanned the hopes of having Jane Dormer live in England. During his stay at the Spanish Court, Howard told the Constable of Castile that Queen Anne was anxious to have the Duchess come and live as her lady-in-waiting at the English Court. What was behind this dubious suggestion was not made clear but shortly afterwards Don Lorenzo commented on it with a trace of his familiar sarcasm to Fitzherbert: "The Constable has lost nothing in reporting this and perhaps we may console ourselves with this plan when that King fails in his promises [to Catholics] which in my opinion are nothing but words spoken to an underling." [85]

This was the last incident in the decade-long intrigue aiming to have Jane Dormer leave Spain and assume a prominent position in Flanders or England. It had been a severe family crisis and it might probably serve to explain why the Duke was usually content with assignments outside the peninsula, where he would avoid the inevitable reproaches of the Duchess. Unfortunately the mother and son were not to meet again, as Don Lorenzo died suddenly in Messina early in 1607 at the age of forty-eight.

[83] W.C.A. Series E, vol. ii, f. 202.
[84] J. W. Stoye, *English Travelers Abroad* (London, 1952), pp. 340ff.
[85] W.C.A. Series E, vol. ii, f. 224 letter of 24 Sept. 1605.

Only recently he had been honored by a special *breve* from the new Pope, Paul V, recalling his many benefactions to the needy English Catholic exiles. In the Duke's private opinion not the least of these would have been his success in preventing his mother from opening a Pandora's box in following the fatuous advice of his aunt, Anne Hungerford. Moreover, Jane Dormer's association with Thomas Morgan, a sinister adventurer to say the least, would easily have spurred a new crisis among the hardpressed exiles.

The last decade of Jane Dormer was spent without the genial companionship of her circle of friends. Sir Francis Englefield had died in 1596, Robert Persons had left Spain early in 1597, Thomas Fitzherbert had moved to Rome early in 1602. Only Father Creswell remained among her older acquaintances, and his cares for the debt-ridden colleges required him to remain at Court regularly. At Court there was only her grandson, who had first taken the title of the Marquis of Vilalba, the town where she and her husband Don Gomez many years before had founded a Franciscan monastery. In 1607 on the death of his father the third Duke of Feria was to become a member of the Council of State.

According to a narrative composed by the last chaplain of her household, ill health began to dominate Jane Dormer's days more and more after 1609. For nearly an entire year before her death in 1612 the Duchess was an invalid confined to bed. She had turned increasingly to her exercises of piety and was fittingly buried in the habit of a Franciscan tertiary.

CHAPTER FIVE

A SOLDIER : *Sir William Stanley*

1548–1630

"Wake, friend from forth thy Lethargie; the Drum
Beates brave, and loude in Europe, and bids come
All that dare rowse: or are not loth to quit
Their vitious ease, and be o'erwhelmed with it . . ."

An Epistle to a Friend, to Perswade him to the Warres.
BEN JONSON

IT IS a favorite metaphor among the historians of the sixteenth
century to view the Low Countries as the chessboard where
the interventions of the western European monarchies were
played through lightly disguised gambits. It was on this scene
of the skills of strategists at other courts that the English
émigrés became the pawns of the Councils of War in Brussels
and the Escorial. Here they played their part in the relentless
siege warfare, the fatiguing marches to one dangerous encounter after the other, and the numbing routine of garrison
duty. Here they formed their own regiment, which was the

source of livelihood for many, and the magnet for whatever militancy existed among them. Here their leaders planned and pleaded for a bewildering variety of "enterprises." The regiment was to include eventually a true cross-section of Elizabethan men of arms. Its muster was made up of hardened adventurers, professional soldiers, wandering deserters, embittered intriguers, mercenaries and crusading idealists. Presiding over this focal point of determined aspirations and disheartening frustrations was a soldier who came to personify the greatness and weakness of the militant English Catholic.

Sir William Stanley was born in 1548 at Hooten Manor by the Mersey estuary in Cheshire. He received the routine formation of the rural gentry of his day: some letters under a neighboring schoolmaster and a thorough training in arms and some polish in the household of his cousin, the third Earl of Derby. It cannot be reliably established whether Sir Rowland Stanley, his father, was a Catholic for there are certain ambiguities in the Stanley record. The family was not indicted for recusancy and Sir Rowland was considered reliable enough to be made high sheriff of Cheshire in 1576. In the nearly fifteen years of his son's service for the Queen in Ireland, the anti-Catholic policy of the pacification of Munster could hardly have escaped him. When William Stanley at the age of thirty-one received his knighthood it was at the hands of the partisan Protestant, Sir William Drury, for his distinguished fighting against the followers of the Catholic Earls of Desmond.[1] Moreover, even after he entered Spanish service in 1587 his wife and children were not mentioned in the extant records for recusancy and, as shall be seen, when they left Cheshire to live in Malines with Sir William in 1606 his grandson was conditionally baptized in their parish church of St. Pierre.

[1] Chetham Society, vol. xxv (1851), pp. ii–iii; D.N.B. *sub* William Stanley.

At the age of nineteen Stanley had his first experience in the profession of arms under the standard of the Duke of Alba in the Low Countries. His willingness to learn the art of war from one of Europe's most famous soldiers was shared by other young Englishmen of his day. One of them, Sir Roger Williams, explained later to his readers: "I do thinke it no disgrace for a poore gentleman that lives by warres, to serve any estate that is in league with his own." [2] It was an excellent apprenticeship, but no more. For late in 1569 with the mounting enmity between England and Spain an ambitious young soldier had to search elsewhere to pursue his career. In Ireland he could make the name which would be the path to the rewards of soldiering. His record in the arduous campaigns was to show that for personal diligence and hardihood Stanley left nothing to chance. Yet favors from court were not forthcoming. Possibly the death of his patron, Sir William Drury, and his family's lack of wealth prevented him from making the required splendid appearance at Court. The long service in Ireland had ended only with his knighthood and the irregular pay usually conferred on any captain of a company. Thus, by 1586, the year of the turning point of his life, Stanley was thirty-eight years of age and a respected soldier. Moreover, in the offing was another arduous campaign, this time in the Low Countries where England had bravely joined the Dutch in facing the splendid army of Parma.

During the final years of Stanley's service in Ireland the penalties against Catholics had prompted an increasing number of English soldiers to take refuge in the Low Countries. Even in 1576 at the time of the hopeful, if confused, planning of an *empresa* featuring Don Juan of Austria,[3] there were enough ablebodied Englishmen there to plan the formation of a few

[2] *A Brief Discourse of Warre* (London, 1590), p. 30.
[3] P. O. de Törne, *Le Cardinal de Come*, pp. 156–57, J. Kretschmar, *Die Invasionsprojecte*, pp. 58f.

companies to fight alongside of the forces of Don Juan. The *empresa* died but the hope of a regiment did not at least for some time. Sir Thomas Copley reported to Lord Burghley, on October 12, 1576, that Geronimo de Roda, the acting Governor of the Low Countries following the unexpected death of Requesens, had approached him "touchinge the levyenge of a company of Englishmen, of such as werr to be founde on this side of the sea, and required me to take on me the charge." Copley was very uneasy at the offer for he was hopeful of avoiding the fate of Englefield and of retaining his estates in England. He had already been rebuked by Queen Elizabeth for holding letters of *marque* in 1575 against the Dutch rebels. He had abandoned this profitable privateering and secured orders from the Spanish army allowing him to live in Brussels "as a gentleman of the coorte, and not as a soldier subject to any commandment further than shall please myself." [4] Copley had continued to receive a pension from the treasury of Spain. [5] Because of Copley's lack of enthusiasm the idea of an English regiment was dormant for a time.

However, as hostilities in the war against the Estates became more intense the plans for a regiment were revived. Early in 1582 Colonel William Semphill, a Scottish-born commander of a company of mercenaries, surrendered the Dutch town of Lier to Parma. Moreover, the Englishmen fighting for Spain had already reached three companies although they were not as yet grouped into a regiment. [6] In fact the numbers were increasing so rapidly that the Duke of Parma summoned Robert Persons to his camp near Antwerp where a large number of "English Catholic gentlemen and

[4] L. C. Christie, *Letters of Sir Thomas Copley*, pp. 90–91; *H.M.C. Seventh Report*, p. 628.
[5] Lechat, *Le Refugiés*, pp. 233ff.; P.R.O., S.P. 12/105/84; E. 2851 n.f. list of pensioners circa 1584.
[6] E 586/71 "paga por tres capitanes de Yngleses."

soldiers" were in need of chaplains.[7] By the end of 1582 Parma estimated that 500 Englishmen had recently left the service of the Dutch rebels.[8] For a time an attempt was made to group all Englishmen under the banner of Charles Lord Neville, the Earl of Westmorland, but he had little to offer but the historic name of his family. He was, according to all his contemporaries, a brooding and incompetent drunkard.[9] Understandably the leadership of the troops fell apart and Philip II wrote to Robert Persons in the autumn of 1584 about "the formation or revival of some companies of English Catholics" but the Jesuit replied that from recent experience "he despaired of success in negotiations of that sort."[10]

It is difficult not to believe that some reports of these developments in the forces of Parma reached the military circles in Ireland where Sir William Stanley served. It is known that at this time over a score of capable military leaders—not famous, but experienced captains and ensigns who would be vital for the sound leadership of troops—crossed the narrow seas to begin their lengthy service in the Spanish forces. For example, on Parma's muster lists appeared for the first time Anthony Chambers, William Bostock, Godfrey Foljambe and John Trevellian. Apparently the formation of an English regiment still remained uncertain for they began to serve with the Italian and Walloon levies which were grouped under Parma's standard at that time.

Sir William Stanley returned to England in October 1585 to convalesce from wounds received in the Munster campaign. In a matter of weeks he was ordered to join the brilliant retinue of soldiers and courtiers who were to accompany the Earl of

---

[7] *C.R.S.* vol. iv, pp. 124–25.
[8] *C.S.P. Spanish, 1580–87*, p. 382.
[9] Even ten years later Versteghen reported: "Some of our country men . . . do talk marvailous broadly of Westmorland and cover not the termes of hidden foule vices." *C.R.S.* vol. lii, p. 199.
[10] *C.R.S.* vol. xxxix, p. 263.

Leicester to buttress the cause of the Dutch rebels. Sir Thomas Heneage, Sir Philip Sydney, Sir Henry Unton, Sir John Norris, Sir Roger Williams were among the company chosen to escort the Queen's favorite.

Stanley could not at first join the glittering entourage of the Earl for in the beginning of March 1586 he had been sent back to Ireland to recruit a new regiment.[11] Even though he was able to promise a good bounty of £3 a man Stanley still had difficulty in raising the required number of 1,000 men. It was not until early in July that his levy began to pass through London on the way to join Leicester for a late summer campaign in Holland. Stanley delayed in England for a short time until all his men were equipped to join the English forces in Flushing.[12] The campaign was already under way when Stanley finally met Leicester again but he was almost continuously in action during September and early October. He earned the complete trust of the Earl who praised his courage after the fierce fighting near Zutphen where Sir Philip Sydney was to receive his fatal wound. "Stanley and old Read," wrote Leicester to Walsingham, "are worth their weight in perle, theie be two as rare captens as anie prince living hath." [13]

[11] Camden Society, vol. xxvii, p. 217, *Acts of the Privy Council*, vol. xiv, p. 62.

[12] Camden Society, vol. xxvii, pp. 344, 360. Early in August 1586 Stanley became the object of one of the falsehoods concocted by "Master" Gifford. For the benefit of Don Bernardino de Mendoza in Paris, he said that Stanley was a "Catholic" who was deliberately delaying his troops to have them ready for a Spanish fleet then proceeding to England (*C.S.P. Spanish 1580–86*, p. 604). However, it was known four months previously that there was no Armada in preparation for that period (letter of Walsingham, 24 March 1586, Camden Society, vol. xxvii, p. 187). At the same time Gifford was alleging that the Howard family, the Earl of Derby and others were ready to place their troops under Spanish service. Unknown to Mendoza, Gifford had become a renegade priest (C.R.S., vol. xxxvii, p. 9); his evidence on Stanley is unreliable.

[13] Camden Society, vol. xxvii, p. 417.

After this battle in which the English won a "sconce," or salient dominating Zutphen, Stanley's brother Edward, then on his first military campaign, was knighted by Leicester.[14] The English troops then turned towards Deventer, five miles away from the "sconce," which commanded the communications by road in the province of Oberysel. It was expected to be an easy capture. Since early in 1586 the Calvinist faction of that town had been in communication with Leicester offering to help in its surrender to the Estates General.[15] The only uncertainty in its seizure was the strength of the faction loyal to Parma which had dominated the town's government since the days when Deventer had declared itself on the side of Don Juan. However, on the night of October 23, 1586, with the town's gates deliberately unguarded, Stanley's troops infiltrated its streets in small bands in disguise. After capturing the town hall they proclaimed Deventer to be under the rule of the faction loyal to the Hague.[16] It was an important victory to close a hard campaign, but it was not sufficiently realized by either Leicester or Stanley that it was owed largely to Deventer's Calvinist "fifth column." [17] This misunderstanding was soon to be of great significance.

Anxious to return to England, Leicester decided to reward Stanley with the post of military governor of the town during his absence. Stanley soon learned the hard realities of his new assignment. His troops had not been paid since they reached

---

[14] Stanley proudly wrote to Leicester of his bravery in repulsing a counterattack on 20 October 1586: ". . . Sir Edward Stanley and my kerns put them to their second gatte, our horsemen had the killinge of their footmen within their gate." B. M., Cotton Galba CX f. 71.

[15] Camden Society, vol. xxvii, p. 223, letter of Walsingham, 11 April 1586.

[16] *Ibid.*, pp. 478–80.

[17] *Correspondentie*, vol. 1, p. 317, "The meanes of obtayning the late possession of the towne grewe by them that are now in office." Wilkes to Stanley, 9/19 December 1586.

the Low Countries, and the Calvinist faction was disturbed at the presence of an English garrison in their midst. Moreover, there remained a sizable Dutch Catholic faction who resented Stanley's occupation and remained loyal to their deposed magistrates. Hardly had Leicester returned to face the anger of the Queen over many of his mistakes when Stanley's troops became the subject of constant protests from the citizens of Deventer.[18]

In addition to accusing Stanley of being a tyrant and of "using them hardly," he was said to be meddling in their liberties by insisting on holding the keys of the town gates and then maintaining strong positions inside the walls. Stanley was adamant in asserting his immunity from the magistrates and even from the orders of the Council of the Estates in the Hague.[19] In reply to a warning from Thomas Wilkes, Leicester's deputy at the Hague, who pointed out that Stanley's commission did not allow him "to meddle any furder then with government of the souldyers and gard of the town," [20] Stanley explained his position. On his hands was a starving, unpaid force of "kerns" in danger of disbanding, since the townspeople refused to give them provisions.[21] Despite the protests of the magistrates Stanley had simply commandeered sufficient food for his men.

The Deventer townspeople were not to be put off. They

---

[18] *Correspondentie*, vol. i, pp. 274–75, 286.

[19] "Stanley did alwaies protest that he would be commanded but by your lordship or her majestie" (*Correspondentie*, vol. ii, p. 62, letter of Wilkes, 24 Jan./3 Feb. 1587). Stanley also informed the Count of Meurs, the Estates Governor of the province, that he could "draw out guarisons from all places there aboutes, yf he sawe cawse to doo some sarvice" (*Ibid.*, vol. ii, p. 39, letter of Gilpin, 13/23 Jan. 1587). He also insisted on his independence of the "commaundement and authoritie" of his rival, Sir John Norris. (*Ibid.*, p. 65.)

[20] *Correspondentie*, vol. i, p. 317.

[21] *Ibid.*, vol. i, p. 331.

continued to complain to the Hague about the activities of
their English garrison which weekly took a levy of "one whole
oxe, three sheepe and one hogg" among other demands.[22] So
great was the clamor that within two months of its capture the
town of Deventer and its unwelcome garrison had become a
cause célèbre in the deliberations of the Council of the Estates
in the Hague.

At this time the first suspicious note appeared in the attitude
of Wilkes toward Stanley. He inquired about the truth of a
"conceit" of the Council of the Duchy of Flanders that a "lieu-
tenant of some Englishe companie at Deventer hath had ac-
cesse to the enemy of Zutphen." Noticing that Stanley's
"kerns" were "for the most part, Papists as it is supposed,"
Wilkes wanted information about a rumor that there was "intelligence with the enemy to betray the towne." [23]

Stanley, however, was quite explicit that there was no
reason to worry. "I would be the sorriest man that lives if, by
my negligence, the place should be lost," he replied grimly.
In another letter he made it clear that he was not allowing
Catholic worship, and he added that "for my person, it is redie
for her majesties service to discharge all honorable actions." [24]

However the situation was still deteriorating. Within four
weeks the Deventer magistrates were so estranged from him
that they were going to the expense of sending a special envoy
to the Hague and to London insisting on Stanley's dismissal.
To them he seemed to be "evell in religion" and consorting
with "notorious and daringe papistes." [25] Their charge implied that Stanley had found friends within the ousted Catholic
faction in Deventer. However, if Stanley had been well paid

[22] *Ibid.,* vol. ii, p. 48, p. 70.
[23] *Ibid.,* vol. i, p. 341, letter of 17/27 December 1586.
[24] *Ibid.,* vol. i, p. 331, letter of 1424 Dec. 1586; Motley,
The United Netherlands (ed. 1904), vol. ii, p. 182.
[25] *Correspondentie,* vol. ii, p. 48, letter of 19/29 January
1587.

and provisioned, it is questionable whether the crisis in De-venter would have arisen.[26]

Facing this impasse Stanley finally turned to sounding out the Spanish commander of troops in nearby Zutphen. The exact date of his decision is not known, but it was apparently when he openly broke with the magistrates of Deventer in mid-January. The most reliable Spanish source is obviously the account by the Duke of Parma who did not write to Philip II until February 12, 1587. At that time he summarized con-cisely all the principal details on two pages.

The principal figure in the negotiations for the surrender of Deventer was Juan Baptista de Taxis who received assurances that Stanley was at present "a Catholic gentleman" as were the majority of his Irish levy. After hurrying to Parma's camp to receive written authorization to make terms, Taxis had found it easy to reach an understanding. Parma wrote:

He demanded neither articles nor signature of mine other than the letter of credence that Taxis carried. He planned noth-ing more than that the said Taxis should enter the town with your Majesty's troops . . . the deed was accomplished on Thursday, the 28th of the past month at five in the morning. Taxis entered at the head of your majesty's troops, which were 600 men and four companies of horse, two of lances and two of arquebuses, through the gate which the colonel opened. There was the least possible disorder as he set up his camp as it were in the lands of friends.[27]

At the same time Sir Rowland Yorke surrendered the English position on the nearby "sconce" at Zutphen.

[26] Writing to Walsingham one year later, Leicester remarked: "The lack of good paiement to the soldyors wyll hazard all that the Queenes Majesty hath here for her serenytie. Stanley's parte wyll make jelous of all, spetyall whear want ys." *Ibid.*, vol. iii, p. 260. See also J. Neale, "Elizabeth and the Netherlands," *E.H.R.* (1930), vol. xlv, pp. 203ff.
[27] E 592/41 despatch from Brussels.

Nearly all the gains of the recent campaign of Leicester were dissipated, for Parma now held the strategic initiative in the province. As part of Stanley's agreement all English troops who did not wish to follow him were permitted to remain under the English standard and about 300 marched away under Sir Edmund Cary.[28] The rest, totaling about 600, including Sir Edward Stanley, Captain Parker and others, proceeded into Spanish service. Significantly, with Taxis at his side, the first act of Sir William Stanley was to summon the new magistrates and demand three months' pay.[29]

The effect of this bloodless surrender was dramatic in the extreme. Thomas Wilkes, who blamed Rowland Yorke for influencing Stanley's decision, reported in amazement to Leicester, "I knew her Majestie reposed as great a trust in him as in any gentleman of his sorte in all her realme," and to Burghley he confided, "I know not whom we maye trust." [30] To the furious letter of the Estates General charging him with neglect, Leicester chose to reply, rather lamely, that his confidence in Stanley had been shared by the Queen, for she had intended to entrust "whole kingdoms" to his care.[31] By this he hinted that a soldier whom the Dutch had been determined to dismiss had been in fact in line for far higher posts. It was ridiculous to expect the Estates to be satisfied with such a reply, nor is there any other evidence that the Queen contemplated such an honor for Stanley. In a more level-headed manner the Privy Council soon ordered an inquiry into the character of the levy of troops that had served with Stanley.[32] But at the Hague feelings still ran high over the affair, for Wilkes re-

[28] They were deployed back to Ireland. *Acts of the Privy Council*, vol. xiv, p. 377.
[29] *Correspondentie*, vol. ii, p. 62.
[30] *Ibid.*, vol. ii, pp. 63–64.
[31] *Ibid.*, vol. ii, p. 86.
[32] *Acts of the Privy Council*, vol. xiv, p. 331.

ported in exasperation that they had "nothing in their mouthes but the treasons and disorders of the English." [33]

It was galling to the English Court to endure such re-proaches. Not merely were the Dutch quite dependent on the Queen, but there had been several other notable defections from the Estates within easy memory. A few months after Stanley's surrender a small book was circulated in London which offered this cold comfort. Entitled *"A Short Ad-monition or Warning"* . . . it was a translation from a Dutch tract reminding the partisans of the Estates of several no-table defectors. There was, the Prince of Chimay who, "pro-fessing the reformed religion, yea comming from the Lord's supper, did not onlie betraie and deliver into the hands of the enemie the town of Bridges, but also the whole government of Flanders." It cited other instances and then ended with the deliberate irony: "We omit the Generall that toke in Brussels treacherouslie and the Low Countrie colonell that would have betraied Bergehen op Zoome but through his unskilfulnesse could not deliver it." [34]

Stanley's change of allegiance was to be imitated by sev-eral others among his contemporaries. Within two years the English troops at Gertruidenberg sold that town to the Span-ish for their back pay, and shortly after that, part of the forces under Sir John Norris surrendered Ghent. The pattern con-tinued with the sale of the town of Alost to Parma by the English captain William Pigot.[35] The advantages to Spain were ultimately more psychological than strategic. The town of Deventer was to remain in Parma's hands for only four years, when the Count van den Bergh recovered it for the Estates in 1591.

[33] *Correspondentie*, vol. ii, pp. 65, 76.

[34] *A Short Admonition or warning upon the detestable treason* . . . (London, 1587), pp. 1–2.

[35] P. Geyl, *The Revolt of the Netherlands* (2nd ed.), p. 201; *Sadler's Papers*, vol. ii, pp. 220–21.

Stanley's surrender of Deventer and his conversion to Catholicism have always remained, however, a controversial case which Stanley's silence, in the midst of the pamphlet war surrounding Deventer, has never adequately explained. On the one side there was the timely warning of Wilkes, nearly six weeks before his decision: "You are to consider that we are not come into these countries for their defense only, but for the defense of her Majesty and our own natyve country knowing that the preservacion of bothe dependeth altogether uppon the preserving of theis." [36] On the other side was the cool appraisal of the Duke of Parma that Stanley was "quite lacking in any sort of ambition." [37] The Spaniards were as mystified as the English. Don Alonso Vasquez, a captain in Parma's army and later an historian of the wars, related, clearly from hearsay, that Stanley's action was caused by his disagreements with Leicester and by his conviction that Deventer was King Philip's by right. [38] There is no evidence in Stanley's correspondence to support this interpretation. He was facing the ruin of his career owing to the Dutch animosity and he was also desperate for food and pay for his men; there is nothing else provable in the extant sources. Quite separate from these urgent reasons, Stanley and his brother declared themselves to be Catholics, but this was never part of the conditions of surrender. On this count Dr. William Allen came to his defense. However, his celebrated book *"Concern-inge the Yeildinge up of the citie of Dauentrie"* was written before the two Englishmen had met. Allen did not see him until late in 1589, and even Father Robert Persons did not meet him until the spring of 1590 in Spain. Nor did the Jesuit publish any comment on Stanley's action until 1602. Allen's book was prompted by an inquiry from one of

[36] *Correspondentie*, vol. 1, p. 318.
[37] E 592/41.
[38] *Colección de Documentos Inéditos*, vol. lxxiii, pp. 232ff.

Stanley's captains, a Roger Ashton, on behalf of those "to whom the matter touches in conscience and honor . . . how they ought to carry themselves under similar circumstances." [39] Allen wisely did not attempt to make any special plea for Stanley but rather to explain the principles that Allen wished to guide any Englishman in the wars. One of its most striking passages makes his viewpoint quite explicit:

> In these warres and al others, that may at any time fal for religion, against heretics, or other infidels euerie Catholic man is bound in conscience to enforme himself for the justice of the cause, the which when it is doubtful or toucheth religion, as is said, he ought to imploy his person and forces, by direction of such as are vertuous, and intelligent in such cases, but specially by the general pastor of our soules being Christes vicar on earth. [40]

While Allen did not assert that Stanley was motivated by "conscience" in January 1587, or that the Pope had obliged the faithful in conscience to support the cause of Spain, he did insist on the duty to inquire into the justice of the cause of war. A Protestant could have the same problem as did in fact the contemporary soldier, John Smith, later to be the famous explorer of Virginia, who as a young man also left Leicester's army. His biographer explained that he went to join the army of Henry of Navarre "because of the obvious injustice of the war being waged by the States." [41]

Allen's book provoked a reaction among Catholics as much as in the rest of England. Some months after its appearance a Jesuit working in London reported to Robert Persons that some of his friends were disturbed that such notions could have been written by a man of Allen's distinction. They told

[39] Chetham Society, vol. xxv, pp. xxii, note 4, 4–7.
[40] *Ibid.*, p. 27.
[41] *The Life of John Smith, English soldier*, by Henry Wharton (London, 1685), L. Striker ed. (Chapel Hill, 1957), p. 40.

him flatly that everyone fought the Spanish "as being enemies
of England and not as Catholicks," and that "no law either
divine or human bindeth to restitution when the same can
not be done without detriment of our honour, danger of our
life, hazard of our friends, etc." [42] An English Protestant published the *Briefe Discoverie of Doctor Allen's Seditious
Driftes* to argue in the same vein. He admitted that the argument of conscience was devised by "a greater, learned, and
far more cunning allurer than myselfe" but he insisted that
Deventer was "justly obtained." He echoed many of his
compatriots by noting that soldiers were but "ministers" of
their ruler's instructions and not "judges" of them.[43] A candid
aside by Robert Persons, fifteen years later, shows that the
issue of Deventer remained largely one of partisan feeling
among the Elizabethans. He advised his readers:

Suppose any Spaniard . . . should hold any toune at this
daye in Ireland of the Earl of Tyrone . . . and becoming a
Protestant should therewith thinke himself bound in conscience
to yeld the same freely and frankly without reward . . . to
her Maiestie as the true owner, would our men (trow you) cry
out heere of treachery?

It is certain that Stanley resented deeply the label of traitor,
so liberally applied to him for the rest of his career. Even in
1600 he visited the English commissioners to the conference
at Boulogne to show them his patent from Leicester allowing
him "to leave the service of the States at his pleasure." [44]
This patent of Stanley's service has yet to be discovered.
While every one admitted that Stanley did not sell Deventer
by any means, it is obvious that he could not believe Wilkes'
advice:

[42] T. F. Knox, *Allen*, pp. 300–01.
[43] G.B., *A Briefe Discoverie* . . . (London, 1588).
[44] R. Persons, *A Manifestation of the Great Follie* . . . (Antwerp, 1602), pp. 44–45.

You are to consider that neither I nor any of our nation here that I know, hathe theis mens purces at commandment, and therfore whosoever will resolve to serve here, must be contented to lack when it is not to be had . . .[45]

Whatever the complexity of hidden motives that prompted Stanley's change of allegiance, once he had made his decision, he never looked back. His energy and considerable talents were now completely at the service of a new loyalty, but there was no important place for him as yet. For a period of a year he remained Governor of Deventer, but later as the Armada crisis developed in the spring of 1588, he obviously expected to be consulted. He was not. Sources both hostile and favorable to him make it clear that at that time Spain did not esteem highly his leadership or advice. Anthony Copley reported later with some asperity: "Even then, when the embarking was supposed, it grieved the better sort . . . yea they sorrowed to see how they were even then disdained of the Spaniard." This is confirmed by Robert Persons who reminded Spanish officials three years after the Armada that on that occasion they had "showed no confidence in any living person of our nation both within and without the kingdom."[46]

Upon entering Parma's army Stanley was granted a pension of 300 escudos a month, which he later remarked had been lower than his pay under Queen Elizabeth. In further compensation Parma wrote to Philip II in September 1587 recommending the Englishman for a membership in the order of Santiago.[47] He did not succeed and it was to be several years before Stanley began to be rewarded more generously.

The principal problem facing Stanley was to be the morale of his regiment. To maintain this, he had but two hopes: to

[45] *Correspondentie*, vol. i, p. 345, letter of 18 Dec. 1586.
[46] Strype, *Annals*, vol. iv, p. 391; T. F. Knox, *Allen*, p. 330.
[47] E 592/116.

keep it employed and to keep it paid. In this unenviable task he was due to face many disappointments. Father Henry Walpole, one of the regiment's chaplains, wrote in August 1589 that "our regiment stands in difficulties and danger of dissolving." [48] Stanley was experiencing the same troubles as in Deventer, for when assigned to garrison duties again, the pay was usually in arrears. There were reports that Juan Baptista de Taxis, the former agent for Stanley's surrender, was using his powers as *Veedor General* to restrict his regiment's growth.[49]

By the close of the summer campaigns of 1589 Stanley had every normal reason to rue his decision at Deventer. He was still encouraged, however, by the sympathetic Duke of Parma to go to the Court of Philip II to explain the urgency of making better use of his men. With Hugh Owen as his companion Stanley left the Low Countries to travel first to Rome, where he finally met Cardinal Allen, and then on to Spain in the early weeks of 1590. Although Parma had taken pains to write to the king: "Please God that your Majesty may realize that from these men there will be services that procure the advance of the Catholic religion," [50] Philip was not too enthusiastic. After granting Stanley an audience in February 1590 the King wrote to Parma that the English colonel could not be put "under the assistance of that army." He ordered instead that the regiment should be promptly paid from the revenues of Flanders. He added the slight consolation that Stanley's absence was not to cause him any loss of pay.[51] In his refusal to place Stanley's forces under the direct assistance of the Spanish treasury, or to give it a special

[48] Stonyhurst MS Anglia A I f. 15.
[49] *C.S.P. Add. 1580–1625*, pp. 265, 291; *C.S.P. For., 1589*, p. 338.
[50] E 598/23.
[51] A.H.N. Estado lib. 251d n.f.

assignment, the King had placed Stanley in a quandary. With his future still bleak the English colonel decided to remain in Spain and still press for better arrangements for his regiment. He was a stubborn man, and was to spend well over a year trying for a better hearing.

In Flanders, meanwhile, the regiment's morale dipped lower than before. From its entrenchments near Antwerp Father Henry Walpole reported in discouragement. "By want and by division ministered by spies, it is even on the point breaking into Irish or nothing." [52] Obviously the familiar rivalry between the English and the western Irish had now broken out among the exiles. The fact that Stanley had served for fifteen years against them in Ireland only increased the tension, although most of Stanley's original companies of Deventer had been levied there. In five years the problem had become so urgent that the Archduke Albert was to separate all Irish soldiers from the regiment and create a separate company under "John de Claramont." He stated in the patent, issued on July 15, 1596, that they could serve best under an Irish leader.[53] The problem was not solved so easily, however. Later, Thomas Fitzherbert recalled the English-Irish mistrust at the court of Philip III in the preparations for the Kinsale expedition. He remarked that Tyrone's agent, a Hugh Boye, "never yet broke the matter with him, nor was willing that any Englishman at all should be privy therunto, as men whome both he and other Irishmen treating therabout presumed to be contrary to their desires and designments therin." [54]

However, the persistent rumors about Spanish help to the Irish in the early 1590's remained linked with Stanley's name. Even such a knowledgeable informer as the English

[52] Stonyhurst MS Anglia A I f. 45.
[53] A.G.R., S.E.G. livre 16, f. 112v–114.
[54] T. Fitzherbert, *A Defense of the Catholyke Cause*, p. 5.

priest, John Cecil, reported to the Privy Council, while Stanley was still in Spain, that he was "hoping to be sent with 1,000 men and 30 ships to Ireland." There is nothing in Spanish sources to confirm this. Instead Stanley was working with the governor of Ferrol in August 1590 advising him and certainly earning his respect, for he wrote in praise of his abilities to the Secretary of the Council.[55]

Early in the spring of 1591 Stanley visited the Spanish Court again and entrusted to Father Robert Persons a new plan. He hoped to use his English troops in an expedition to seize Alderney in the Channel Isles. He was confident enough of its feasibility to leave before a final decision was made, so that he could make ready his troops. This time he was encouraged by a warm letter of praise from Philip II.

The Alderney *empresa*, written out in Persons' hand, represents Stanley's first efforts to strike out on his own. It is a document that only an experienced soldier could prepare. It began by giving the physical aspects of the island: "Midway between St. Malo and Portland . . . ," "three leagues and a half in length and one and a half in width . . . ," "its shape is exactly like an animal's kidney," with "four small villages." Its lord was an English knight named "Thomas"[56] Chamberlain. It was stated that Chamberlain had told Stanley that "he desires the island to be in the hands of Catholics" but that he would leave to Philip II "to decide what reward would be suitable after the island is captured." Stanley believed that the one harbor on the island could be easily defended by 600 men at two points near its mouth. He reminded Philip of the advantages of having a good haven for ships passing to Flanders and it could also be a base for rapid raids of reprisal against England. He noted also that Elizabeth

[55] E, K 1574 n.f.
[56] The Christian name is an error, probably for George, in Stanley's notes. E 2851 n.f. 6 July 1591.

might be obliged to spend money on fortifications in England such as those that had to be erected in the Indies by Spain.

About the actual *empresa*'s operations Stanley was typically concise. It was to be timed for the month of October or November of that year so that the Spanish forces would use the following winter to fortify their position. He did not expect the Queen to break her custom of keeping her fleet in port during the winter storms. Stanley wished permission to use 300 "very select" men of his regiment and 200 from the *tercios* of Parma. They were to sail under an English flag until the port was taken "without giving a greater role to the lord of the island." After the landing Captain Edward Stanley was to bring a small force of 200 English and Spanish soldiers to complete the occupation of Alderney. His statement ended with a note on the ships and supplies needed for the expedition. There was one vague item of 5,000 ducats "for the occasions which are offered in those regions through necessity." This could either be a special payment for his troops or a reward for Chamberlain.

Alderney, dubbed with local pride by the historians of the Channel Isles, "the Gibraltar of the North," was to remain an island of strategic importance long after the reign of Elizabeth. As late as 1794 its capture was known to be the first step in Napoleon's plan for the invasion of England. Conscious of this strategy it was to be highly fortified by the English Admiralty later in the nineteenth century.

Previous to Stanley's ambitious *empresa*, Alderney had not often appeared in the calculations of the military leaders of the time. In June of 1558 it had been occupied by the French as a move to counter the dominance of the English and Spanish fleets near Gravelines. At the peace settlement of Ardres it had been returned to England and early in the reign of Elizabeth it had been conferred on Sir George Chamberlain, the brother of the Governor of the Isle of Guernsey.

However, in 1584 because of George Chamberlain's defection to Spain it was granted to another brother, John and his heirs, *in capite* for a knight's fee. In May 1586 the Privy Council had requested Sir John as "Captain of Alderney" to see to its proper defenses.[57]

In these years the suspicions of England were directed against France. Even Don Bernardino de Mendoza, the Spanish envoy in Paris, wondered at the interest among the French courtiers "whether the Queen of England's fortresses in Jersey and Guernsey" were strong. Eventually in March 1590 John Chamberlain agreed to an indenture with Essex surrendering to the earl his rights to the island for £1,500.[58] It was apparently an ordinary business transaction for Essex placed another brother, William Chamberlain, as his bailiff on the island.

Yet within a year the area assumed a prime importance in English military activities, and was thus an excellent target for Stanley's *empresa*. The Spanish invasion of Brittany under Juan de Aguila with 3,000 men had already begun in October 1590, three months after Stanley had visited the port of Ferrol. To counter this threat the Breton Estates asked Queen Elizabeth for help in May 1591. Even while Stanley's notes were being finished in Spain, Sir John Norris had led 3,000 men to Paimpol in north Brittany and the Earl of Essex was leading 3,600 men to Dieppe, where it was planned to proceed up the Seine valley to help Henry IV at Rouen. The seizure of Alderney by a well trained force of

[57] J. D. Mackie, *The Earlier Tudors*, p. 559; F. B. Tupper, *The History of Guernsey* (Guernsey, 1876), p. 165; E. F. Carey, *The Channel Islands*, p. 181; *Acts of the Privy Council*, vol. xiv, pp. 129–30.

[58] *C.S.P. Spanish 1587–1603*, pp. 81–82; P.R.O. Close Roles, Indenture of March 25, 1590 of Essex, Lord Rich and another (I am indebted to Mr. L. W. Henry for this reference); E. M. Carey, *The Channel Islands*, pp. 176–77.

English exiles could develop into a serious threat to Eliza-beth's French campaign. A squadron from Stanley's base in Alderney could threaten the supply line of the English ex-pedition or even raid the English shores on the channel. The basic merit of the plan had occurred to several of Stanley's contemporaries. For example, a port near the enemy coastline was suggested by both Mendoza, who looked to the Scilly Isles as a base against England, and the Earl of Essex, who urged the occupation of a port in Andalucia, to harass the Spanish convoys.[59]

Despite the merits of Stanley's plan, the Spanish Council of War was reticent for many months about the Alderney *empresa*. Eventually nothing was done about it and Stanley had to remain with his regiment and simply hope for a change of luck.[60] Yet there are two interesting points to probe on this first ambitious project of Stanley: what was the reason for his special interest in Alderney, and what were Spain's motives for ignoring such an attractive plan.

The selection of Alderney undoubtedly had its origin in a family quarrel among the Chamberlains. It was well known that not all of that family conformed to the established church in England.[61] Since at least 1573 Sir George Chamberlain, the original incumbent of the rights of Alderney, had been a Spanish pensioner in exile, and later he had become a good friend of Father Robert Persons, to whom he had loaned his splendid Captain's garments of "buff laid with gold" as a disguise for Persons to enter England in 1580. His son, George, was a soldier in Stanley's company and he was to

[59] J. Corbett, *Drake and the Tudor Navy*, vol. i, pp. 197–98; L. Henry, "The Earl of Essex as a Strategist and Military Organ-izer," *E.H.R.*, vol. lxvi (1953), pp. 363ff.

[60] William Chamberlain remained Essex's bailiff as before, and the island reverted to him on Essex's attainder in 1601 (Tupper, *op. cit.*, p. 168).

[61] C.R.S., vol. xiii, p. 102.

serve in the Spanish forces until 1600 when he resigned to become a priest.[62] Eventually, George was to be chosen the bishop of Ypres. It was quite likely that the detailed knowledge of the island's defenses came from Sir George Chamberlain or his son. Clearly the knight also hoped to recover his inheritance from his brothers.

It is apparent that Stanley had not as yet won the full confidence of the Council of War. Father Henry Walpole, the former chaplain of the regiment, later related a conversation he had had with Don Juan de Idiaquez in the spring of 1593 in which the great Spanish councilor told him he still had Stanley's memorial, "but could not geve him any answer therunto." It had evidently been discussed at the Court for Anthony Standen informed Anthony Bacon, in September 1592, that "all the drift in Spain" was towards Brittany and that a "watchful eye" on the Channel Isles was in order.[63] Undoubtedly the problem of finance and the initial success of the Spanish campaign in Brittany had made the seizure of Alderney appear superfluous.

When Stanley returned to Flanders late in the summer of 1591 he was still without a command which would give him the distinction to attract new men to his banner. Not unexpectedly the regiment stayed in its sorry state. Henry Walpole continued to note quarreling and desertions. A typical instance was a "Mr. Holker" who told the authorities that he was "willing to serve as a soldier in Italy or Spain, or to serve otherwise or abide any penury rather than return to the regiment."[64] A special reason for bitterness had been Stanley's choice of a deputy during his absence, in the *teniente colonel*, Giacomo de Franceschi, or "Captain Jacques." This

[62] C.R.S. vol. xxxix, p. xv; E 617/56 "entretenidos Ingleses."
[63] C.R.S., vol. v, p. 254; T. Birch, *Memoirs*, vol. i, p. 82. See also Strype, *Annals*, vol. iv, p. 392.
[64] Stonyhurst MS Anglia A. I f. 65. Holker was in Rome in September. Foley, *Records*, vol. vi, p. 564, *Liber Peregrinorum*.

quarrelsome figure, whom Stanley had first known in Ireland, was to be trusted by the English colonel, against the advice of all of his friends, until 1596.[65]

However, Stanley's troubles with his regiment were not unique within the military customs of the day. During these years desertions plagued the forces of Spain, England and France. The opposing forces encouraged it by giving safe conducts to deserters and some officers took bribes to connive in it.[66] Whenever some left, others would join. Thus, when Stanley returned to Flanders, he found "divers captains and gentlemen come from the Earl of Essex in France."[67] But there was little to offer these promising new arrivals.

A year later Stanley's frustrations broke out in his direct appeal to the King. "The true witness of the zeal I have borne towards your majesty," he wrote, "in addition to what I have already shown by my past services, I believe now well established in these six years of tribulation in deep misery . . . Were it not for the hope of improvement, it would be impossible to go on . . ." He then informed Philip that he had received the report that Sir John Norris would return to Brittany with 6,000 men and would then dominate the entire province. In an eloquent plea for action he advised: "the most certain way to change everything is to create fear in England, and bring the war home to them. Then will follow the disruption of their plans, making them withdraw their forces . . ." He reminded the King that this offensive against England would cost the expense of but one month's warfare in France.[68]

This warning was met with the reaction that Philip reserved for any enthusiasm, silence. After a small part in the

[65] Strype, *Annals*, vol. iv, p. 389.
[66] G. Cruickshank, *Elizabeth's Army* (Oxford, 1946), pp. 106–07.
[67] Stonyhurst MS Anglia A I f. 64.
[68] E 606/213.

seige of Gertuidenberg the regiment had the same repute as before. There were Philip's orders to pay the regiment faithfully but nothing more. In the tergiversations of the Court the place of Stanley's English Catholic regiment was being made clear. There were to be no spectacular raids, it was to be only a part of Spanish military operations in the war in Flanders. The decision that faced Spain was not an easy one. If its energies were to be devoted to the action in the Low Countries, or in France, any further attack on England could possibly increase the English military involvement against Spain. Stanley would have to bide his time for a suitable opportunity. It was never to come, but he would keep stubbornly trying to make his viewpoint appreciated.

Stanley's contemporary in the Elizabethan wars, Sir Roger Williams, had put his finger on another familiar difficulty of the English regiment with his famous remark: "Experience and Learning must confesse all warres are maintained with these three principles: a good chiefe, a good purse and good Justice." [69] The preoccupation of Stanley with a "good purse" was well known, for he faced an added difficulty in that any failure in the Spanish payments was usually judged to be a mark of the crown's insincerity.

It was not actually a policy of discrimination against foreigners on the part of the Spanish Court. It was a problem that arose from a bureaucratic, and corrupt treasury system which prevented adequate and regular payments to most of the Spanish forces. As far back as 1583 Cardinal Granvelle had composed a strong indictment of the inspectors of the Spanish army who paid salaries to officers who never mobilized their troops, or pretended to keep the fleet at full readiness even during the winter when it could not be used. Meanwhile Florentine banks received the high profits to be made

[69] Roger Williams, *A Brief Discourse of Warre*, p. 1; *Sadler Papers*, vol. ii, pp. 236ff.

by expediting the shipments of money throughout Europe. The Cardinal estimated that only one quarter of the money destined for the Low Countries would be actually paid to the troops.[70]

Aware of the problem, the Council of State demanded regular reports on the finances of the armies in the Low Countries. However, these papers demonstrate that very little, in fact, was done to improve a deteriorating situation. They also establish clearly that Stanley's regiment received as many payments as were normal throughout the armed forces of the Archdukes. These reports are also a valuable record of the number of pensioners who were annexed to Stanley's muster and the fluctuating composition of his personnel.

A full picture for the month of July 1592 is available in a special report which gives the details of every feature of Stanley's regiment at a time when its morale was not high and its English character was on the verge of disappearing.[71] The total pay of the regiment was 11,473 florins a month. There were 1,000 florins for Stanley including his household and staff; his own company of 66 soldiers and 23 pensioners [72] received 2,322 florins. Sir Edward Stanley, a captain with 44 soldiers and 3 pensioners received 950 florins. Robert Bostock's company of 45 soldiers and 4 pensioners received 1,043 florins. A Captain Edward Stanley—a first cousin of the Colonel—received 893 florins for 42 men and 3 pensioners. "Lawrence Funlan's" company of 63 men and 7

[70] M. Van Durme, *El Cardinal Granvella* (Barcelona, 1957), p. 363.

[71] E 603/89 Lewis Lewkenor reported: "The olde English and Irish soldiers being worne out, Stanley was faine to fill up his regiment with Walloons and Dutchmen." *Sadler Papers*, vol. ii, p. 240.

[72] These did not serve in the wars. In Elizabeth's forces they were intended to be a permanent reserve of men resident abroad in Ireland for emergencies. See C. G. Cruickshank, *op. cit.*, pp. 47ff.

pensioners received 1,306 florins. Lastly, there was the hated "Captain Jacques" who was given 2,572 florins for 62 soldiers and 32 pensioners. The total strength was 427 officers and men with 78 pensioners. A Spanish officer penned a note on the bottom of the report: "This regiment on the march does not have 350 soldiers according to a count." His comment reflects the number of absentees and deserters that made the fighting strength of the regiment appear unreliable.

The report composed over a year later was a useful basis for comparison. The regiment had gradually increased its membership to 10 companies, owing to a larger number of Scots, Irish and Walloons.[73] The next two years showed a dip in membership. A report on March 20, 1595 listed only four companies and 318 men, who were described loosely as "Walloons." The regiment was not always paid in full according to its due allotment. The use of the *socorro*, or "aid," in place of the regular pay was quite frequent as well as a *paga media*, or "half pay." [74] The importance of keeping the regiment in active service, which also assured the pensioners of their funds, can be seen in the entries later for the period from January to November 1600. The summary read: "A payment of 17,851 escudos was made for 10 companies; 2 payments for 7 companies, 3 payments for 2 companies and five payments for the remainder." [75] Clearly the differences in salaries came from the variety of small assignments that were made available to parts of the English regiment.

One of the good qualities of Stanley's leadership of the regiment was his honest appraisal of its condition. This, more than his enthusiasm, would build his reputation with the

[73] E 606/100; E 605/93.
[74] E 599/58; E 603/84; E 610/39.
[75] E 617/180; E 622/206.

professional soldiers of Flanders. In the spring of 1596 he was asked to give a report on his officers as part of a move to reform the various foreign regiments in the Archduke's service. In reply, he compiled a list of thirty-one Englishmen who served as officers for pensions of 15 escudos a month or more. He requested the dismissal of all others with the blunt comment:

I have not named here several other English, Scottish and Irish persons who are still with the mutineers at Tirlemont. It is evident that no other decision ought to be made concerning them except to pay them what is still due and not to make any further use of them at any price.[76]

For the cadre of thirty-one remaining Stanley had limited praise for nineteen in active service. Even then, three were part-time chaplains who lived at Douai and came occasionally to minister to the troops. Concerning the twelve other officers, who were not approved, Stanley had several revealing comments. For a George Barrett, who had been given a pass to travel to Rome, there was the note: "It will be a small loss if he does not come back." Two were described as spending all their time with other regiments so that it would be better to remove their pensions to their preferred places. Three others were found to be living in Brussels on various excuses. One of them, a Josiah Barney, who had been appointed the agent for the regiment's business at the Court in Brussels, had not reported to Stanley in six months. Ten others spent all their time haggling with the Spanish treasury officials over the irregularities in their patents of appointment.

His incisive criticism must have had a salutary effect for by the end of the year the regiment reached the total of nine companies and 1,084 men.[77] Even allowing for some desertions, which inevitably occur, it was in good condition when

[76] E 613/126.
[77] E 611/169.

the welcome news arrived that Philip II had finally given approval for some independent action against England. On April 2, 1597 the King wrote to the Archduke that he could allow Stanley to prepare a squadron of seven ships with 1,200 men to raid the coastline of England. The orders re-quired that the Englishman would have his base at Dunkirk and the forces were to be "partly from his own regiment and partly from another at your own discretion." [78] There is little doubt that Philip's approval was influenced by the famous raid of Don Carlos de Amesquita on the Cornish coast which had alarmed the area so thoroughly in the preceeding year. Moreover, the port selected had been the former base for the "Dunkirkers," the fierce rivals of the "Sea Beggars," who had sailed with letters of *marque* from the Duke of Parma. They had been suppressed after the Flemish towns had protested over the effect of their raids in their own dwindling commerce.[79]

Brussels took a very different view of releasing Stanley for such activity, for it would divert personnel from the com-ing summer offensive in the north. Crestfallen, Stanley faced once again the frustration of his ambition for an *empresa*. The demoralizing effect on his regiment was noticeable at once. By the autumn of the same year the membership of his regiment dipped so alarmingly that in exasperation he had to let it be totally disbanded for a time and its members scat-tered among other active units. Stanley was never to resume its leadership again, for when it was revived in 1599 a new colonel was selected. Yet despite this rebuff Stanley was far from retirement from military affairs.

He apparently turned with zest to contribute to the po-litical discussions then current among the English exiles. The

[78] E 2224/1 f. 238.
[79] P. Geyl, *The Revolt of the Netherlands*, pp. 234–35; *C.S.P. Spanish 1587–1603*, p. 630.

publication of the *Conference about the next Succession* and the usual rumors of Elizabeth's ill health spurred speculation about their policy in the event that the reign of the great queen was nearing its end. A military force, ready to move from the Spanish Low Countries had always been one of his fixed convictions. Stanley hoped that should James VI of Scotland be found unacceptable, then an English Catholic military force, manned by his willing soldiers, could strengthen the claim of any other pretender. As an English regiment it was expected to remove the hesitancy that any purely foreign intrigue would inspire. Such, in brief, were the plans that Sir William Stanley discussed with the exiles during the next four years. Without their delineation, most of his later activities would be unintelligible.

The Spanish Court was not enthusiastic over their schemes, Brussels even less. A good illustration of this difference in outlook was a private letter of Philip II to the Archduke Albert in which he asked the advice of "the experienced men around your Highness" on an enterprise which the King recalled to have been "at one time favored by Colonel Stanley." [80] Philip's words implied that Stanley had doubts at present on the feasibility of the operation. In any case the plan first originated with an anonymous English exile who was very likely a native of Hartlepool.

Apparently as part of the preliminary operations for the Armada to be sent northward later in the year it was planned to have a diversionary force of 3,000 men landed at a prearranged site on the Humber river. After their safe landing an attack on Hartlepool could be launched. The unknown strategist was filled with fanciful optimism: "The countryside is Catholic," he advised, and could easily be aroused if arms were ready for ten or twelve thousand men. A local cavalry force could then be easily readied, "for the people therabouts

[80] E 2224(1)/240, letter of 5 April 1597.

] 158 [

are the most skilled horsemen in England." The strategist concluded with the remark that the same success would come to his attack that had come to Warwick and Richmond who had returned "at the head of 3,000 Frenchmen, and assisted by the people, overthrew Edward the fourth and Richard the tyrant." [81] The Archduke refused to consider the plan for the same reasons that had prompted his veto of Stanley's ambitious plan for a squadron against England before.

During the rest of that year, as the discussions of the possible candidacy of the Infanta of Spain for the English throne developed in detail, Sir William Stanley began a review of his military needs for such an event. Together with Hugh Owen, Richard Stanyhurst, and some assistance from Father William Holt, a survey of the resources of the exiles in Flanders was prepared "in the event that your Majesty has the intention of proceeding further in the claiming of the realms of England and Ireland for the Infanta." [82]

The new opinions of Stanley, after the dispersal of his regiment, reflect all the presuppositions of the exiles' plan of the succession. First Stanley and his friends requested that the Infanta should reside in the Low Countries as soon as possible, for only in her name should any decisions be announced. Before she left Spain, the King and Prince Philip were urged to renounce in her favor any hereditary titles to England so that, upon her arrival, she could announce her claims without any rivalry among the Hapsburgs. Books to justify and propagandize her title would then be prepared, a sign that they considered their famous *Conference* too general a discussion. They asked that a council could be set up among the English exiles to advise the Infanta which would be an assurance that it was not foreign or Spanish advice that was being followed. They were optimistic that many English-

[81] E 2224/1 f. 242 "Discurso sobre la Empresa de Inglaterra."
[82] E 2288 n.f. despatch of 5 May 1598.

men would soon come to the Low Countries anxious to serve in the regiment. They also hinted that it was well known that many leading English nobles were ambitious and they might well be satisfied by advising the Infanta.

Naturally, the longest part of their report was taken up with the reconstruction of the English regiment. It was obviously the personal concern of Sir William and understandably he emphasized his plans for recruitment. "Once a regiment of foot is set up and maintained over here," he wrote, "it will be but a short time before its numbers increase sixfold." He noted that every recruit would have a "relative, a friend, or a neighbor" and the word would spread swiftly about each shire. Moreover, there were other possibilities: "There are always men at large without a leader who wish a change and who would more readily rally to someone they already know than to a stranger . . . such people can easily deceive an outsider whereas they fail with one of their countrymen." He believed these hardy adventurers would be of more use than "three regiments from a foreign nation." He then touched upon the familiar problems of prompt payment and good treatment. He commented, from rueful experience, that those who return to England after poor treatment always leave everything in a worse state than before.

This survey by Stanley and his fellow-exiles is a significant appraisal of the stages of their study of the problem. Although it was never to be implemented it was by no means a sterile exercise. Until their failure became certain, it was to be the forerunner of a number of plans discussing the diversion of Spanish might directly to the assistance of the English Catholics. Eventually the proliferation of ideas was to become so bewildering to the Council of State that it fell to Father Joseph Creswell to review the trends within the various memoranda submitted. Few of the original papers he mentioned survive, so that their content can only be known from his summaries. His report to the Council was entitled simply, and aptly, "What has been represented in all papers on this question." [83]

Creswell reduced the suggestions to three basic patterns. The first was a military *empresa* involving the preparation of 15,000 troops in the Low Countries for an invasion of England after the death of Elizabeth. These were not to be partisan supporters of any one contender for "there will be no word of the crown or of the successor until victory is assured on behalf of the Catholics." Afterwards, he noted, in a new parliament the most suitable person could be selected by common consent. The second pattern was to have an expeditionary force seize and fortify certain English locations that could be defended "so as to prevent the heretics from getting them first." This project would entail placing Colonel Stanley at the head of the "enterprise," and, as in the former plan, a parliament was to be held where the new ruler would be proclaimed. The third pattern was styled by Creswell as "the one proposed by Father Persons in 1596." This was quite different from the two preceding suggestions. Persons stated quite frankly that the Spanish Crown was not in a position to give sufficient armed forces to the support of the English Catholics. Therefore he suggested the mere proclamation of "the rights of the Infanta and the reliance on the strong reasons, which, of their own, will be of more force within and without England." This was not a military solution, nor did it plan for an armed rising in England, although its appreciation of Philip's military intentions was far more shrewd and realistic.

Since Creswell merely stated the three possible courses of action and did not indicate any of the Council of State's previous comments on them, the vital question of Spanish reaction to them can only be answered in a study of subse-

[83] E 2288 n.f.

quent events. In this instance, the declining health of Philip II, his bankruptcy and desire for peace negotiations with France, did not give a favorable forecast to the ambitious plans of Stanley and his military friends.

With the accession of Philip III in September 1598 there was new hope that the young king would reconsider the *empresa* sympathetically. In November 1598 he even asked Father Creswell for another review of the question. At hand were two letters from England, which Creswell left anonymous in this report, advising as before, a twofold military campaign. There was to be a force of seven or eight thousand men to be mustered in Spain "and in all secrecy embark them for the part of England that will be named." At the same time a similar force was to be readied in Flanders and after a rendezvous at sea they were to land "where they will find an easy entrance and the land full of Catholics." The correspondents of Creswell advised that, just as the Moriscos of Spain would certainly help an invading moslem force, "so much the more will the oppressed Catholics arise." The location for the landing, though unnamed, was described as one that could be defended for months.[84]

Whether there was a continuity of authorship, or only an identity of military ideas was only a point of speculation. Yet there was clearly a pattern established in all of these letters to the Spanish Court in 1597 and 1598. There was to be the gathering of a force in the Low Countries, or Spain, or both; the quick dash to a defensible position somewhere in England, and the confident hope that Sir William Stanley's talents would finally be employed to advantage. They were the typical facile plans of the partisan enthusiast. Philip III and his Council did not show any appreciable difference from his father in his reaction.

Events at last seemed to encourage Stanley and his follow-

[84] E 2851 n.f. memorial of 7 November 1598.

ers. The Spanish intervention in Ireland was viewed with great interest as a possible way of getting more favorable terms from England. Early in 1599 Stanley sent fresh advice from Flanders to Creswell to be drafted into a paper for King Philip's consideration. This time his reasoning pursued both historical and military lines.

Taking note of the rumors of possible peace overtures with England he observed that any such discussion of peace should follow the example of Francis I's dealing with Henry VIII. For the French King had first harassed the English coastline, "through the ships of Pedro and Leon Strozzi, as the chronicles of England and Pablo Luis in his History tell us." Because of their naval strength, Stanley recalled, the French secured very favorable terms. King Philip was then urged to act at once. He suggested that Sir William Stanley was readily available for advice. Moreover, he was told that there was little hope of success unless word was sent secretly to the leading Catholics of England.[85] There was still no reaction at the Spanish Court, but, curiously, the Archduke was sufficiently interested in the employment of the military-minded exiles to allow the regiment to be re-established for active service. Late in 1599 Colonel Robert Bostock assumed command and he was to lead it until his death in action at the siege of Nieuport over a year later.[86] However, Albert wished to organize the exiles for his own northern campaigns.

Moreover, the exiles' concern over the peace overtures between England and Spain continued as lively as ever. Even though military suggestions were unpopular, Creswell, for example, urged King Philip to use the conference at Boulogne

[85] Ghent, Archive d'État, Liasse 74, ff. 69–77, draft in Creswell's hand.
[86] E 617/180, E 2764 n.f. letter of June 19, 1601. His widow, a Catherine Carondelet, was granted a pension of 25 escudos (A.H.N. Estado, lib. 254 n.f. order of 4 Nov. 1603).

in June 1600 as the place to demand some measure of liberty for the Catholics. He even advised the King to order his commissioners there to announce the claims of the Infanta for the English throne. His reason, he said, was that it would be proper to stop confusing the Catholics of England with only secret assurances.[87] While Philip could hardly be considered hostile to the idea of helping the Catholics, he feared that an open declaration of the Infanta's claims would probably stimulate more anti-Spanish sentiment in England with nothing in return.

Stanley, however, remained convinced of his own viewpoint. On February 3, 1600 he asked Creswell to present a paper which was in effect a return to his projected squadron of the spring of 1597. Again he boldly planned to animate his fellow exiles serving in the Spanish army by some victory through the use of some fast, lightly armed ships. Creswell explained the idea as follows: "These vessels would be kept under Stanley's orders and be commanded, in his name, by Captain Crisp."[88] Stanley even wanted immediate authority to begin to equip the vessels. "In order to encourage and attract more captains and mariners, Stanley asks that your Majesty would be pleased to grant as a gift the fifth portion coming from any prizes taken from the enemy." Stanley also asked for accommodations for his crews and he assured Philip that his men would be carefully screened, for they would be selected from those who had served Spain for seven years or "had lost all their property in England."[89]

This time Philip was more impressed and he passed the letter to his Council of War. There Don Esteban de Ybarra advised that the implications of the plan were too large and

[87] E 1743 n.f. (*ca*. Dec. 1599).
[88] He was serving in the Spanish fleets since *ca*. 1594. Strype, *Annals*, vol. iv, p. 388.
[89] E 1743 n.f. 3 Feb. 1600.

he requested that the Council of State look into it: "To their Lordships here this seems to be a matter in which it is better to examine more deeply." The Council of State was equally worried about it. It quietly advised: "It is to be reserved to the Archduke to decide on the employment of English soldiers on the seas, since the Archduke after his experience of affairs, will know what ought to be done." [90] This was tantamount to the veto. But the exiles were not to be put aside so quickly.

In a report which was sent to the Council of State at this time, under the title, "What can be said at the present on the affairs of England," King Philip was advised to consider the advantage of supporting a faction in England. After this was prepared, and when the Queen should die, Philip must order Colonel Stanley "to go and assist the Catholics and support them until his Majesty can send larger forces." The report continued: "To this purpose, it will be very important to keep troops in Flanders under cover and to vote money for this purpose." [91] Typically it concluded that as far as the precise enterprise is concerned "there can not be specified any particular thing at the moment except to wait on events." Thus another impasse faced the English exiles, for to be well prepared required money and public announcements in Spain, yet Spain was reluctant to endanger its other objectives.

However, the belief that something ought to be done to prepare for the probable succession crisis was shared by some Spanish observers. For example, Don Baltazar de Zúñiga, at that time on a mission to the Archduke's Court, became convinced that the English Catholic problem could not be ignored. However, the only suggestion he had to offer in a letter of April 7, 1600 was to enclose another copy of the survey of Stanley, Owen, Stanyhurst and Holt that had been pre-

[90] E 2855 n.f.
[91] E, K 1631/11.

sented two years before.[92] The suggestion was received in the same way as before, so that the impasse between Stanley and the Council of State continued.

The news of a proposed force of English Catholic soldiers also came to the notice of the papal nuncio in Brussels. His observer at the Boulogne conference, Dr. Robert Taylor, informed him of it in addition to other developments on the succession. The nuncio, Bishop Ottavio Frangipani, reported to Rome, late in June, that James VI was reacting by assuring some leading English Catholics that there would be liberty of conscience for them. He commented that they were listening more readily as the reality of Spanish aid was diminishing. Dr. Taylor had observed that some of the English exiles were constantly encouraging the Archduke that he could bring about the accession of his wife, the Infanta, to the English throne. For this, as always, they advised the assignment of "three regiments . . . to be sent across quickly after the death of the queen. . . . To this his Highness will only reply that the matter is under consideration." [93] Inevitably, from Spain's inaction, a split in the ranks of the English Catholics appeared over the best course to pursue. In Rome, meanwhile, Father Robert Persons continued his correspondence with England. Since he had seen no prospect of military support four years ago, he was advising his friends to watch carefully for any Protestant leaders who might become friendly to the Catholics.[94]

By the autumn of 1600 Don Baltazar de Zúñiga had had further opportunity to reflect on the merits of Stanley's survey which he had urged Philip to reconsider in the previous spring. The collapse of the conference at Boulogne had given

[92] E 2288 n.f. Holt had died in April 1599.
[93] A. O. Meyer, *England und die katolische Kirche* (Rome, 1911), appendix, pp. 461–63.
[94] Stonyhurst MS Anglia II f. 62.

courage to "the Stanley clique" at the Brussels Court to push their "enterprise" energetically. He had discussed it with the leading exiles, Zúñiga reported to Philip, and they had assured him that they were in touch with others in England so that the "enterprise" should procede smoothly "by negotiating with some leading persons." He observed however:

The plan they reveal for their purpose, in which your Majesty would be committed another time, does not seem to offer much. It does not seem bad to me to negotiate with certain lords and leading persons in any case, but for this a large amount of money is needed. We will be running the risks that similar dealings always involve.[95]

When the Council of State reviewed his despatch on November 30, 1600, it was rather eager to reflect Zúñiga's scepticism of the *empresa*. It noted:

There is nothing to be done except to continue the consideration of the affair, for experience has shown the impossibility of conquering that kingdom by a coup, even if there were more substance to that project than there is now.

It was anxious that King James VI should come to the throne under some obligation to Spain, otherwise he would be free to turn into an enemy. It approved the idea that the Catholics should be encouraged to make friends among "leading personages" in England. For this it was later to approve a grant of money to be entrusted to Don Baltazar,[96] although in fact he did not receive it.

Thus by the December of 1600 the Council of State had quietly rejected the proposed expeditions of Sir William Stanley. His troops were still to be employed exclusively in the campaigns of the Archduke in the north. Mindful of this opposition at the Spanish Court, Sir William Stanley and his

[95] E 617/110–118.
[96] E 2033/3.

brother, Sir Edward, until recently a captain in Bostock's regiment, decided to go to Spain to see what could be done to change the policy of the king.

Sir Edward was very anxious to receive the command of the regiment. In his reports to the Council of State the troubled morale of the soldiers was heavily emphasized. Apparently there had been many casualties and desertions soon after the death of Colonel Robert Bostock. Sir Edward had gathered all of the surviving soldiers into his own company but even then its effective strength was not sufficient so that the company was "re-formed." Clearly sharing his brother's burning hope of building up the regiment for a new role, Sir Edward asked Philip III for a new patent to re-establish it "since little by little the number of Englishmen is increasing and they are necessary for any enterprise." Since he had by then served in the Spanish army for fourteen years he felt he would be able to give the new arrivals a good training and discipline "for from these men can be selected the officers and captains to guide the Catholics in England when they rally to defend the cause of religion in due time." As the first step he urged that he be ordered to return to Flanders with authority to collect all English soldiers serving in other regiments and place them in one regiment under a Spanish *Maestro de Campo*. Moreover, he wished permission to enroll other Englishmen who would arrive in the Low Countries, provided they were first approved by "reliable men" in Brussels.[97]

The plan of Sir Edward Stanley was more than a roundabout way of readying the exiles for the death of Elizabeth; it was the creation of a Praetorian Guard among them. The reluctance of the Council to agree was seen at once in its hesitant response. Three months later came the evasive decision: "Let the Archduke be advised." This was hardly encourag-

[97] E 1743 n.f. memorial of 17 Feb. 1601.

ing, but the Council was generous to Sir Edward personally, giving him 50 escudos a month in pension and a grant of 500 escudos for his travel and a recommendation that "if there was a company of his nation" the Archduke should confer it upon him.[98]

It was undoubtedly the invasion overtones of the plan of Sir Edward which worried the Council as much as the Archduke. For, only four days after the Council's decision, far away in Brussels the Archduke gave the command of the regiment to Sir Henry Flood on May 30, 1601. His patent stated:

We elect and name you Captain for all the English and Scottish soldiers that now serve in the Spanish infantry and for all the rest elsewhere in our said army, or who ever shall come to it. You are to keep a company of pikesmen to the number of 200, setting up the standard and naming the officers. By these you are granted all the honours, dignities, pay and prerogatives pertaining thereunto.[99]

This was a hard blow to Sir Edward's pride. At the age of thirty-six he had hoped to have the honor of leading his brother's former regiment. On seeing his small prospect of advancement in Flanders he asked Father Creswell to send a letter on his behalf to the Council of State. It was a blunt request for a transfer.

Seeing that I was not rewarded with the regiment which was leaderless after Colonel Bostock's death, although I had the longest service in it, nor have I been given a company of horsemen as I requested, I wish to be transferred to the Spanish forces in Milan.

The Council, in obvious relief, agreed and King Philip issued orders to Don Pedro de Franqueza to transfer Captain

[98] E 2764 n.f. consulta of 26 May 1601.
[99] A.G.R., S.E.G. liv. 20 f. 45–45ᵛ. Henry Flood had first appeared on Stanley's muster in March 1596 (E 612/126).

Stanley's patent to Italy in September 1601.[100] Sir Edward was to serve in the Spanish army for eight years more, until in 1609 he resigned and entered the Roman College to study for the priesthood.

Meanwhile Sir William Stanley had not been idle at the Spanish Court. He was intent on collecting the arrears in salary owed to him and, of course, to find another opportunity for his services. In his report to the Councilors he reminded them rather pointedly that he had received less pay since Deventer than before, and at the present his wife and children were suffering want in England. The Council reacted with evident sympathy for his privations when it recommended that he be given a higher salary and the enormous grant of 6,000 escudos.[101] The King halved their allotment but he was careful to send a warm letter of approval to the Archduke insisting that Stanley's services be continued.[102] For Sir William it was the familiar, rather disheartening story. He remained in Spain hoping for some actual payments during the autumn of that year, but he had a lengthy stay since the King had promised his grant on the condition that it be taken from the proceeds of confiscated English shipping. In December 1601, after the capture of the English vessel *Unicorn*, Stanley made another try, the Council agreed to look into the matter but an order conferring the amount was not drawn until April 8, 1602 and Stanley had left Spain six months before.[103] What had really sped his departure was the decision of the Council to commit the Spanish forces to the

---

[100] E 2764 n.f. letter of August 1601; E 187 n.f. order of 3 Sept. 1601.

[101] E 2764 n.f. consulta of 36 May 1601; E 1743 n.f. letter of 3 Aug. 1601.

[102] E 2741 orders of 12 July and 27 Aug. 1601.

[103] A.H.N. Estado lib. 254/18, Father Blackfan of St. Alban's College was made his agent for the bills of exchange (S.A.C. Serie II legajo 6).

campaign in Ireland. This had closed the door on his own
hopes for an *empresa* to prepare for the succession crisis.
His former regiment was now under another's command, and
it was earning the Archduke's approval for its loyal service
in his campaigns.[104]

Leaving Spain early in January 1602 Stanley traveled to
Rome to consult the Duke of Sessa and Father Robert Persons. The ambassador was careful to report his arrival and the
substance of their talks in a letter to Philip III. They both
were convinced that French influence was increasing at the
Papal Court and that the Pope believed there was nothing
that would impede the peaceful accession of James VI to the
throne of England. Moreover, Henry IV was unalterably
opposed to allowing the Archduke to have any voice in the
future of English Catholicism.[105] This was hardly encouraging news to the already disheartened Stanley; he had no choice
but to return to Brussels to await events.

The summer of 1602 was one of especial frustration to
him. He watched the resources of Spain being mismanaged
in the Irish debacle at Kinsale with obvious bitterness. In the
autumn of that year he sent letters to Father Creswell to present to Philip III directly. On October 14, 1602 his new
appeal to gain a hearing was made. "Your Majesty should
reflect," Creswell wrote, "how sound was the advice of Colonel Stanley and what, through his efforts, was requested by
the Catholics of England. They wished that an order be
given to ready his forces in this year of 1602 and to wage
one war in the place of several." Stanley reminded the king
that he had neither counsel, preparation, nor a clear policy
in handling the English war and this was preventing its
proper solution. Stanley advised that galleys should be sent

[104] A.G.R., S.E.G. liv. 20 f. 116, 31 Oct. 1601. An order
for a special award (*ventaja*) to be distributed among its members.
[105] E, K 1631 f. 23 letter of 23 Jan. 1602.

to Flanders at once and a commission be given to him to have his men ready to pass over the channel so that "in the event the Queen should die before your Majesty can assemble more help, he may encourage and rally the Catholics in the interim." [106] He warned that "the rebels" of Holland had already prepared an identical plan to be used without hesitation in support of James VI.

After a second letter from Stanley, Creswell approached the Duke of Lerma with further details of the Englishman's criticism of Spanish policy. The Jesuit noted that Stanley was "very disheartened at the bad results in Ireland, as there was ready at hand a man well informed on that country, but of all that could have been suggested or done there was never requested a word." After this partisan comment, he informed Lerma that Stanley planned to collect secretly the needed galleys by choosing sailors from Genoa and other foreigners in "hired ships from Ragusa or Germany." These mariners could draw their supplies from special ports in Italy or Spain "under color of an expedition against the Turks." The ships could then proceed slowly towards northern ports so that all would be ready in the early spring "so as to have matters in hand when the queen is still alive." [107] Stanley's companies would also be training in the interval.

A week later Creswell submitted a new memorandum, inspired in part by Stanley, which he entitled "The resolution of the Catholics of England to continue their devotion to your Majesty." The title was both vague and misleading, since the contents were only a summary of his most recent correspondence. He began by stating that "the Catholics"— a vague term—requested that Stanley must be brought to Spain again "as they have communicated to him various important matters touching the public good." The rest of the

[106] E 2512/61.
[107] E 2512/64 letter of 18 Oct. 1602.

paper was devoted to revealing what he excitedly introduced as an important letter "from the person who sends letters secretly from the Catholics of England to Spain." The missing identity was regrettable since the message remained vague without identifying the author. It read:

> If the Catholic King would make peace, we would like to urge him to make war, . . . Were our danger and security not also his, then his Majesty and his council could well leave us to our fate . . . but they help themselves who help us.

Spain had wasted its resources foolishly in the past and now "the Catholics" did not have any accurate word on Spain's intentions. There must be an end to indecision so that they could go on alone if necessary.[108]

In the same memorandum Creswell enclosed a copy of a letter from Sir William Stanley written on November 1, 1602 in Ghent. The English soldier told of conversations with "some one from England" and that he had also received letters from the Duke of Sessa in Rome. He had become convinced that "the cause of God" was threatened unless Spain could "work a sign." He wrote ambiguously of his new ideas: "I once had conversations with the Duke of Sessa in Rome when returning from Spain, and over these same matters there has come a new beginning from which a fine result can be expected. Yet it is not a matter for paper, so I leave it to another opportunity." He closed with an appeal for a change in Spain's policy, otherwise everyone would be ruined "while going from bad to worse." [108a]

Who was the Englishman passing through Ghent whose name Stanley was reluctant to put on paper? What was the "new beginning" that raised his hopes? What was its connection with his conversations in Rome with the Duke of Sessa

---

[108] E 2512/71–75, letters of 23 Oct. 1602.
[108a] *Ibid.* enclosure of November 1, 1602.

several months previously? There was to be a despatch in cipher from the Duke of Sessa four months later which would clear up the obscurity with some remarkable information.

Thomas Sackville, son of the Lord Treasurer of England, had visited the Duke of Sessa early in 1603. He informed the Spaniard that he had become a Catholic on an earlier visit to Italy and that he had returned from England with important news. He began by urging that Spain should continue to assist the Irish rebels as a show of force. Then he reported that the sentiment of the Queen's Privy Council was against James VI, "for being a Scot and a Puritan." He declared that the Council wished to know what was the likelihood of support by the Catholic princes abroad for another candidate who would be a Catholic and acceptable to Philip III "according to the disposition of affairs at that time." Sackville then gave a thorough endorsement of the long cherished *empresa* of Stanley:

> It is of the greatest importance that a commission be given at once in Flanders that, at the moment of the Queen's death, Colonel Stanley should cross over to England . . . to give assistance in the place to which he will be called. This will encourage the councilors greatly to make a decision and the Catholics to be united in their defense. The arrival of the Colonel with such a small force will not cause much unrest, yet it will clear the way for all the rest.[109]

It is difficult to avoid the conclusion that Sackville was Stanley's visitor in Ghent in November 1602. He indeed carried advice that to Stanley would appear to be a "new beginning," and he shortly after in Rome endorsed a military strategy that was identical with the plans of the veteran English soldier. Yet there are questions of a larger dimension to be probed. What authority, if any, did Sackville really have? With Sir Robert Cecil and the Earl of Northampton in se-

[109] E 977 n.f. Sessa to King, letter of 13 March 1603.

cret correspondence with James VI, how could the Privy Council, with its Protestant majority, be conceivably in favor of another candidate? Since the despatch of Sessa reached the Spanish Court at the very time of King James' peaceful accession, the contrast in the evidence is startling. Even more so was the spectacle of Elizabeth's former councilors proceeding to ingratiate themselves with the new king. In March the Council of State gave its typically sceptical appraisal of Sessa's information: "There is nothing to do but keep the Catholics in good faith and assure them of support." [110] However, by then time had already run out.

It is not possible to find out how much more than this was communicated by Stanley to Creswell in the autumn of 1602. At least the news would present a likely explanation for the Jesuit's melodramatic request for a private interview with the King and the secretary, Don Andres de Prada, in a letter of November 28, 1602. He explained only that: "I see that it is essential to keep this concealed, not only because of enemy spies . . . but also because of other people for reasons which I will present to your Excellency." [111] It is quite certain that his audience with the king, if it was granted at all, was of no avail, for the decision of the Council of State on Stanley's correspondence was announced on December 5, 1602. In the most explicit rejection of Stanley's military force that had been made after its presentation in various forms for over five years, it wrote flatly: "Things here are in such a condition as to make it impossible." [112] The days of planning were over, a chapter in the career of Stanley was definitely closed.

It was left to Father Creswell to inform Stanley and his

[110] E 1857/9 consulta of 17 June 1603.
[111] E 2512/58.
[112] E 840/39 consulta of 5 Dec. 1602; See also *C.S.P. Spanish, 1587–1603*, pp. 717ff.

correspondents in England. He duly reported to the King at a later date that the English Catholics remained grateful for Spain's interest in them. However, his correspondents were "saddened over this misfortune. What they cannot begin to understand is that enterprises which are announced publicly for their relief, have produced nothing but their obvious ruin." He still suggested, but rather diffidently, that his friends hoped that "Colonel Stanley will return to Spain a third time." [113] This only signified to the Spanish Court another review of the discarded *empresa* and so it was not granted.

Meanwhile in Brussels Sir William was still waiting at the Archduke's court. In an obvious effort to soothe his pride and still to reward his clear devotion it was decided to elevate him to the Council of War.[114] *Elevetur ut amoveatur.* Stanley was fifty-five years old, the decision of the Spanish Council of State had removed the possibility of active service, yet his prestige among the exiles surely required some recognition.

The early months of 1603 were filled with rumors as the Council of State toyed briefly with a new appraisal of the possibility of a candidate to the English throne who would be suitable to the interests of Spain, France and the Papacy. It was only the beginning of a complex diplomatic *detente*, which became immediately out of date by the death of the queen in March 1603. Even in the midst of these new diplomatic overtures the Council of State had made it clear that military support for such a candidacy was not to be arranged until the diplomatic situation had become more favorable.[115] It had, in effect, never reversed its decision of December 1602.

The peace proclaimed between England and Spain on

[113] E 2512/64–70 (Stanley had been in Spain in 1591 and 1601).
[114] A.G.R., S.E.G. liv. 21 f. 159. Patent of 8 Feb. 1603.
[115] *C.S.P. Spanish 1587–1603*, pp. 729–37.

James' accession was finally dedicated a year later at the treaty of London of August 1605. The first three years of the reign of the king, so despised in the calculations of the exiles for over a decade, were to prove, ironically, the time of greatest prosperity in the recruitment of the English regiment. Since the treaty gave Englishmen "equal liberty to serve all Princes," the enrollment climbed rapidly to 1,500 men and Thomas Lord Arundell of Wardour was appointed the Colonel at the generous pension of 4,000 florins.[116] Volunteers were crossing the Channel in such numbers that a separate regiment for the Scots was finally planned.

The rapid recruitment of such a force was soon to excite the angry suspicions of the House of Commons. The old reports of Stanley's discarded *empresa* were undoubtedly known in England for there had been little secrecy about them at that time. The House proceeded to pass a law which made it a felony to enroll in a foreign army after June 1606 without previously taking the oaths of supremacy and allegiance. However, the Archduke was not seriously affected by this measure since he had already granted full liberty of conscience to English Protestants serving in his forces.[117] In any case within two years the willingness of the Archduke and the Estates of Holland to negotiate was to lead to the Truce of 1609. The English regiment was again to be disbanded.

However, a nemesis had been still following with limping foot the career of Sir William Stanley. After abandoning hopelessly in the autumn of 1602 his practice of submitting his plans for a quick invasion of England, he was suddenly denounced by one of his former ensigns, the notorious Guy Fawkes, as being ready to do that very thing in November

[116] Winwood, *Memorials*, vol. ii, pp. 28, 111; A.G.R., S.E.G. liv 22, patent of 18 Oct. 1605.
[117] E 2584/3 report of Pedro de Zúñiga, 17 Jan. 1606. *Statutes of the Realm*, 3 Jac. I cap. 14, n. 13.

1605. There was, of course, no regiment available to him since he had not had in fact an active command since 1599. Moreover, since early 1603 he had been installed in the completely advisory post of a member of the Council of War at the Court of the Archduke. However, with the same bungling confusion that had placed Hugh Owen in prison, Stanley was placed under arrest to placate King James.[118] It was easier for the Baron de Hoboken and Pedro de Zúñiga to assert the soldier's innocence since his actual career was public knowledge. Although Zúñiga had never met Stanley, he remarked to the king in London that Fawkes' charges must be ridiculous since they were so impractical. He inquired sarcastically the whereabouts of the fleet to carry over the troops, especially with the Dutch squadrons so dominant in the channel. He noted also that such a project would be permitted only with the approval of a prince who was not engaged elsewhere.[119]

The furor in Brussels had died down by January 30, 1606, when Sir Thomas Edmondes, the English envoy, was told that King James agreed to Stanley's release from arrest "until further matter be sent to charge him." [120] Nothing was eventually sent, and Sir William was to be excluded from the attainder enacted later by Parliament.

Stanley was not the man to ignore such a calumny. In April 1606 he drew attention to his vindication by having a solemn service of thanksgiving in the church of St. Pierre in Malines. He had been living there as the Archduke's governor. It was a most elaborate ceremony, made more splendid by the choristers of the Archduke directed by his friend Peter Philips, the master of the Chapel Royal. The celebration had been deliberately delayed to coincide with the liberty of Hugh

---

[118] Winwood, *Memorials*, vol. ii, p. 184.
[119] E 2585/2 despatch to Philip, 17 Jan. 1606.
[120] Winwood, *Memorials*, vol. ii, p. 189.

Owen and Father William Baldwin.[121] When the news reached London the Earl of Salisbury was piqued by the entire affair. When he railed to the Baron Hoboken about the deliberate insult to King James, he was blandly assured that the battle-scarred veteran of Elizabeth's and Philip's wars was very devout and quite interested in music.[122]

Until this time Sir William's family had lived in England without suffering any vindictive reprisal after the dramatic surrender of Deventer. However, it was time for a reunion and the peaceful possession of the honored position he now enjoyed in Malines. His wife Elizabeth, William II his son, and his grandchildren had continued to live at Hooten Manor with the aged Sir Rowland Stanley.[123] Their reunion in Malines after nearly twenty years was a happy one, but Sir William was not to be allowed full leisure. Because of his reputation as a soldier, Pope Paul V wrote two letters to Philip III asking for his services in the imminent papal war against Venice early in 1607. Spain hesitated and then refused the request. It had no love for Venice but it was conscious of the suspicions any new military role for Stanley would arouse in England.

However, late in May 1608 Sir William traveled for his third and last time to the Spanish Court. He had been sent by the Archduke to reveal the full details of the secret alliance of James I and the Estates General and he was to offer his advice on the terms of the truce that was to be negotiated in the following months.[124] He also obtained full assurances over his Spanish pensions for even in the great reform of English

[121] Philips had dedicated his *Madrigalls for Eight Voices* to Stanley in 1599.

[122] *Revue d'histoire ecclésiastique*, vol. xix (1923), p. 356.

[123] The parish register of St. Pierre lists the baptism of the grandson, William III, at the age of seventeen.

[124] Winwood, *Memorials*, vol. ii, pp. 416–17; *C.S.P. Dom. 1603–10*, p. 652.

pensioners in September 1609 special instructions were issued that Stanley was to be exempt "because of his many services." [125]

From 1611 to 1614 various personal sorrows afflicted the English soldier who had at long last achieved respect and security with his family's companionship. His son, William II, died in 1611 at the age of forty-one, so that Sir William and his wife Elizabeth undertook the raising of their seven grandchildren. However, in 1614 his wife was to follow his son to the grave. Meanwhile, Sir Edward Stanley, after twenty-three years of soldiering abandoned his career in Italy and entered the Roman College to study for two years. He was ordained a priest by the great adversary of King James, Cardinal Bellarmine.[126] In 1612 he returned secretly to England to work among the recusants, yet it is not recorded whether he was with his father, Sir Rowland, "the oldest knight in England" at his death in 1613. He was to return to the Low Countries after seven years in England to enter the Jesuit order. He then devoted his time to help in establishing colleges for young English students in Louvain and Liege.

In 1626 Stanley's grandson, William III, decided to return with his family to Hooten Manor in Cheshire so that only Sir William and Father Edward remained in the Spanish Low Countries. His famous residence at Malines was sold and four years later he was to die at the age of eighty in Ghent. His brother was undoubtedly at his bedside as he was the Vice-Rector of the Jesuit college in that town.[127]

Sir William Stanley's funeral at Notre Dame in Malines drew most of the court of Brussels to mourn in the elaborate baroque ceremonies cherished by the notables of the period. For thirty days the church was draped in black with "every

[125] E 626/89 list of pensions.
[126] C.R.S. vol. xxxvii, p. 156.
[127] *Revue d'histoire ecclésiastique*, vol. xix (1923), pp. 362ff.

day masse of Requiem being said for him." There were 100 musketeers and 100 pikemen marching in the burial procession in company with the 100 poor men carrying lighted candles who preceded the nobles and distinguished men who had come to do him homage.[128]

Thus, there passed from the company of the English exiles the most colorful soldier that had served among them in the wars of Spain. He had never been a man of divided loyalties. He had remained the blunt, hard-headed soldier to the end, trying to explain hopefully the professional military possibilities of the several *empresas* in which he believed so much could be achieved. His ambition to mold a strong regiment of distinction, whose actions would attract recruits was doomed to frustration. He failed by attempting the impossible; he could not find a place in the Hapsburg determination to recover the Low Countries. Eventually he had to relinquish his regiment to others, but he retained a position among the exiles which the Hapsburgs clearly respected. The value of his regiment, a small force of men quite unworthy of a man with Stanley's record, should not be ignored. It was to remain the gathering place for the *émigrés* who sought a soldier's life, while it became the excuse for the pensions of other refugees "who served outside it" as the fiction of the paymaster's roles put it. Few can fail to appreciate the attitude of the English Court towards him, even if the prominence of his name in the reports of English informers is an indication of only potential, rather than an actual danger.

[128] Chetham Society, vol. xxv, pp. lvii–lxi.

CHAPTER SIX

"A Seminarie" : *Joseph Creswell, S.J.*

1556–1623

"King Philip dothe in shield a lion beare
The Inglish armes of lions three depend,
Whose countries children they with pawes do teare,
The other dothe them with his pawes defend.
One dothe them from the other free,
One lion then more stronger is then three . . ."

A Student's verse from *A Relation of*
the King of Spaines Receiuing in
Valliodolid and in the Inglish College
of the same Towne. (Antwerp, 1592)

A HISTORY of the Spanish Elizabethans would be incomplete without a study of their famous colleges below the Pyrenees. This was their *santa empresa*, as it was called at times even in the debates of the Council of State.

While the establishment of the colleges of St. Alban in Valladolid and St. Gregory in Seville was largely the labor of Robert Persons to whom Philip II reserved a unique confidence, their subsequent history is dominated by another and far different personality. Joseph Creswell's twenty-three years of attention to college maintenance and financing, as well as his energetic propagandizing for them at the Spanish Court, offer a rare insight into these institutions and their first genera- tion of students. From the first months of his stay in Spain Creswell was inducted into the anxieties of financing a college in an alien land. Five years later, after Persons left, Creswell was already protecting the interests of English students with a singleminded preoccupation. He was also on the way to be- coming, during the first half of the reign of Philip III, virtu- ally an *éminence noire* in advising the Council of State on Catholicism in England.

Joseph Creswell, who apparently had the Christian name Arthur until he entered the Jesuit order, was born in London in 1556, a son of Percival Creswell, a servant of the famous financier Sir Richard Gresham. Aside from the fact that his family were solid recusants,[1] little is known of his early career except that, after his father's death his mother married a York- shire gentleman named William Lacy. In June 1580, after his wife's death, Lacy left England to travel to the college of Douai which had been moved to Rheims temporarily only two years before. A month later when Edmund Campion and Robert Persons were beginning their famous secret journeys in England to minister to the recusants, Creswell served in the first dramatic weeks as one of their escorts. However, by the end of August he had decided to join his stepfather in France. Both Englishmen were intent on studying for the priesthood. Since there was no room in the makeshift quarters in Rheims, Lacy traveled eastward to the university at Pont-à-Mousson,

[1] H. Aveling, "Yorkshire Notes," *Recusant History* vol. vi (1962) pp. 238–40. H. Foley, *Records*, vol. vii p. 182, believes Arthur was another member of the family who entered the Jesuit order, however, the career of "Joseph" matches the entry of the *Liber Ruber* of the English College under "Arthurus Creswellus."

while Creswell applied for admittance at the English college in Rome in November 1580.[2]

At the age of twenty-four Creswell began a course of studies which would span six years. After attending lectures in philosophy for three years, he entered the Jesuit order, and after three further years mastering the theological curriculum, he was ordained a priest. His first assignment in February 1588 was in Flanders in company with his former Rector at the English college, William Holt. The two Englishmen were answering a request from Cardinal Allen and the Count of Olivares for chaplains for the increasing numbers of their compatriots who were serving under the Duke of Parma. In his instructions for this work Father Robert Persons, the Superior of the English Jesuits, warned them to avoid political issues while serving Parma's forces, and in England as well, "should it happen that God gives us back that kingdom." [3] Although his work was sorely needed, Creswell's chaplaincy was short-lived for, after the Armada disaster of the same year, Persons decided to recall him to Rome to become the Rector of his former college. It was a very difficult post to fill and it was made more so for Creswell when Persons left shortly afterwards for Spain. Creswell, at the age of thirty-two, could have used Person's advice on the problems that were still plaguing the college in its early years.

Although the strong rivalry between its Welsh and English students had recently been pacified there was still a danger that it would flare up. Other students were from the first suspicious of Creswell because he was a Jesuit, although the fact that he had been a student there shortly before would quiet their resentment somewhat. Creswell's principal worry

[2] Lacy, who was ordained in Rome in March 1581, was captured in Yorkshire and executed on August 22, 1582. Knox, *Douai Diaries* pp. 167, 169, 191, 192; *Recusant History* vol. iv (1957) p. 139.

[3] C.R.S. vol. xxxix, pp. 184–85, 314, 363.

was over the security of the students. No matter what measures were taken there would still be visitors such as John Gale,
who visited there as a "pilgrim" in Rome and later revealed
the identities of all the students to the Privy Council.[4] Gale
was to contribute to the greatest crisis of Creswell's rectorship.

In the final year of his tenure, the college together with
those at Rheims and Valladolid were violently denounced by
a royal proclamation in England in the autumn of 1591.
Creswell found his college portrayed to the English people
as a "receptacle" where

> certain principal seditious heads . . . gather together with
> great labor . . . a multitude of dissolute young men . . . and
> thus to be instructed in school points of sedition, and from thence
> to be secretly and by stealth conveyed into our kingdom with
> ample authority from Rome to move, stir up and persuade as
> many of our subjects as they dare deal withal . . .[5]

Deeply disturbed and alarmed by the attack, Creswell as
Rector of a "receptacle," hurried to justify his labors in print.
His *Exemplar Litterarum*, published in Rome early in the
spring of 1592, was, however, a rather dull Latin essay of
186 pages composed without any divisions or chapters. The
theme that Creswell developed with such prolixity was that
the proclamation was but another example of the folly ac-
companying the war between England and the Hapsburgs.
He charged that if there was unrest and disunity among the
people of England, it was prompted by the Queen's advisers
who could not prove the collegians were conspirators. What
were the details, he asked, who precisely was inciting to re-
bellion? Who was to gain power? He pleaded instead that
peace between England and its neighbors would allow the
opportunity to show the wisdom of toleration for Catholics.

[4] P.R.O., S.P. 12/243/29; See also H. Foley, *Records*, vol.
vi, p. 564.
[5] Strype, *Annals*, vol. iv, pp. 73ff.

It was an earnest, if bombastic, effort to save the reputation of the college.[6] It denied the substance of the proclamation effectively, but not all of its argument was to the point. Its most evident quality had been the author's sincere belief in the ideals of the college.

It was this single-minded devotion that prompted Persons to summon Creswell to Spain to become his assistant. Philip II had finally become reconciled to the presence of alien students in Castile and was even privately subsidizing the foundation of the college in Valladolid. Accordingly in mid-April 1592 Creswell set out from Rome with a gift of 200 escudos for his voyage from the Count of Olivares.[7] Cardinal Allen, aware that an unknown Englishman could encounter suspicions at the Spanish Court, took pains to write a special letter to Philip II assuring him that Creswell came

by order of his superiors and at my request . . . to serve only as the assistant to Robert Persons in the necessary affairs of England, and particularly in the college which through the royal munificence had been begun in Valladolid.[8]

When he finally saw Persons in May 1592 Creswell found his friend anxiously preparing for the King's arrival on a royal progress to the city of his birth. For the future of the English students much would depend on the favorable impression of the King and his Court. Philip had, as yet, never seen the strange new college. Moreover, contrary to the impression which even Allen shared, that all was well with the finances of St. Alban's, the visit would be vital to its very survival. In order to understand the significance of Philip's favor the three early years of the college's existence should be briefly recalled.

[6] J. Perney (Creswell), *Exemplar Litterarum ad D. Gulielmum Cecilium* (Rome, 1592), pp. 9, 50–51, 92, 111.

[7] E, K 1630/3.

[8] E 960 n.f. holograph, 24 April 1592.

Although the plan for a college as a residence for English students who could attend a university's theological lectures, yet live together under a special rigorous discipline, had been recommended as far back as the Synod of London in February 1556,[9] the Elizabethan settlement had postponed the establishment of such a *seminarium*. Dr. William Allen and his circle had revived the plan in his college at Douai in 1568. Its success was to lead to a similar foundation in Rome ten years later. However, the hurried exodus of the Douai students to Rheims and the financial straits of the second foundation in Rome had forced many prospective students to take the roads to Spain.

Only a few weeks after the final news of the disaster to the Spanish fleet, fourteen English and Irish students were addressing a petition to the town council of Valladolid for help. They begged permission to remain at the university where they had been studying "for over a year." Meeting a cold response from the *ayuntamiento* they appealed as a last resort, to Philip II. The King was generous to the hapless aliens for he ordered the town council to give them 100 escudos for the next four years. In June 1589 the council's *fiscal* gave them their first Spanish benefaction;[10] it was a pittance but the precedent had been set. However, there were already other students en route to the city.

The college of Rheims was threatened once again by the reversal of the fortunes of the Guises in the spring of 1589 and was in an even worse position to accept new students. Moreover, because of the maritime war it was considered particularly unsafe to let the young priests return to England in that year. The Rector of the College, Dr. Thomas Worthington, decided to send two small groups of priests and stu-

[9] W. Schenk, *Cardinal Pole* (London, 1950), p. 144.
[10] S.A.C. Miscellaneous Papers, Transcript of the Minute Book of the *Ayuntamiento*, for 24 Oct. 1588; 21 June 1589.

] 187 [

dents to look for aid in the university cities of Spain. In the spring of 1589 when a group of five reached Valladolid they were arrested by the Inquisition.[11] Shortly after this the second party of three reached Burgos and were also promptly imprisoned under suspicion of being "followers of Drake." Although a letter from one of the students, John Blackfan, to the superior of the Jesuit residence had brought about their liberty in Burgos, both incidents were soon reported to the Court of Philip II.

For the preceding five months Robert Persons had been residing near the Court on a private mission from the Father General of the Jesuits, Claudio Aquaviva, but the trials of the increasing number of English students in Spain attracted his notice. He later recorded his intervention on behalf of his compatriots with King Philip in these words:

> The king gave royal letters that the said preestes and scholers should not onlie be set at libertie and protected, but also most tenderlie cherished and favored . . . and he appointed that the said father should presentlie go downe to Valladolid, and gather together such English as weare theare and provide for them, until the weather and tyme and other opportunities did serve for them to follow their intended iorney unto England.[12]

While the only aim of Robert Persons in June 1589 was to arrange a temporary shelter, in a matter of six weeks he seems to have decided to try to arrange for a college as well. Characteristically, Persons resorted to a series of temporary expedients until a better foundation could be made. At first, some students were sheltered in the Jesuit college, others in hospices. In order to give publicity to his purpose he circulated a simple, but effective tract called an *Información* to explain his needs. Here he tried to counter the rumors that were cur-

[11] C.R.S. vol. xxx, p. 6.
[12] R. Persons, *A Relation of the King of Spaines Receiuing*, pp. 9–10.

rent in Castile over the novel experience of finding students from a hostile nation. They were here only to study and not to seek a benefice in Spain, he wrote, for they would return to assist their compatriots. He reminded his Spanish readers that, in the midst of their poverty, English Catholics had helped the Spanish mariners who were found among them after the dispersal of the Armada.[13] He also assured them that the authorities would be able to scrutinize the testimonials that each student carried.

Even while this appeal was being published, other students from the College in Rome, where Creswell was still Rector, were hoping to travel to Spain. One of these, James Yonger, declared after his capture in England later, that

ff. Persons wrote out of Spayne to the Rector . . . that he should send no priests into England that yeare, but, if they would accept of it as a benefitt, to send them into Spayne for that he had obteyned in Valladolid a new college . . . the year 1589 at michaelmas tyme I together with fower other priests took shipping at Genua and landed at Alicante.[14]

The contingent from Rome was to remain until it was felt safe to travel to England. Shortly before their departure Persons described their activities to a friend at Rheims in these words: "They have done themselves much good by this year's staying here, for they had time to review their books and learn the language and manners of this nation."[15]

The first year had been anything but serene. Although some friends, such as the Duchess of Feria and Englefield could be counted upon for gifts, there were many exasperating quarrels with the authorities in Valladolid. Persons was very afraid that the students would earn too much ill-will if the

[13] *Información que de la Padre Personio,* pp. 73–74ᵛ, contained in the *Relación de Algunos Martyrios* . . . (Madrid, 1590).
[14] B. M., Lansdowne MS, vol. 96, f. 152.
[15] *H.M.C. Salisbury MS,* vol. iv, p. 569.

situation continued much longer.[16] Eventually he succeeded in renting two houses on the edge of the ruined town walls which he and the students dedicated to the memory of St. Alban. This ancient English cult had become dear to the Elizabethan recusants, for his legend described his martyrdom early in the fourth century near Verulamium in England for sheltering a priest.

For the next year the college managed to struggle along through the gifts of Spanish sympathizers but it was still heavily in debt. The year 1591 was to be the turning point in its fortunes. These brighter prospects were an entirely unexpected by-product of the proclamation of the autumn of 1591 that had so disturbed Creswell in Rome. Curiously this sudden official notoriety had stimulated an interest among the young Catholics of England and it quickly rallied support, hitherto not conspicuous, in the Spanish Court. One observer of the new students arriving in 1592 put this development succinctly. He reported that after asking the students why they had traveled so far, "divers of them answered me that the late proclamation set out by the Quene in November last against this seminarie did first of all give them notice thereof, as also appetite to see the place." [17] King Philip's anger at the proclamation which would prompt his subsidy of Robert Persons' famous book *Responsio ad Edictum,* also incited further curiosity in the Court to see the notorious "receptacle."

It was at this juncture that Creswell was summoned to Spain. He readily appreciated that the royal favor would certainly make their problem of finances far less hopeless. It was not an imposing place in Creswell's eyes; since October 1590 it had consisted simply of "two large houses with a garden, and a garden in between." [18] When the Court arrived in Val-

---

[16] E 166/135.
[17] *A Relation of the King of Spaines Receiuing,* p. 12.
[18] *C.S.P. Dom. Add. 1580–1625,* p. 311.

ladolid an invitation to the King was presented by the Rector of the college, Rodrigo de Cabredo, in an address of welcome at the *ayuntamiento* of Valladolid. The King accepted at once and the young English students spent days in decorating their quarters for the solemn reception of the Spanish monarch. Every possible talent in language and heraldry was drawn upon for the great moment.

On entering the college, Philip II was greeted by a young student who addressed the assembly in English comparing the King of Spain to the royal saints of the Old Testament. He lingered on Abdias, the king who said to Elias: "Have you heard perchance what I did in tymes past when Yesabel the wicked queen did persecute . . . the prophets of God almighty? How I did save a hundred of their lives together by hyding fifty in a cave and fifty in another and feeding them with bread and water?" The bounty of the Catholic King was then suitably extolled. When the royal party had passed on into the unfinished dining hall they found it covered with a canvas roof but "hanged verie decently with grene and red tafatie and adorned with abundance of verses of many languages, Emblemes, Hieroglyphics and other learned inventions." Then began short academic orations by ten students on the verse of the seventy-first psalm *"Deus judicium tuum regi da,"* in Hebrew, Greek, Latin, English, Scots, Welsh, Spanish, French, Italian and Flemish. Philip was apparently delighted because he ordered all the emblems sent to his palace for further examination by the Court.[19]

The visit was a singular success, but more tangible proofs of the royal favor soon began. Shortly after this Philip II wrote to the Cardinal of Seville and the Duke of Medina Sidonia declaring his support for another college for Englishmen in Seville. The intention to found a new college there was originally sparked by the precarious existence of the college of

[19] *A Relation* . . . , pp. 23–24, 52–53.

St. Alban. In the winter of 1589 two of the students had journeyed to Andalucia to beg alms with a royal license and they had reported that they were given a better reception there than anywhere else.[20]

Seville was a wealthy city, the administrative center of the great overseas domains of Philip, and it was far more cosmopolitan that any city of Castile. In the autumn of 1590 Robert Persons had traveled southward with six priests, who were to continue secretly on their journey to England, to consider the feasibility of transferring the college to Seville. He was warned by the authorities that there would still be difficulties in finding a house and revenues to support his students. There was one bright moment in the journey at that time. The surviving members of the English merchant fraternity of St. George donated their chapel and meeting house in San Lucar de Barrameda as a hospice for English priests and students *en route* to and from England. But nothing more could be done until Philip II wrote his letters to the authorities in Seville on September 12, 1592.

In this personal letter to the Cardinal Archbishop the King announced that Persons was coming to visit his city and that his "good work" needed no recommendation. In a typical sentence the monarch asked the prelate to help the college *"con el secreto y dissimulación necessaria."* [21]

On this second journey to Andalucia Persons brought his new assistant of four months, Joseph Creswell, who wrote to the Jesuit Father General on December 1, 1592 with his not infrequent glowing optimism. He felt that the hard-pressed students would find more assistance there than in any other part of Spain or France. He felt it was due to "the ancient amity and trade with England that has lingered here." The laborious task of getting permissions and securing some suit-

[20] C.R.S. vol. xiv, p. 2.
[21] E 1855 n.f. letter of 12 Sept. 1592.

able quarters went far more smoothly on this occasion, for Persons recalled years later that "within two months there was in being a large community gathered in the manner of a splendid college." [22] When Persons returned to Castile and the court of Philip II, Joseph Creswell remained in Seville to direct the beginnings of the new college. So many students were coming to Spain that it had been decided not to close the earlier foundation in Valladolid.

For the next four years Creswell learned the problems of administering the finances of the hard-pressed colleges in Spain. He visited the Court and traveled regularly to learn the causes of any discontent that appeared among the students. St. Alban's was constantly a trouble spot because of the incompatibility of its Spanish Jesuit rectors with the English. His stay at the Escorial became lengthier when Philip II began to look to his opinion on the affairs of the English Catholics, when Robert Persons was absent.

In a letter of July 15, 1593 Persons reported to Rome that Creswell was showing a special aptitude for the tiresome duties of bookkeeping and begging. He observed that his talent for business was "greater perhaps than dealing with young men in a college, as we are already beginning to find out." He noted that Creswell was building on his experience and creating a good impression at the royal Court "and especially with the leading personages there." [23] In these years a pattern of administration was being informally arranged. Robert Persons was to remain as superior of all the English Jesuits, but with his men scattered in so many places, he used three deputies to make the ordinary decisions. Henry Garnet was in charge of England after his arrival in 1586, Joseph Creswell was responsible for the English Jesuits in the Iberian peninsula and William Holt was to direct his compatriots of the Society in

[22] C.R.S., vol. xiv, p. 6.
[23] A.R.S.J. Castila vol. 136, f. 138.

the Low Countries. Creswell did not bring any notable flair to his office. He was known to be industrious and attentive to detail, but some of his contemporaries also found him aggressive, impatient with delay, and at times devoid of feeling. His correspondence was enormous. One of the papal nuncios in Spain asked him to prepare regular reports on English affairs and he also sent despatches to the Papal Secretary of State. As his reputation grew, he was soon receiving many letters from discontented exiles asking his help in Flanders. He even found time to help English prisoners of war.

His difficulties in dealing with the time-consuming procedures of a bureaucracy in the richest kingdom in Europe can readily be understood. Robert Persons once commented in exasperation over the failure of the English exiles to appreciate that their petitions required considerable attention. He noted that merely sending letters was a "very feeble method to use with these dilatory officials." Because of the amount of correspondence connected with the gifts and revenues of the colleges, complaints of students and the general reports to be made at times to the Council of State, Creswell began to have a small secretariate at Court. From 1594 he entrusted minor details to Francis Fowler, the brother of John Fowler, the famous English printer in Flanders.[24]

As Creswell's residence in Spain lengthened he gradually acquired greater prominence in the Court. This was particularly true after the accession of Philip III in September 1598. The English spy, Giles van Hardwicke, reported to London in April 1599 that "the Jesuite Creswell hath so good intelligence that their waggeth not a strawe in the Inglishe

---

[24] Francis Fowler had been a soldier in the Spanish army from 1584–1588 and then in the navy for five more years. He was secretary to Creswell from 1594 to 1605 when with Philip III's approval he retired on 15 escudos a month "payable in one of the presidios of Spain" (E 2742 n.f. consulta 5 May 1605; Knox, *Allen*, pp. 216–17).

court but he heareth of it . . . this Creswell hath weekly a porter's burden of letters of intelligence from all places which is the cause of his estimation in this land."[25] After making allowances for the exaggerated rumors that Hardwicke was relaying it was evident that Creswell was holding the solid confidence of many. The mass of his papers in the files of the Council of State show that he usually was more inclined to suggest policy than offer specific information. For example, in 1600 Juan de Velasco, the Constable of Castile, asked him to find "two reliable people" in London to send out reports "on what would be of advantage to the Catholic religion." Two people had been engaged, as well as another informant in Antwerp, but the Constable had not made arrangements for their proper payment and so Creswell had to bring up the whole matter to the Council.[26]

However, Creswell's personal favor with the King did not always guarantee the admiration of every one at Court. In a short letter to King Philip written on April 24, 1599, the Jesuit discreetly described the opposition he had found among some of the Council. "There was a member of the Council of State," he confided, "who a few months ago said to me among other inane things that Spain has been hurt by giving aid to the English Catholics . . . Another said in public that it was treason to advise your Majesty to try on another occasion to send help there, seeing that it was impossible."[27] Creswell was, without doubt, a crusading idealist, but he was careful to distinguish his convictions from some of Spain's previous specific failures elsewhere. He particularly disliked the comparing of the English exiles to the "Leaguers" of France. The League, he carefully reminded the Council of State on one occasion, was really based on the personal jealousies of the lead-

[25] P.R.O., S.P. 94/6/212–13.
[26] E 617/226.
[27] E 2851 n.f. letter of 24 April 1599.

ing French nobles, "besides, many Catholics used religion as a reasonable excuse to draw the cities and people of France to their party." [27A] He warned that should Spain seek similar political advantages in England every Protestant would become its enemy.

Creswell was, as most of the exiles of his day, ardently dreaming of a Catholic ruler for England, but again he warned Philip against Spain's past mistakes.

It is obligatory that a Catholic ruler . . . never resort to violence in matters of religion but only proceed . . . by the path of reason and gentleness. The majority of Englishmen who walk in the error of heresy are born to it. The fault is in the leaders rather than in private beliefs. Thus it is wrong to act as they do now in Spain, and as they once did in England in the days of Queen Mary, against heretics who have left the Church. [28]

It was the voice of an independent thinker that would dare to speak out contrary to the prevailing climate of opinion at the Spanish Court, especially when it was to Creswell's interest to encourage support. It would account for the fact that when Creswell fell under suspicion a decade later, he proved to have fewer friends at Court than many expected. Yet during the turn of the century the admiration of Don Juan de Idiaquez assured Creswell of a hearing. This useful *entrée* had begun as early as 1595; Robert Persons once reported to Rome that Creswell was seeing that councilor regularly and that "he is the person to whom the King entrusts all the business of the lands beyond the mountains." He added significantly that Idiaquez "will only take reports from the hand of some one he already knows." [29]

Since Creswell had become responsible for maintaining the small but vital flow of aid to support the Spanish colleges for

[27A] E 2851 n.f. letters of 15 and 23 Sept. 1599.
[28] E 840/95 para. 2.
[29] A.R.S.J. Hispania, vol. 138, f. 249.

English students, he was adept in suggesting ways to put them on a more secure basis. He had been only a year in Spain when he visited the Escorial together with Robert Persons to suggest to Philip II how to improve the situation.[30] He had yet to learn that any suggestion of applying vacant benefices, or of using the returns from the auction of confiscated English shipping, were invariably rejected. In the autumn of 1601 he came up with a typically ingenious, if impractical, idea. Apparently he had been receiving letters on the need of a safe route for the young students to travel from England to the continent. He suggested to the Council of State that the Catholic clergy who had been selecting students "in London, the northern shires as far as Scotland, and in the nearer parts of Ireland" wished the King of Spain to give a special license "to a Flemish merchant, or one of the others trading with Spain." With this authority the merchant could sail two or three ships to trade profitably on the coasts of England, Scotland or Ireland and still "carry away six or more of the students" to the continent.[31]

He was so taken with the plan that he again offered a modified version of it on behalf of an English merchant living in St. Malo. He explained to the Council that Francis Naylor who had done "great service for the colleges in bringing priests to England" was looking for a license to trade in England for lead, brass and cloth to bring to Spain. "He promises, in addition to carrying over the students to Saint Omer, to put ashore the priests that we will send there and so be a great help to the colleges."[32]

On October 25, 1601 the Council debated Creswell's suggestion to use licensed merchants to bring students to Flan-

[30] A.R.S.J. Hispania, vol. 135, f. 372, letter of September 1593.
[31] E 2851 n.f. memorandum c. October 1601.
[32] E 617/225.

ders and Spain. They noted that "while the work he wishes to aid is most deserving of assistance," there were too many dangers in the plan to allow it.[33] Their decision was surely justified since any ship, exempt from the embargo, would quickly become known and its activities in England watched more closely—and easily—than any other. It would have been a trap for the unwary.

The variety of Creswell's plans is noticeable for he looked into every aspect of the students' life. For example, he decided to try to increase the official gift of money for travel expenses —usually called a *viaticum*—for the young priests to England. In a letter to the Council he explained that the amount granted to those bound for the Indies was always greater, yet while he admitted the distance to England was shorter, there were far greater difficulties involved. No one can go directly to the north, he argued, for in order to avoid discovery, they had to change their means of travel at least twice. "Some priests must stay many months in the ports of France and Holland before finding a safe route." Then, on arrival, there were risks before encountering their friends. "This is the reason why many are captured in the ports, for they do not have the money to bribe the officials, who never accuse any one with money." [34]

The Council was again sympathetic to Creswell's reasons, but it would not raise the allowance beyond the normal 50 escudos. There was, however, a special letter from the Duke of Lerma to Juan de Ybarra, of the royal treasury, reminding him to pay the money promptly to priests en route to England. "Let it be with all secrecy for it is important that they be not noticed here, as Father Creswell . . . will inform you." [35]

[33] E 2764 n.f. consulta.
[34] E 2855 n.f. letter of February 1600.
[35] E 2764 n.f. letter of 23 Feb. 1600.

Not merely were the colleges below the Pyrenees under Creswell's care but he also had to help the Douai college for which 2,000 escudos a year had been promised since 1582. This vital grant was usually in arrears, so that at times Persons or Creswell were negotiating for a draft that was at least two years old. However, occasionally payments for two or three years would be made in one instance.[36] It was Creswell's task to keep the already hard-pressed Spanish treasury conscious of the royal commitment. There was an understandable note of satisfaction in a review of the finances of all his colleges in 1600 when he added that the Spanish grant to Douai was paid in full until that date.[37]

Another of his cares was the college at Saint Omer. This had been hurriedly planned in 1593 after the English Catholics learned that a law was being introduced in the Parliament requiring the children of recusants to be placed in homes of Protestants for instruction. Their fears were proved groundless as the bill was never passed, but the plan for a college for young students had already been approved by King Philip on March 13, 1593. In a letter to the Count of Mansfeldt, the acting Governor of the Low Countries, he ordered that arrangements be made to support sixteen students at the cost of 10 escudos a month. The funds were to be raised by granting licenses to import cloth or "other convenient merchandise" from England.[38] This did not commit Spain to any direct support of the college, but the licenses were apparently not issued, and Robert Persons had to borrow 400 escudos "from people

---

[36] For example, in 1594 a draft on the "Bank of Malvendi" was secured for 4,000 escudos and sent to the Rector at Rheims. He lost it and searched for two months before it was found (A.S.V., Nunziatura di Fiandra, vol. 3/II f. 327; A.R.S.J. Hispania, vol. 136 f. 245).

[37] E 2764 n.f.

[38] A.H.N. Estado libro 251 n.f.; libro 253 n.f. letter of 29 July 1593.

who will not be in a hurry to ask for its return" to send to the struggling college. This was in December 1593, and he had already sent 800 escudos during the preceding months. When the original plan for the licenses for merchandise had proved unworkable, it was changed to an allotment of 200 escudos on the Customs of the port of Gravelines. Unfortunately the Customs of that port had already been farmed out, and so the early years of this college were like the others—ones of debt and uncertain benefaction.[39]

The college of Saint Omer continued in this unhappy state for several more years. In April 1596 Philip II sent an urgent appeal to the Court at Brussels to find the funds to maintain it, but it was of little effect.[40] In desperation the bishop of Saint Omer, Jean de Vernois wrote to ask leave to send some of the young scholars to beg at the Spanish Court.[41] The prime difficulty was not merely its uncertain revenue but, owing to its popularity with the English recusants, it was hopelessly overcrowded. In a summary of the English colleges drawn up for the Council in November 1598, Creswell stated that there were ninety students—not the sixteen of Philip's original order —and an annual debt of 3,000 escudos. The problem was indeed serious, yet the only action taken upon it was a letter from the Duke of Lerma to a treasury official, the Marquis of Poza, announcing the King's decision to grant 4,000 escudos a year in Flanders "in a secure place where they are to be well paid."[42] Any survey of the Spanish involvement in the Low

[39] A.R.S.J. Hispania, vol. 136 ff. 136 and 245.
[40] For further information on the early history of this school see L. Hicks, "The Foundation of the College of St. Omers," *Archivum Historicum Societatis Jesu*, vol. xix, pp. 146–80; H. Chadwick, "Le Collège Anglais á Saint Omer" *Les Establissements des Jesuites en France*, fasc. xvi pp. 886ff.; and his excellent survey *St. Omers to Stonyhurst*, London, 1962, pp. 11–18.
[41] A.H.N. Estado lib. 253 n.f.; E 610/212, 213 letters to the Archduke and the Infante.
[42] E 2851 n.f.; E 185 n.f. letter of 23 Feb. 1600.

Countries at that time would reveal that all "secure" places had been already assigned to other urgent needs.

Somehow amidst the currents of suspicion, disapproval and neglect, Creswell had managed to keep the colleges going. Yet Richard Versteghen candidly reported to friends in Spain that "some here do murmur at the erection of new seminaries aledging them to be a meanes to withdrawe his majesties benevolence from relieving the body of our nation." [43] To a destitute Englishman whose unpaid "entertainment" was vital for survival, the colleges could easily appear to be absorbing too much Spanish pension money. Many of the English were unaware that the colleges were on different funds than the army which sustained the pensioners in Flanders. Moreover, the principal reason for the new foundations in Spain was to ease the burden on the trouble-ridden colleges elsewhere. This was readily grasped by the Cardinal Secretary of State in Rome.

In his instruction for the nuncio to Spain, Camillo Caetani, Cardinal Aldobrandino reminded him that one of the evils of the long war in Flanders was that the collection of the revenues for education in Flanders was disrupted. They were either impossible to obtain or confiscated for military needs.[44] Thus Spain's support for the colleges was more necessary than ever if their ideal was to be pursued.

There was another facet to the attitude of contemporaries to the colleges which may be less readily appreciated. Many exiles retained a clear conviction that their residence abroad was temporary, and many incidents in a college's development have a distinct air of improvisation. Planned for only a few years' duration, they were housed at first in rented buildings with only a slight alteration for their own minimum needs. In

[43] Stonyhurst MS Collectanea B f. 103.
[44] R. de Hinojosa, *Los Despachos de la Diplomacia Pontifica en España* (Madrid, 1896), p. 354.

1595 when Joseph Creswell reported to Cardinal Aldobrandino on his first three years in Spain he remarked that funds
given to the colleges would be "for the ten or even seven
years that the persecution continues." [45] Similarly he planned
the begging of funds on a year to year basis, in 1603 he drew
up a list of 32 students who were supported by private patrons
for that year at the Spanish Court. [46] Some of the original licenses handed to the young English scholars to go about Castile and Portugal to collect alms even mentioned that their
need was for a short period of time. [47]

Eventually this collection of funds became part of the regular routine for students in a college in Spain. An early seven-
teenth-century English traveler left a vivid picture of a student
that he had seen in Seville.

There is an English youth that walkes up and downe the
citie in a gowne, and a boxe in his hand all day long and begs
from doore to doore for the Englishe college. Yet hee comes to
one place but once a weeke for the citie is great and spacious.
They have many good benefactors that bestow upon them a
certaine set pension or stipend monthly or weekly, some in
money and others in Bread, Wine or oyle . . . they have also
a greate boxe in every ship that saileth either from Sivill or
St. Lucas or Cales to the West Indies with the picture of
St. Thomas Becket upon it and with this superscription *Sancte
Thomas Cantuarensis ora pro nobis* . . . which boxe is tied
up with a great chaine unto the maste of the ship and in the lid
is a hole for people to put their devotion in . . .[48]

The College of St. Gregory at Seville had continued to live
up to the promise of its first days when Persons had written
that when the city officials approved their foundation in April

[45] A.S.V. Fondo Borghese III 124g2 f. 63.
[46] C.R.S. vol. xxx, Introd.
[47] S.A.C. Serie II legajo 1, original letters.
[48] Lewis Owen, *The Running Register* . . . (London, 1626),
p. 68.

1594 "there was not a single vote against us." [49] In various reports on that college it was apparent that its regular expenditures totaled approximately 6,000 escudos, yet there were few debts. For instance, the Duke of Medina Sidonia gave a full share of the water supply of his palace, while the city officials paid the rental of the buildings, and other friends supplied food and books. [50]

The experience of Saint Alban's at Valladolid was never as happy. Without Philip II's subsidy of 140 escudos a month from the *Alcabalos* of Leon the college might very probably have ceased to exist. In June 1595 it was noted that of 4,000 escudos spent thus far only 18 had come from the city. [51] Occasionally Philip II would give secret gifts to the students. From an auction of confiscated English goods in Fuentarabia in September 1592 he gave 4,000 escudos. [52]

While holding the line against financial ruin during normal times, the slightest dip in the Spanish economy meant great danger to the plans of Creswell. In 1598, while the effects of the current crown bankruptcy were being felt, he informed the Council of State that St. Alban's was heavily in debt up to 1,500 escudos. "The cost of upkeep has almost doubled in Castile," he commented, "and there are even now fifteen new students coming from Saint Omer." [53] It was the same story in Seville whenever the yearly convoys from the Indies were mauled by storms or piracy. The year 1599 was particularly bad in this respect so that Philip III offered a special secret gift of 1,000 escudos to keep the students alive. [54]

Thus the nature of Creswell's primary concern in Spain can be appreciated for what it was. He was not a diplomat, nor

[49] A.R.S.J. Hispania vol. 136, f. 184.
[50] See also C.R.S. vol. xiv, pp. 6 ff.
[51] A.R.S.J. Hispania vol. 138 f. 399.
[52] A.R.S.J. Fondo Gesuitico 691, letter of 7 Oct. 1592.
[53] E 2851 n.f.
[54] E 185 n.f. consulta of 23 February 1600.

a great educator. Instead he worked tirelessly in the manifold details of somehow keeping the colleges going. His constant reports and reminders assured the royal grants and the approval of the Council of State and the Court; undoubtedly his work was essential to the survival of the colleges. Yet was this uninteresting administrative eminence his only concern? It would be unfair to his career to omit some other aspects of his dedicated personality.

During his first visit to Seville in 1592 Creswell learned of the case of some starving prisoners of war whose leader, a Captain Robert Frost, he befriended. Frost was in grave difficulties. He had already fought in the Cadiz expedition of Drake in 1587, and the following year he had captained a vessel of 200 tons in Howard's squadron against the Armada. Four years later he had sailed from Fowey in England for the West Indies hoping to make his fortune in privateering. However, in June 1592 he was captured near Cartajena where his ship had foundered off shore.[55] Brought to Seville to await a trial before the Council of the Indies, he and some of his crew were in a wretched state.

Creswell appealed to the Council to allow Frost and his fourteen companions to come to his new college every day for a meal. After their case was left undecided for many months, in July 1594, Creswell made a special complaint to Philip II over the neglect of the officials conducting the trial. Prodded by the King, the lower court of the Council of the Indies sentenced the prisoners in August 1594 to be exiled. This was virtually the same as exchanging them. However the *fiscal* of the lower court appealed the sentence as too lenient. After a review the Council of the Indies declared that Frost and his

[55] K. R. Andrews: "English Privateering Voyages, 1588–95," *Hakluyt Society* (Series II), vol. cxi, pp. 175–76; I. Wright, "Further English Voyages to Spanish America," *Hakluyt Society* (Series II), vol. xcix, pp. 290, 297–300.

comrades were "corsairs and robbers . . . and deserve to be executed." They admitted, however, that there were "difficulties which could occur in matters of state." [56] They were apparently adverting to the fact that Creswell had already informed the King that Frost and seven of his friends had offered to serve in the Spanish navy. However, Philip was not impressed, for he endorsed their dossier: "Let sentence be passed according to law." Creswell then urged Frost to appeal directly to the King.

The English captain wrote a short but eloquent letter explaining that he had gone to sea only under the Queen's orders. "Subjects are not obliged, nor are they able, to examine whether a war is just or not . . . ," he wrote. His appeal did have some effect, for soon after the *fiscal* wrote to Creswell inquiring whether his friends were "persons of quality." The possibility of a ransom or exchange was again being considered. In February 1595 from his secretariate at Court Creswell wrote in reply that ransom was out of the question but that the Council should simply "treat them as every one else." The Council agreed and had the sentence altered to let Frost be exchanged as other prisoners of war. Although Creswell had clearly helped to alter the sentence, an exchange was never easy to arrange. Three years later Robert Frost was still petitioning the Spanish Court asking that his exchange be expedited. [57] It is not known when Frost returned to England, but it was Creswell's intervention that had averted a senseless tragedy of war.

Another self-imposed task for Creswell was his occasional efforts to propagandize the needs of his students and of the English recusants to the Spanish reading public. His first Spanish book was also a personal tribute to a friend who had written

[56] Archivo General de Indias, Sección Quinta, Santa Fe legajo 1 n. 113.
[57] E 182 n.f. letter to the Infante, 22 June 1598.

to him often when serving as a chaplain of Sir William Stanley's regiment. Late in 1595 he wrote a brief account of the
tragic ending of Father Henry Walpole. Written in un-
adorned Spanish, it told the story of a Jesuit who had studied
at St. Alban's for a year before traveling to his betrayal in England. His forty-eight page *Historia de la vida y Martyrio que
padescio este año 1595 el P. Henrico Valpolo*, left un-
touched the inherent drama of the facts but it also stressed the
unique role that St. Alban's hoped to fulfill. In his preface he
praised the generosity of their benefactors and then urged the
Catholics of England to ponder "the great expectations of seeing the remedy and end to their troubles." Perhaps this was
an optimistic allusion to the Armada being contemplated at
that time.

The success of the little book was sufficient to produce a
French translation of it at Arras in 1597; but it also encouraged him to undertake a far more ambitious publication.
Shortly after this, Bishop Diego de Yepez, a Hieronimite friar,
and a former confessor to Philip II, asked Robert Persons for
more details of the recent history of the Catholics of England.
"I beg you," he wrote, "to put into writing every narrative
available." [58] Since Persons was to leave Spain early in 1597
Creswell inherited the task. During the following two years
Yepez was given materials from which he composed a basic
draft. This he duly handed to Creswell to revise. "He has
done this in such a fashion," the bishop later acknowledged to
Robert Persons, "that he has added many important matters,
yet he left it to be printed under my name." [59]

Thus late in 1599 the famous *Historia Particular de la
Persecución en Inglaterra* came off the press. It was a massive
anthology from all the varied short histories, private reports
and letters in circulation among the English exiles. It con-

[58] W.C.A. Series A, vol. v f. 253, letter of 3 Oct. 1596.
[59] A.R.S.J. Anglia, vol. 37 f. 263, letter of 6 Aug. 1599.

tained, for example, two long accounts by Elizabeth Sanders of the harried existence of the nuns, formerly at Syon Abbey, before they settled in Portugal. These were already available in two small Spanish editions. There was also a brief account of the life of a young English student who had died in the college at Seville which was composed in Spanish by its Rector, Francisco de Peralta.[60] There were also liberal excerpts from Dr. Allen's history of Edmund Campion, as well as many other contemporary accounts.

The book was of considerable popularity at the Spanish Court. Shortly after its appearance, the Duke of Feria wrote to Thomas Fitzherbert who was then with Creswell at the Spanish Court, thanking him for sending a copy and commenting enthusiastically on Creswell's work. I have received the book of Father Creswell," he wrote, "it is a work that deserves to be seen. No less a good idea was the plan of the author in that same book to place it under the name of the Bishop Fray Diego de Yepez. In my opinion it has nothing else of his." [61]

Although Creswell was not to lose his interest in publication the mounting difficulties of his office were to interrupt his writing for nearly eleven years. His supervision of the colleges was becoming a more complex operation all the time. He was still very concerned about the risks of the journey back to England. Yet there was little that could be done about it. It was no longer possible for young Englishmen to pass as casually across the narrow seas as they once were observed in 1583, enroute to a new college at Eu. At that time Nicholas Faunt reported that "the young gentlemen go over by heaps from hence, out of all places and most by the creeks and in fisher

[60] See C.R.S., vol. xiv, p. 16 note, *Relación de Algunos Martyrios* (Madrid, 1590), Palau y Dulcet, *Manuel del Librero Hispanoamericano*, vol. vi, p. 236.
[61] W.C.A. Series E, vol. ii, f. 132 letter of 4 Feb. 1600.

boats, carrying with them great provisions of all neces-saries." [62]

The direct passage between England and Spain was, of course, long out of the question. The route was now an ex-pensive challenge to the ingenuity of each student. The aliases and changes of disguise had become frequent. William War-ford, for example, took two months to go from Seville to Am-sterdam in the spring of 1591. He told his friends in Spain that careful consideration had to be given to clothes:

. . . which should not seem Spanish, and they could use Irish, Scotch, German, Polish or any other nation's name rather than English because the name attracts the attention of all who hear it. All Englishmen are considered either great heretics or determined Catholics, and both the one and the other of these things have a danger of their own on these roads. [63]

It was this uncertainty that made the journey by the southern ports of Spain become more frequent. The fortu-nate gift of the residence at San Lucar by the Brotherhood of St. George as a hospice only accelerated its popularity. As early as December 1592 Creswell had confided to Pope Clement VIII that the frequent ships en route for Scotland, Ireland, Flanders and Brittany were willing to take the stu-dents on a first stage of the journey. Lisbon was considered a useful port of entry and exit. The English spy, Giles van Hardwicke, reported in February 1599 that the young Eng-lishmen were going by way of Waterford in Ireland "and from thence in the Trinitee or Jonas Shipps of that place" to an agent waiting for them in the port. [64] In another letter he reported that the young priests were going to England dis-guised "as prisoners of this castle." He had even overheard some of them discussing the hazards of the trip, "their danger

[62] T. Birch, *Memoirs*, vol. i, p. 41.
[63] S.A.C. Serie II, legajo 1, letter of 15 May 1591.
[64] P.R.O., S.P. 94/6/192.

they report is all in their landinge, for yf they get out to be 6 houers on shore in anie place in England, they have re-ceyvers and harbourers of them. There are a great store of them there." [65] The English Privy Council had learned of the disguise of the exchanged prisoners of war before. One captured English priest had admitted in 1591 that he knew of four priests who had come "under pretense of galli slaves in the Portugall action." [66]

Lisbon was soon to boast the same type of hospice as San Lucar to serve the travelers for the colleges. They were busy places during the war. Robert Persons praised their useful-ness in providing "hospitality to such priests of the seminaryes as are to imbark towards Ingland, who lye there without charges and say Mass every daye, and have their shypps pro-vided for them as also necessarye apparell for their journey and finally the viaticum of fifty crownes." [67]

Yet there were real dangers in Lisbon and elsewhere which the ingenuity of the students had to circumvent in a variety of ways. In January 1596 the Rector of St. Alban's informed Creswell that in the past year "the College has sent a total of twelve priests to the mission, of whom two were sent by the ports of Biscay, another two by San Lucar de Barrameda, six are on route through Madrid for Andalucia ports and two other still await the first convenient way to travel." [68] He could not safely be more explicit, for it was clear that all information on friendly ships was regularly passed from Lisbon and elsewhere to the colleges so that the danger-ous period of waiting in the ports could be kept to a mini-mum.

While the hazards of the voyage were vivid to Creswell

[65] P.R.O., S.P. 94/6/212.
[66] B.M., Lansdowne, vol. 96, f. 152.
[67] Stonyhurst MS Collectanea N–II f. 125.
[68] A.R.S.J. Fondo Gesuitico 651.

few narratives of the actual journey survive at present. There
is one typically adventurous account in the unfinished auto-
biography of Father Oswald Tesimond. From this it was
learned that his journey from Valladolid to London required
four months. He chose a route through northern Spain by
foot to Bilbao. There he was so careful to board the ship at
the last moment that he had neither food nor water, which he
had subsequently to beg from the ship's company. The only
available space for him was near the stove. "What caused me
the greatest and almost incredible annoyance was the smoke,
so that I could not open my eyes, into which the pungency of
the smoke brought incessant tears." After nine days his ship
arrived off Calais where, in maneuvering to escape some
Dutch marauders, it ran aground on a sand bar. Tesimond
and the panic-stricken passengers had to wade ashore. Choosing carefully a route away from the scattered campaigns of
the French wars and the sieges of the Low Countries he
made his way on foot to Middleburg and then to Flushing.
There he assumed the garb of an English merchant for a
four-day sail to England with a suspicious companion who
turned out to be a Puritan. Entering the Thames in a convoy
of forty ships Tesimond had a narrow escape at a checkpoint
near Gravesend, where he forced his reluctant companion to
ask so many questions about some friends nearby, "that they
on the galleon, instead of examining us, were examined by
us" as they sailed past.[69] Tesimond landed safely and eventually labored in London for several years before escaping
successfully to the continent again.

Before a young priest returned to England, what kind of
experience had he acquired in Spain as a student? A contemporary observer of the scholars of Valladolid noted prin-
cipally that they had a special curriculum.

[69] Printed in J. Morris, *Troubles of Our Catholic Forefathers*
(London 1872–77), pp. 157–83.

There is a peculiar order of studies, . . . for supplying diuers poyntes of learning necessarie for this enterprise . . . in matters of controversie and diligent reading of the text of the scriptures, with skyll of the Hebrue and Greek languages and other lyke poyntes besides the ordinarie course of diuinitie and philosophie which most learnedly are read in this universitie.[70]

Another unusual feature of the Spanish colleges was that an oath was required of the students that they would seek to go back to England to minister to the Catholics. This was taken only after a period of time, but it was a distinctive part of the college rules.[71] It was insisted upon so that the funds given by their Spanish benefactors were spent to support those willing to fulfill the ideal of the college.

Mindful of some unfortunate experiences in Rome and Rheims, the colleges in Spain conducted a rigorous scrutiny of those who tried to enter as students. Although they had to carry letters of introduction from priests known to the faculty, after their arrival an elaborate screening was begun. At first the new student was kept apart for a few days so that he could be questioned in detail about his place of birth, his parents, his position in life, his earlier studies, the origin of his Catholic faith and the people he knew. His answers were to be reviewed for any divergences and doubts which were to be discussed with any other students from the same shire. If

---

[70] *A Relation of the king of Spaines Receiuing* . . . , pp. 22–23.

[71] The constitutions of St. Alban's were explicit: "Instruuntur ii tantum qui spiritualibus Angliae necessitatibus . . . opitulari possint, velintque." (Cap. I para. 3 C.R.S., vol. xxx, pp. 252–53.) Since 1579 the authorities of the English College in Rome had required the oath after overcoming the resistance of several who wished to be the incumbents of an academic sinecure. See A. Kenny, "From Hospice to College" in *The English Hospice in Rome* (*The Venerabile*, Sexcentenary Issue, Exeter, 1962) pp. 242ff. When Douai College began to require the oath in March 1600, several had to leave. (C.R.S. vol. x, 14, 26.)

he was accepted he could then be enrolled subsequently as a student with the approval of the Rector.[72]

It was unfortunate that the financial straits of the colleges did not permit encouraging the student who wished to devote his entire career to study. For at that time they could hear in Valladolid and Salamanca some of the great lecturers of the Spanish theological renaissance. Francisco Suarez and some of his brightest disciples were teaching at the flourishing colleges of Santa Cruz and San Ambrosio in Valladolid. The young English students at St. Alban's were not by any means a passive audience to these new intellectual currents. On one occasion, in July 1594, Robert Persons noted their dislike for a Spanish Jesuit lecturer to whom they were obligated to listen at San Ambrosio. He commented frankly:

> I find it impossible to instill in the students any respect for his methods. I have tried everything with them, from persuasion to severity, but nothing succeeds. . . . The reason they reply is because each lecture comes to this: does Saint Thomas teach this or not? Is the statement probable or not? Is Saint Thomas' argument convincing or not? Well-founded or not? It is impossible to get rid of this reaction to him, and besides the Jesuit students at San Ambrosio feel the same way . . .[73]

From other reports Persons had learned that the young English students were stimulated by a disciple of Suarez named Antonio de Padilla whose brilliant lectures they were anxious to have continued. However, a bitter academic feud had developed within the faculty of St. Alban's over Padilla. The English students were so taken with the newer school of Suarez that Persons was afraid to take either side, out of fear of fomenting more resentment in the college.

The students were also kept abreast of contemporary de-

[72] The full text of the *Liber Primi Examinis* is in C.R.S., vol. xxx, pp. 1-3.
[73] A.R.S.J. Hispania, vol. 137, f. 24.

velopments in the running controversies between English Catholic and Protestant theologians. In an inventory of books sent in 1593 to Spain by Richard Versteghen a shipment of this controversial literature was included. Among the books were "Sutclif against the Puritans . . . one of Mr. Reynolds books against Bruce" and Versteghen's own *Speculum pro Christianis Seductis*.[74] There is every indication that the list was typical and that their interest in these polemical theological debates continued throughout this period.

In keeping with its ideal the College at Valladolid was governed by rules that ordered the students' days completely. There were fixed periods of the day for lectures and study, while special days for relaxation were set aside "even if the weather is bad." The students were told that they must avoid being seen in the city of Valladolid in any large numbers. There were even customs to be observed if the students were traveling to other cities in Spain.[75] Less information survives about the college of St. Gregory in Seville. However, there does exist a series of consultations by the faculty on small points of order within the college which implies that its regime was quite similar to its sister foundation in Castile.[76]

Such, in brief, were the principal features of the colleges to whose maintenance Creswell devoted his talents and considerable energies. He left the details of their government to their faculties but he prepared reports on their condition for Cardinal Aldobrandino, the Secretary of State, whom he had known in Rome when he was Rector of the English College.

[74] Stonyhurst MS Collectanea B f. 137; Matthew Sutcliffe: *De catholica, orthodoxa et vera Christi ecclesia libri duo* (London, 1592); William Rainolds: *A Treatise conteyning the true Catholike faith of the Holy Sacrifice ordeyned by Christ* (Antwerp, 1593).
[75] S.A.C. Serie II, legajo 16, Manuscript, "Diario de Costumbres."
[76] S.A.C. Sevilla, legajo 17c/641.

No little part of the success of his work was due to the strong support that Camillo Caetani, the papal nuncio in Spain gave openly to the pleading of the English Jesuit.

Creswell needed all the help he could get. Constantly writing letters, interviewing the royal bureaucrats, or looking to find new benefactors, trying to compose books to evoke sympathy for the cause of the English students, worrying about their safety after leaving for England, and becoming increasingly the spokesman for the exiles at Court, he had set for himself an incredibly complex task. An English spy who watched his secretariate with interest at this time found great activity "with three or four Englishmen who go and come." [77] Creswell was constantly preoccupied with improving his relations with the Court since everything depended upon this. After nearly six years in his work he reported to his superiors in Rome that "several ministers have disengaged themselves of their first impressions and are showing it in action." [78] The most tangible proof of this was the elaborate visit of the young King Philip III to the college in Valladolid in August 1600. As before, the royal visit assured the prestige of the King's favor for the present. For nearly two years the faculty had looked forward to the visit for, as the Rector reminded the monarch on his accession, "help is needed to keep the young plant growing which was once fostered by your father." [79]

The visit was gratifying to Creswell and it was duly reported in books in both Spanish and English. Again there were orations, and the usual display of emblems and 270 "hierogliphickes." There was, however, a greater emphasis on music. For as King Philip and his young Queen Margarita entered the chapel "the students above in the quire sang *Te Deum* in their accustomed ecclesiastical Musicke which

[77] *H.M.C. Salisbury MSS*, vol. viii, p. 185.
[78] A.R.S.J. Toletano Series 5–II, letter of Jan. 1600.
[79] E 181 n.f. letter of 5 Oct. 1598.

contented so much." Then proceeding into the hall "the musicians in the other room adioyning . . . began to play upon their viols and virginals with a very grand and pleasant song of eight partes" to escort the royal retinue.[80] The chapel had recently been enlarged through a gift of the King in response to earlier appeal from the Rector, which stated that their chapel was small and without any musical instruments.[81]

Not merely was there the assurance of the continued royal favor but apparently there was the inner satisfaction to Creswell of sending more and more students in England. As early as November 1598 he had calculated that the *viaticum*, or travel allowance, was reaching a total each year of "800 or 1,000 escudos, and some years more, according to the numbers sent."[82] This would be sufficient for 16 to 20 graduates each year and the numbers were increasing.

In England as the reign of the great Queen drew on with increasing rumors over her poor health, Creswell and his friends among the exile clergy were gradually faced with the hard conclusion that Spain could do nothing, beyond assisting the "seminaries," to change the lot of the Catholics. There had been many warnings of this which Creswell reluctantly had to recognize. The English Jesuit had shared the disappointment of Sir William Stanley, when his plans were decisively rejected several months before the death of the Queen. Moreover, there had been the persistent official coolness to the suggested candidacy of the Infanta as a Catholic pretender to the English throne. Instead of facing a comforting prospect

[80] Antonio Ortiz, *A Relation of the Solemnitie wherewith the Catholike princes . . . were receyuved in the Inglish Colledge . . .* (Antwerp, 1601. Translated by Francisco de Ribera, Francis Rivers).

[81] E 182 n.f. P. Rodriguez de Toro to the Infante, 3 March 1598: "y en el choro aun no auen los tres juegos de violones y clauizimbolo . . ."

[82] E 2851 n.f.

that the troubles of the English recusants were at an end, he had been forced to plan as if they were to continue indefinitely.

Yet the unabashed optimism that Creswell possessed in 1595 when he wrote to the Cardinal Secretary of State of the "ten to even seven years" that the persecution would continue, never left him. He encouraged Philip III's secret and novel attempts to negotiate a partial repeal of the recusancy laws as part of the Treaty of London of August 1604. This diplomatic "enterprise" would produce little of lasting importance to assist the Catholics of England. Still he hoped that the presence of Charles Lord Howard of Effingham at the Spanish Court in the spring of 1605 to secure the ratification of the treaty would be a useful opportunity to speak privately on toleration. Months in advance he had secured a special grant of money from the Council of State to repair the college buildings at Valladolid and buy new clothes for the students.[83]

When Lord Howard arrived in Spain late in March the new English resident ambassador to Spain, Sir Charles Cornwallis, was in his retinue. Lord Howard visited St. Alban's and spoke courteously to the students whom he greeted as "from his nation." [84] There he hinted broadly of his sympathy for the Catholics but nothing of substance was promised. According to Howard's official interpreter, Giles Porter, Creswell visited the residence of Howard frequently and it was undoubtedly these conversations [85] which stimulated a remarkable approach to the Earl of Salisbury which Creswell penned the day that Howard left the shores of Spain.

He began with the unexpected remark that at present he

[83] E 624 n.f. letter of 19 November 1604.
[84] A.R.S.J. Anglia, vol. 36 f. 235–38; J. W. Stoye, *English Travelers Abroad*, p. 332ff.
[85] Winwood, *Memorials*, vol. ii, p. 76.

believed that Sir Robert Cecil had been evidently following his father's deathbed advice "to procure to reunite kingdom of England to the rest of the body of Christendome" for
Cecil had been "so principall an Instrument . . . in con-
tryving of this peace." He offered the opinion, in line with
his *Exemplar Litterarum* that the "short and secure way" to
maintain the peace would be to procure that "subjects at
home may have peace among themselves, and those be favored who have peaceable minds, without forcing them to
more dangerous intrinsecall warre with God and their own
consciences." He warned that any enforced conformity would
be a failure for they who "seeme to conforme themselves are
never the nearer to the purpose pretended, but further off by
doing that which they doe with interior hartburninge, re-
pugnance and mislike." Such a policy, he concluded, would
allow true love for the prince to grow.[86]

That the letter reflected Creswell's honest conviction was
confirmed in the correspondence of the English ambassador,
Sir Charles Cornwallis. At this time he was reporting to
Salisbury that he had found Creswell to be a loyal Englishman, for through his conversations with the Jesuit, he had
"understood much of the harts and dispositions of the greatest." He even boasted that Creswell's prominence made him
a "conduit" to tell the Spanish Court "anything that I desire
they should give belief unto."[87]

For over a year this fine impression would continue. Occasionally Cornwallis would try to remind Cecil of Creswell's
assistance, but it is doubtful whether he was very much impressed. In a letter of June 1606 he discussed a rivalry between Creswell and Persons which he imagined to exist. He
had decided that they were both ambitious but that Creswell

[86] B.M., Cotton Vespasian C XIII f. 207, also P.R.O., S.P.
94/14/48.
[87] Winwood, *Memorials*, vol. ii, p. 131.

"would gladly take hold of the advantage of the tyme and build the foundation of his greatness in preaching and per-swading of obedience and temperance, and becoming a meanes to combyne the two great monarchs of Great Britain and Spain."[88]

Cornwallis was correct in hinting that there was a differ-ence between the two friends but he had missed the reason completely. An outbreak of serious discontent in St. Alban's had exceeded its usual limits. Creswell, preoccupied with his work and never too sensitive to the human factor in his out-look in any case, had never realized the state of affairs at Valladolid until a near riot among the students had occurred. The focus of their complaints centered on the incompetence of certain Spanish Jesuits who were college officials.[89] How-ever Creswell was in a poor position to handle the crisis since he had been bickering for over a year with the few English Jesuits still at the college. Even in May 1605, during How-ard's stay at Court Creswell had had a violent and silly quarrel with Father Richard Walpole, who was the brother of the man whose eulogy he had published ten years before. The Father General of the Jesuits received reports that Creswell had been acting independently and crudely in his dealings with his subordinates.

In October 1605 Creswell was asked to go to Rome to explain his conduct to his superiors. When leaving Spain early in December 1605, one of the few kind remarks made about the harried Jesuit came from Cornwallis who wrote him an affectionate note wishing him "all the happiness that a man of your sorte upon this earth can desire."[90] Un-

---

[88] Winwood, *Memorials*, vol. ii, p. 226.
[89] C.R.S., vol. xxx, pp. 90–96.
[90] A.R.S.J. Castilla, vol. 7–I ff. 158, 262, 313, letters of Claudio Aquaviva; B.M., Harleian 1875 f. 292 letter of Corn-wallis, Dec. 22, 1605.

doubtedly Creswell valued the gesture, although events were soon to give it an ironical memory for him. For not merely were there serious troubles in the colleges, but charges were being prepared in England which placed Creswell, with Stanley, Owen and Baldwin, in the ring of exiles abetting the Gunpowder conspiracy. However, when the news first reached the Spanish Court, Creswell was absent in Rome discussing his administration, and the morale of his colleges. Creswell was always an honest man, and the problem facing him was did he really have the ability to alter the deteriorating morale of the young students.

He returned to Spain in April 1606 with the formidable task of putting his affairs in order as superior of the English Jesuits in Spain. The many letters he wrote to Rome after this time were exclusively concerned with the various petty problems of assignments, finances and the still restless college of St. Alban's.[91]

Yet, even though Creswell was eventually not to be indicted in London for the "Gunpowder" treason, Cornwallis observed that there was a change in his outlook. "Sithence he saw his name in printe in the late statutes," wrote the ambassador referring to the preamble, "I understand . . . that he hath blotted it out of the Book of Well Wishing to his country."[92] Later the break between them was complete when Cornwallis met Creswell at the residence of the Florentine ambassador. There they had an angry exchange over the guilt of Hugh Owen which Creswell vehemently refused to believe. After this time the English envoy was to view Creswell with the same wary eye that he had hitherto reserved for Robert Persons.

Creswell's reconciliation with his superiors in Rome did

[91] A.R.S.J. Toletano, vol. 6–II f. 457, letter of 14 Nov. 1606 reviewing his correspondence.
[92] Winwood, *Memorials*, vol. ii, pp. 273, 283.

not guarantee that he could assume the unfamiliar role of a peacemaker. He was soon involved in a petty dispute with his Spanish brethren which he allowed, typically, to become magnified by neglect and rumor. Sometime before his death Philip II had given to Creswell a residence in the crown's possession for his secretariate and any English students staying in Madrid on business. The grant had been renewed by Philip III after a Court chamberlain had tried to evict them.[93] In 1607 the Jesuits in Madrid began to complain to Rome that Creswell was living at Court in what they were con-vinced was unbecoming luxury. Aquaviva, the Father Gen-eral, was prudent in his handling of the affair, which was ac-tually a sign of Creswell's isolation from his own Spanish community, by merely advising him to avoid any cause of scandal.[94]

Creswell had far more on his mind than his Madrid resi-dence. During the preceding year the college of St. Alban's had continued to be in virtual chaos. There had been a serious and uncontrolled outbreak of the plague and the result had been several deaths and the severe illness of most of the stu-dents and faculty. The official in charge of the students' health had neglected his duties and the whole affair was described in a common letter to Robert Persons from the handful of re-sentful English students still surviving amid the disorganized squalor.[95]

In September 1607 Creswell visited the college but he was handicapped by his own incompatibility with the Span-ish Jesuits on the faculty who were being blamed for most of the troubles. Moreover, he did not show a skill sufficient to reassure the young men by a deft and sympathetic relation-

[93] E 1743 n.f. orders of 9 March 1600.
[94] A.R.S.J. Toletano, Epistolae Generalium, 1600–10, f. 500.
[95] C.R.S., vol. xxx, pp. xxii, 90–96; A.R.S.J. Toletano, vol. 6–II, ff. 543, 549, 558.

ship. The damage largely attributable to his overall neglect would take over six years to repair at Valladolid. He did not see that his time-consuming and important post at Court obligated him to find reliable assistants to watch over his other responsibilities. He never achieved a balance between his familiarity with the debates in the Council of State and the judicious handling of delicate problems of a college for aliens in a rather hostile land. His summons to Rome had not come any too soon, yet apparently it had had little effect in changing him radically into a successful superior.

From 1607 to 1610 Creswell remained in residence at the Court in Madrid. He had still been receiving considerable correspondence from England, but his relations with Cornwallis had gradually begun to take on the character of a feud. The English Jesuit was employing in his secretariate Wadsworth and Fowler, both formerly of Cornwallis' embassy, as "his right and left hands," and a fear that the young and gifted Francis Cottington would imitate their defection made the ambassador even more irascible.[96]

There were even greater misfortunes awaiting Creswell, which developed from a seemingly innocuous source. The King's physician, a Florentine named Don Cesare Bogacio, had long been an admirer of the ideals of the colleges for English students. He decided to leave in his will a bequest to establish in Madrid a small college supporting twelve students a year. They were to study the arts curriculum, to relieve the overcrowded school at St. Omers, before going on to Seville or Valladolid for higher studies. Unfortunately the wording of the bequest had not been carefully prepared, so that on Bogacio's death there began a suit by the disappointed heirs of the physician to block the essential royal approval of the college.[97] Creswell met this obstacle with typical head-on

[96] Winwood, *Memorials*, vol. ii, p. 321; vol. iii, p. 37.
[97] A.R.S.J. Toletano, vol. 6–II, f. 939.

brusqueness. Determined to meet the terms of the bequest he ordered twelve young students to come to Madrid even though the funds were not as yet available to support them. Because of his high position at Court, his handling of Bogacio's bequest became a *cause célèbre*.

Digby, the new English envoy, did his part by spreading rumors damaging to the college, while some of the Spanish courtiers on the side of the heirs of Bogacio repeated their belief that the young men were not students, but spies. King Philip, although he had shown confidence in Creswell for over fifteen years, decided to withhold approval. Yet Creswell had a special reason for insisting on his rights. The law courts had interpreted the bequest to require that the students had to be in residence for the year of 1611 to be considered the beneficiary at all.[98] As the furor mounted the luckless students were expelled from Madrid, and the position of Creswell, and even the entire future of all the colleges was suddenly placed in jeopardy. The charges against one group of students could be repeated against the others all too easily.

It was no longer simply a question of Creswell's intractable personality now, and he had to work to save everything he had labored for years to maintain. In a long personal letter to King Philip he attacked the notion that his young Englishmen were spies at the center of the Spanish empire. He noted sarcastically that there were already enough foreigners living openly in Madrid who would be more capable of doing the work. He attributed the animus against the college largely to those Spanish courtiers who curried the friendship of Sir John Digby, the new English envoy in Madrid. He remarked rather cynically that since there were "many hidden Catholics at the English Court so it is not improbable that here there are hidden heretics." [99]

[98] C.R.S., vol. xxix, pp. 80–82 MS History of the college.
[99] *Ibid.*, pp. 167–79.

Not satisfied merely with his personal appeal he tried to rally support among the Spanish nobility and hierarchy. However, his former patrons, Don Juan de Idiaquez, and the first Count of Olivares, and Bishop Diego Yepez were dead, and the all-powerful Duke of Lerma had announced that he had received reports that Creswell's correspondence with England was anti-Spanish. In the face of such serious charges Creswell decided to put in writing his sentiments on the oath of allegiance controversy in England. The move was planned at the same time to diminish the popularity of Digby's faction at the Spanish Court. Under the alias of Bernard de Clermont he prepared a short book entitled simply *A Proclamation published under the name of James, King of Great Brittany. With a briefe & moderate answere therunto*, which he had printed at Saint Omer. In his preface he warned that "the Christian and discreet Reader will perceave by this Proclamation into what hands the kingdome of England . . . is now fallen." He then printed the text of the proclaimed oath of allegiance [100] with his comments in side heads. They were directed toward showing that the new recusancy laws were "against the laws of God and nature." He then added four short chapters advising English Catholics how to penetrate the deceptions in the oath as proposed by King James.

In this unusual context at Madrid the book was particularly effective. It was an indirect attack on King James' ambition to have Sir John Digby open negotiations for a possible marriage alliance with the Infanta. The question of toleration for English Catholics, which was always to be the most obstinate issue to be resolved in any alliance, was being put forth early to counter Digby's actions. In effect, he reminded the Court that if James was sincere he could not object to a small English college in Madrid. Creswell did not stop there.

[100] R. Steele, *Tudor and Stuart Proclamations*, vol. i, no. 1093, act of 2 June 1610.

Pope Paul V, with whom he had corresponded ever since the special nunciature of that pontiff in Spain early in 1594, agreed to take the new college under Papal protection and away from the direct supervision of the Archbishop of Toledo.[101]

Meanwhile some testimonials in favor of the ideal of the English colleges were finally appearing for the consideration of the Council of State. Don Francisco de Tejada y Mendoza and even the famous Marquis Ambrosio Spinola, Philip's brilliant military commander in the Low Countries, were among the names endorsing Creswell's college. Spinola added a remark, worthy of the Emperor Charles V, that he would like to retire some day and end his days in a monastery with the young students.[102]

The tide gradually began to turn in favor of the dogged English Jesuit and a temporary permission for the college was granted. Creswell commented on this decision on September 29, 1613 to the Archbishop of Toledo:

> With the favor and license for the students to return to their houses, although but for a short time, the scandal and the different stories excited by their departure, some ascribing it to our faults, others to the ministers who consented to it, and others to those who succeeded by secret negotiations, all have ceased.[103]

Creswell's analysis of his predicament was an understatement for a far more malicious intrigue was reposing in the files of the Council of State.

Due to the rumors and misinformation about the new college the integrity of Creswell had remained under the hostile scrutiny of the Duke of Lerma. In February 1613 the powerful favorite of the King had ordered secret inquiries into all the English Jesuit's activities and especially his relations with

---

101 C.R.S., vol. xxix, p. 192.
102 E 2858 / 12,13.
103 C.R.S., vol. xxix, p. 197.

the embassy of Digby in Madrid. What the cynical and corrupt Duke hoped to gain was not too clear, but his inquiry
was thorough and discreet. Even the Duke of Escalona, who
had been the Spanish envoy in Rome when Creswell was
summoned there by the Father General of the Jesuits seven
years before, was questioned and duly reported that Creswell
had only discussed the condition of the college of St. Alban.
"I brought him to greet his Holiness in a regular audience
. . . and he spoke about the reasons for his coming, and they
were the very same as those he had told me previously, and
his Holiness gave him his blessing." [104] The Marquis del Valle
reported to Lerma on his inquiries with the *Alcalde* of Alcala
de Henares over the conduct of the English students who had
lived there after their sudden expulsion from Madrid. Their
behavior was reported to be honest, and a deposition to that
effect was enclosed.[105]

Lerma finally convoked a session of the Council of State
on April 1, 1613 to consider the evidence against the English Jesuit. It was decided to let him remain in Madrid until
further information was available. The Council advised the
King: "Creswell has always been considered a virtuous man
and zealous for the service of God and your Majesty," and it
then added rather pettily: "even if he is long-winded in his
way of negotiating his business." [106] The affair could not end
on this note nor was it to be allowed to do so. Creswell remained under a cloud for several months further. The Marquis del Valle kept him under surveillance and in August he
reported in triumph to the Duke of Lerma that he had seen
Creswell have secret conferences with Sir John Digby. He
had observed the priest riding with the envoy "in his coach
with the curtains drawn for two hours." This had occurred

[104] E 2027 n.f. letter of 10 March 1613.
[105] E 2027 n.f. letter of 1 March 1613.
[106] E 2027 n.f. consulta of 1 April 1613.

the day after Simon Digby had arrived at Court with an urgent despatch from England. The Marquis remarked that, from his experience, such a secret conference always occurred whenever an English pensioner, dissatisfied with Spain, would try to see the ambassador.[107]

What had Creswell been trying to do? By April 1613, when the Council of State had reluctantly decided to let Creswell remain in Madrid, it was openly asserted at the Court that Digby had prevented the college's foundation. Apparently Creswell had decided to see his adversary and persuade him that he was hurting his own purposes in Spain by attacking the college. Creswell described the meeting in his letter to the Archbishop of Toledo:

> I would not wish, however important the seminary, not to have obtained under his signature the manifestation of the bad service he [Digby] rendered us in secret, for it will be of use in its own time. I have sent copies of his letter and my letter to England where they will be better understood.[108]

Still disturbed at the hostility of the Council, Creswell confided the whole matter to his friend Don Diego de Sarmiento, the Spanish envoy in London and a secure favorite with King James.

In October 1613 Sarmiento wrote a long letter to Philip III explaining that Creswell's talks with Sir John Digby were only an attempt to remove his objections to the young men studying in Madrid. Sarmiento, who was as deep in the confidence of Philip as he was in that of James, added a strong personal endorsement of the priest: "He is a holy man," he wrote, "a great person and very useful for the seminaries." [109]

[107] E 2027 n.f. letter of 12 Aug. 1613; *C.S.P. Venetian, 1610–13*, p. 517.
[108] C.R.S., vol. xxix, p. 198.
[109] *Documentos Inéditos para la Historia de España*, vol. iii, p. 142.

Yet Sarmiento's assurances were too late to save Creswell. The Father General of the Jesuits now had deep misgivings over the future usefulness of Creswell after over two years of calumnies and suspicions among the powerful courtiers of Philip III. It would embarrass his difficult task with the struggling colleges and possibly lead to further friction to have him remain in Spain. Late in 1613 Claudio Aquaviva sent two letters to Joseph Creswell. In the first he was ordered to reside in Flanders, while in the second, he allowed him time if he wished to clear his name. The hesitancy to move abruptly was caused by the fact that Creswell had never been handed a formal accusation. In a letter to the Council Creswell bluntly reminded them of that essential propriety. "I only ask," he wrote, "that I be allowed to leave Spain with no less reputation than when I arrived here twenty years before." [110]

With the prospect of Creswell's departure imminent it was King Philip's task to make amends to one whom he had once honored with many confidences on English affairs. The monarch had also been generous, as his father had been, to the hard-pressed colleges. His letter to the departing Jesuit was a kindly one but it did not advert to the last two futile years of troublesome suspicions. In February 1614 he wrote to Sarmiento in London that Father Creswell was going to Flanders

so that he can manage more fruitfully the affairs of the seminaries and the Catholics of England. . . . I continue to be satisfied deeply with the good that the said Father Creswell has done and of his high virtue and of his devotion to God's service and mine. Thus you are given to understand that when he arrives there you may hold full correspondence with him. [111]

[110] E 2027 n.f. endorsed: "Carta de Padre General de la Compania."
[111] E 2571/30 letter of 7 Feb. 1614.

In effect the King removed any stigma marking the name of Creswell, but the college of Madrid still needed final royal approval.

For over a year Creswell had to conduct the remaining litigation over the new foundation in Madrid by letter. It was a laborious way of negotiating as Creswell knew all too well. Finally, on November 29, 1614 the Council of State approved the new college at Madrid and in effect it exonerated the absent Jesuit. Moreover, it decreed that there was to be no further litigation about it if possible.[112] It was at best only a personal vindication for Creswell as the troubles of the new English foundation in Madrid were to continue during most of its subsequent history. Moreover, after Creswell's departure no new and energetic servant of the interests of the English colleges appeared at Court.

Creswell, in virtual retirement in the Low Countries, could not exert an influential role in English Catholic affairs. His own generation of English exiles in high positions was passing. His long-time friend, Robert Persons, had died four years before and Jane Dormer only two years previously, while Hugh Owen was living in quiet retirement in Rome. Only Sir William Stanley, possessing an honorable sinecure in Malines, could recall the high hopes and frustrations of former days.

Creswell turned to the writing of devotional literature and counseling the young students at St. Omers. From this period of more reflective seclusion emerged probably his finest book. Ever preoccupied with the troubles of his harassed friends in England, he made the first English translation of the fifth century Christian classic, Salvian's *Quis dives salvus, How a Rich Man May be Saved*.[113] It was a tract for the times whose ancient advice on the folly of greed and the duty of the rich

[112] E 844/87, 88.
[113] Under the initials N.T., at Antwerp, 1618.

to help the poor he wanted to recall to his coreligionists. He offered the work, he explained in the preface, "as a sovereign counterpoyse against the feare and shame whereof the persecutor maketh his advantage to draw many soules from the love of Christ." He recalled to his English readers the poverty of the primitive church which still flourished in the midst of its tribulation. It was a precise translation, faithful to the spirit of the original, yet its simple language enhanced its topical value. It was to be his last message to those who shared his convictions. In 1622 Creswell was asked to become the rector of a new college founded at Ghent where Sir William Stanley was both a regular visitor and benefactor. Apparently the task was too much for his health for he died in January of the following year at the age of sixty-six.

His career had been an unusual one. Despite the limitations of his personality, he had borne almost single-handedly, for over two decades, the drudgery of the detailed correspondence concerning the needs of three colleges below the Pyrenees and the subsidy for two more in Flanders. His work was essential, and in it he was revealed to be tireless, devoted, blunt and consistently optimistic. In his honest letter to the Earl of Salisbury in June 1605 he had written with an affecting candor of his unusual gratitude to the late Queen "and those that governed in her tyme." For through their actions, he wrote, he had enjoyed for more than twenty years, "an inestimable treasure." He esteemed his calling higher "than yf they had given him the crowne of England and all the crownes in this world." [114]

[114] Letter cited in note 86.

CHAPTER SEVEN

THE SPANISH ELIZABETHANS IN HISTORY

AFTER STUDYING the principal problems facing the English diaspora in Spanish Hapsburg lands, some assessment should be attempted of their imprint on the politics of the Courts of Spain and England. Their prominent place in official documents has suggested the unavoidable conclusion that they had earned a reluctant hearing at one, and provoked an outspoken animus at the other.

At the outset, however, a few easy misconceptions can be discarded. First, the impact of personalities of the calibre of Owen, Stanley, or Englefield did not come from merely the emotion-dappled predicament of their exile. They, and the other Spanish Elizabethans, were not a unique phenomenon in sixteenth-century history. They were simply one group of people who were uprooted by the alteration in the religious traditions of their native land. Every western European kingdom had these unfortunate casualties of circumstances. In England the pendulum had previously swung in another di-

rection during the reign of Queen Mary to produce a different group of exiles in Zurich, Strasburg and elsewhere.
Moreover, Queen Elizabeth gave shelter to Protestant exiles
from Flanders, France and even Spain. The mere fact of exile offers no clue to the international interest in the Spanish
Elizabethans. Secondly, Philip's concern for them was not
unexpected. The western European monarchs had been casting themselves in the politically flattering role of "protector"
of the "oppressed" of other nations on several occasions. Intervention and protection were familiar and useful gambits
on the chessboard of European diplomacy.

Thirdly, the word "Catholic" does not promise solidarity
of action among the faithful of England, Scotland and Ireland.
The word can prove in many respects to be a "portmanteau"
term. The Elizabethan Catholic refugees retained many of
their accustomed attitudes and prejudices. They made no
serious effort at *rapprochement* with the Irish or Scottish exiles; on the contrary, there were sparks of rivalry and hostility.
Therefore religion did not prove to be a convenient bond in
any degree for those who were opposed, for various reasons,
to the politics of the English Court. Moreover, the importance
of seeing the subtle differences in the reaction of the various
Catholic princes on the continent to English policy has been
underlined by the experience of the English refugees.

Inevitably there were differences in the leadership of
Philip II, Philip III and the Archduke to which the English
exiles reacted. Thus they must be studied in relation to the
politics of the Court where each resided, and it is an error to
lump them together as dispossessed wanderers, moving indis-
criminately from Court to Court with a fairly predictable tale
of woe. The Spanish Elizabethans were drawn into the greater
issues which dominated the policies of King Philip II. In
seeking his assistance they were diverted into what was already
the magnet for his interests, the war in the Low Countries.

This was the irritant which inflamed the fear and the anger of the English Court. Was the reality of the lot of the refugees properly appreciated in the calculations of Elizabeth and her councilors? Evidently it was not. Yet this mistake resulted from a higher—or shrewder—estimate of the potential of the exiles than the Spanish Council of State bothered to make.

It would be only laboring the obvious to note that the Catholic exiles did not find their adopted countries to be lands of milk and honey. The evidence is far more convincing than Lewknor's book that all exiles strove to be assured of their livelihood. Even when the hurdle of gaining a pension was passed, many spent the rest of their stay in anxiety over whether it would be paid regularly. It was not unlikely that Sir Francis Englefield's efforts to retain his estates in England were spurred by this urgency. Because of this threatened pauperism the refugees were hampered from an energetic pursuit of an independent course of action. Since they were not paying the piper, they could not call his tune.

Secondly, while in the personality of Cardinal Allen the English exiles had undoubtedly a religious leader who expressed their needs with burning sincerity, they never had a military and political leader with the experience and prestige to unite them under his banner. Sir William Stanley was the professional soldier, first and last, but nothing more. The misguided attempt to place the Duchess of Feria in this difficult position of leadership was never seconded by the more intelligent among them.

In the third place, it is now clear that an invariably long apprenticeship preceded the rise of several Englishmen to important positions, where Spain showed considerable confidence in them as individuals. Hugh Owen's eminence was not established until nearly twenty years after his departure from England. Sir William Stanley was not a member of the Archduke's Council of War until sixteen years after his entry into

Spanish service. Similarly, although he came to the Court in 1592, Joseph Creswell's favored place was not assured until the early years of the reign of Philip III. Even then he was to retire after twenty-three years of residence in the midst of litigation and deep misunderstanding. Englefield's useful secretaryship under Philip II came only after many years of minor positions in the Low Countries. Long proven reliability was the basis of Spanish confidence.

Fourthly, the Spanish Court steadfastly preferred its practice of assigning a pension to the exiles in return for a foreseeable service rather than as an alms. In this indirect way the primacy of Spanish political and military aims was guaranteed. Consequently, their military activities were carefully restricted, and despite the pleas of their leading soldier, Sir William Stanley, they never assumed a more suitable crusading character which would have attracted more volunteers at once. The military services of the English regiment—so alarming in concept to the English Court—were limited to the needs of the warfare in Flanders. Clearly the Council of State never deviated from concentrating Spain's resources on their exhausting campaigns on land. Stanley's suggested *empresa* was persistently viewed as a risky and expensive diversion. This was true even of his vital plan to train a regiment to be ready to cross the channel in the event of the death of the Queen. His plans were quickly vetoed by the *Realpolitik* of Brussels.

Fifthly, it is really an exaggeration and a euphemism to call these English refugees a "Spanish Faction" as even some of their contemporaries asserted. Their failure to produce a leader in the true sense, their dispersal into various professions and localities, their financial insolvency, their rivalries over leadership—all prevented the solidarity needed as a prelude to such a development. This was well understood by the more perceptive among them. As late as 1596 it was planned to form a committee to unite "their nation" in the service of

Spain and "to remove the groups, factions and dissensions" among them and thus give "life and spirit to the cause of the Catholics." [1] Significantly, it proved impossible to convene such a *junta*. It was important, of course, that there be the approval and active encouragement of the Courts at Brussels and Valladolid of such steps leading to solidarity. Instead, the anti-Spanish exiles stayed on the same pension lists as the Hispanophiles. In effect, the Hapsburgs proved insensitive to such aspirations, for it viewed them with the same myopic indifference which was displayed towards Stanley's military ambitions.

Finally, while it may be expected that the bond between the exiles in Spanish Hapsburg lands and the Catholics of England would be strong, there were clear hints of support for them in what may be called the crypto-Catholic levels of Elizabethan England. It was an elusive thing and it would be rash to read too much into any one example. Yet to select one valuable clue: the amount of useful information coming to Flanders and Spain from those well informed about the English Court in the 1590's was an indication of sympathy. What was of greater, if at present more elusive, significance was the evidence in the impounded file of Hugh Owen concerning "certain letters of various lords and many leading personages, who undertook by pledges of their persons and fortunes to assist his Majesty and his Highness whenever the opportunity came." [2] While up to the present nothing but the description of Owen's file has come to light, it is clear that the secret knowledge of such an attitude would be a substantial encouragement to the leading *émigrés*. It would also be an unprobed reason for the disquiet of the English Court over the "Spaniolized Papist."

While the true relationship of the English refugees to

[1] E 839/129.
[2] E 624 n.f. letter of 14 Dec. 1605, enclosure.

Spain was completely different from what the ominous proclamations in the Queen's name indicated, still the concern of
Spain for the plight of the English Catholics cannot be lightly
dismissed.

There is little doubt that Philip II was sincere in the sympathetic hearing usually granted to the Englishmen who came
to him, or wrote to his Court. However, the King prudently
followed the advice of only a trusted few. The survival in the
files of the Council of State of so many *consultas* based on
the numerous letters presented through Englefield and Creswell is proof of his active concern. The granting of pensions
and various substantial subsidies to the English colleges was
a more tangible proof of Spanish generosity. As in other matters, King Philip was master of his own decisions. When the
Spanish might was eventually aimed towards England in the
planning of the Armada of 1588, the exiles complained justly
that they were ignored. Their role in the later Armadas of
1596 and 1597 and the Kinsale expedition was even more
unsatisfying, since the strategy of Spain was usually influenced
by the crises within Ireland.

The high expectations of the Catholic exiles faltered because of their impromptu, unofficial position within a Court
preoccupied with a declining continental hegemony. Moreover, Spain's ambitions made it difficult to form alliances with
other Catholic princes. King Philip's relations with Pope Sixtus were notably poor, nor was there any appreciable improvement towards the turn of the century under Pope Clement VIII. The reluctance of King Henry IV of France to
watch Spain acquire the prestige of aiding substantially the
English Catholics was obvious. In any case, a Catholic coali-
tion on the continent never materialized to the evident regret
of the English exiles.

The history of the Spanish Elizabethans emerges as one
where great political expectations stayed unsatisfied, as their

empresas remained unwanted on the table of the Council of State. It was the bleak lot of refugees in many other moments of modern history. Their fate was to be impatient, frustrated spectators of the successful containment of the Catholic resurgence in England. Why then could the young Oliver Cromwell observe the notable "Spaniolized" sentiment among his Catholic countrymen? Later, of course, it would change, as the Hispanophile wave reached its crest during the first decades of the seventeenth century. It would recede to leave deep pools in segments of English Catholic thought. Ultimately their affection for Spain had been simply a tribute from a hard-pressed minority, not so much for getting everything they expected or needed, but for a perceptible aid to their morale. A great power, still pursuing the hardheaded ambitions of its traditions, was seriously concerned about their troubles. That there were mistakes, miscalculations and misunderstandings in Spain's policy can be recognized by all; but evidently the Spanish Court's unique and generous assistance was valued and understood for a time by Catholics in England.

APPENDIX I

A Survey of the Students Registered at St. Alban's College in Valladolid, 1589–1603

In the first table the origin of the students according to their former dioceses is presented as an indication of the geographical distribution of the membership of the college. In the second table is offered a numerical total for each year of students who registered during a twelve-months period, and who eventually returned to minister to their compatriots. It was compiled to estimate the effectiveness of the college in fulfilling the primary purpose of its foundation. Doubtful cases were not included. There was, not unexpectedly, a large variation in the prior education of the students, so that their period of residence at Valladolid differed considerably. Some would return within two years, others after five or more. The principal source for both tables was the evidence available in C.R.S. vol. xxx. There was insufficient material extant to attempt a similar study of St. Gregory's College in Seville.

A. THE ORIGINS OF THE REGISTRANTS

Diocese	Number	Diocese	Number
Bangor	7	Lincoln	11
Bath and Wells	3	London	16
Canterbury	5	Menevia	1
Carlisle	2	Norwich	12
Chester	36	Oxford	5
Durham	8	St. Asaph	3
Ely	2	Salisbury	6
Exeter	8	Winchester	6
Gloucester	3	Worcester	1
Hereford	13	York	19
Lichfield	11		

B. REGISTRANTS KNOWN TO HAVE RETURNED AS PRIESTS TO ENGLAND

Year		Year	
1589	11	1597	3
1590	7	1598	6
1591	8	1599	8
1592	11	1600	7
1593	9	1601	No entrants
1594	8	1602	10
1595	5	1603	3
1596	10		

APPENDIX II

A Profile of the Manpower of Colonel Stanley's Regiment, 1588–1600

THE OFFICIAL STATEMENTS, prepared at irregular intervals, of the deployment of the various regiments under the command of the Duke of Parma and his successors indicate the fluctuations of the size of the force of Sir William Stanley. Unfortunately the statements, prepared by different officials, vary in detail, since there was not apparently a very precise method of reporting. For example, during Stanley's absence in Spain in 1591 his name was not used to designate his forces, for in January 1592 one despatch stated merely that the English soldiers were paid 6,900 florins and "regrouped" (E 602/139).

Date	Numbers	Source
1588	7 Companies 918 soldiers	E 594/192
1590, August	6 Companies 850 soldiers	E 599/58
1592, July	7 Companies 259 men, 68 pensioners	E 603/94
1593, June	7 Companies 350 soldiers	E 605/259
1595, March	4 Companies 318 soldiers	E 610/49
1596, July	9 Companies 1084 men, 64 pensioners	E 611/169
1597, March	10 Companies 984 soldiers	E 614/65
1600, January	10 Companies (Under Colonel Robert Bostock)	E 617/180

A CENSUS OF THE KING'S PENSIONERS
ATTACHED TO THE REGIMENT,
1587–1603 [1]

THE FOLLOWING Englishmen were named in various lists of pensioners prepared for the review of the Spanish Council of State during the war with the Anglo-Dutch *entente*. After its integration into the Spanish Hapsburg forces in 1587, Stanley's regiment became the nucleus for the support of the English *émigré* community, while the King constantly added to its role the major proportion of Englishmen for whom a special maintenance was planned. This census cannot, however, hope to provide a total coverage of every English pensioner since an undetermined number secured appointments elsewhere, for example, in other regiments in the army, or in the navy or in the Archduke's personal service. There was never apparently any request from the Council for the muster lists of the hundreds of foot soldiers or cavalry which formed the ranks of the regiment.

Although each name on this list appeared in Spanish sources, references from English reports are included here when that report was judged to be reliable by comparison with other evidence. Some English despatches apparently lumped together pensioners,

[1] The following brief table of contemporary exchange values may provide an evaluation of the sums involved in the pension system.

Spain	England
1 escudo	5s. 6d.
4 escudos	1£ 2s.

Flanders	England
1 florin	3s. 4d.
6 florins	1£

(From P.R.O., S.P. 12/153/182: "Rates between the monies of England and those of . . . Flanders, . . . and Spaine" 1582.)

travelers, deserters and even persons who were only rumored to be in Spanish employ. However, in a few instances, such as Anthony Rolston's despatch of late 1593 (List G), quite accurate details concerning the pensioners were available to the English Court.

Among the sources listed below two require a special comment. List A (Treasury disbursements in the Low Countries, c. 1573) is used only to indicate that the name was already established as a pensioner but was later transferred to the rolls of Stanley's regiment. List R (The residence certificates, 1597) was valuable solely for the biographical detail, and was not a list of pensioners. After the name and varying amounts of pensions, there is added a calendar of the occasional comments of Spanish officials which were found in these papers. It will be noted that some names leave the lists for a period of time. This could be explained by the fact that, after being "discharged" or "reformed," the pensioner successfully petitioned for a return to the lists. During the two-year period, 1598–1599, when the regiment was disbanded, the pensioners were assigned to other accounts in the Spanish army.

The lists have been lettered alphabetically, and placed in chronological order.

List	Date	Title and Description	Source
A	c.1573–4	Treasury Disbursements in the Low Countries.	Lechat, *Les Refugiés* pp. 230–36
B	1574	"The certyn Nott of . . . Yngles Gentlemen who come to Spayne . ."	B.M. Lansdowne MS vol. xviii f. 174–75
C	c.1583	"English Rebels at Spau" . .	B.M. Lansdowne MS vol. xxxvi f. 151
D	c.1584	"Nobles y Caualleros Yngleses que tienen entretenimientos. . ."	E 2851 n.f.
E	1589	"Names of pensioners in Stanley's Regiment . . ."	P.R.O. S.P. 12/224/113
F	c.1592	Report on the distribution of a month's pay to the forces.	E 603/89

THE SPANISH ELIZABETHANS

G 1593, late "A Note of all suche English as receue stypend of the K. of Spaine." Lambeth Palace MS vol. 651, ff. 41–42

H 1593 Report on pensioners in the Regiment. E 606/100

I 1593 Report on the pensioners. E 606/96

J 1595 "The English in Spain." H.M.C. Salisbury MS vol. iii, p. 357

K 1596 Report on the quality of pensioners for the Archduke. E 612/125–27

L 1596 List of "effectives" among the pensioners of Stanley. E 612/126

M c.1600 Pensioners with the army after the "reform." E 617/56

N 1600 A Second Report on the quality of the pensioners for the Archduke. E 617/24

O 1603 Report on pensioners "near the person or in the army of the Archduke." E 622/205

P 1604 Report on pensioners "of all types and nationalities." E 623/75

Q c.1605 "Names of Gentlemen that serve in Flanders." P.R.O. S.P. 77/7/329ff.

R 1597 "Residence Certificates," not a pension list, containing details of residence prepared by English émigrés on orders from the Archduke in July 1597. A.G.R. P.E.A. 1398/7

1. *Alcock, Walter*
15 escudos G,I,K,M,N,O,P
After serving in the cavalry for a long time, he was given a pension as a reward; a good man and a good soldier. (K)

2. *Allen, Elizabeth*
80 escudos K,M,O,P
The sister of Cardinal Allen; she has three grown daughters to wed. (K)

3. *Allen, Gabriel*
   35 escudos G, 40 escudos I,K
   The brother of Cardinal Allen, he is living in Rome where his pension can be continued profitably; he is not a man of warfare, nor of affairs but is entirely engaged in his devotions. (K)
   "Place Gabriel Allen's pension on the embassy accounts."
   (E 1855 n.f. King to the Duke of Sessa, draft, 1596.)

4. *Amery, Richard*
   20 escudos I,K
   A troublesome man, once involved in the surrender of Alost, where he received his pension; he is a *teniente,* and serves in the regiment. (K)

5. *Ansley, Edward*
   20 escudos H

6. *Bagshaw, Thomas*
   12 escudos G,K
   Recommended by Madame de Fressin; he is deceased. (K)

7. *Barrett, William*
   12 escudos G, 20 escudos H,I,K,L,M,N
   He was, with Amery (No. 4), instrumental in the surrender of Alost; he has the pay of an *alférez.* (K) "The Count of Fuentes gave him a licence to travel to Rome; it will be a small loss if he does not return." (L)
   "He asks an exemption from a tax of the town of Dormond for his wife and children."
   (A.G.R., P.E.A. 1830/3 n.f. petition of 9 October 1590)

8. *Barney, Josiah*
   35 escudos G, 40 escudos I,K,L
   A Captain, he came at the head of 500 soldiers from the enemy; after the reform of the company he was given only 25 escudos; at present he is serving in the regiment. (K) He has moved to Brussels from the regiment and for six months he had handled its affairs there. (L)

9. *Bates, Thomas*
   15 escudos D,G,I,K,N,O
   He is a good man and a loyal soldier. (N)

10. *Bayley, Richard*
    30 escudos G, 25 escudos I,K.

He was employed because of the reports of M. de la Motte; his service is in matters of secrecy; at present he is employed by Juan de Ribas, the Governor of the Ecluse; a very fine man, he is married and a good worker. (K)

11. *Berrington, John*
25 escudos H

12. *Bone, Abraham*
20 escudos I,K
He was formerly majordomo in the household of Madame de Fressin; at present he is a Canon at Tournai, and does not need a pension. (K)

13. *Bostock, Robert*
40 escudos F (as Captain), 200 escudos (Colonel, 1599–1601)
Catherine de Carondelet, widow of Colonel Bostock, asks a pension in view of her husband's services of 14 years as captain, sergeant major, and colonel until his death at Nieuport.
(E 2764 n.f. Petition of 19 June 1601.)

14. *Bridgewater, John*
25 escudos G,I,K,M,N
He is of the Scottish faction, has property by inheritance and is of little service. (K) He is a priest, aging but well-to-do. (N) He left England in 1576, and has been a pensioner since 1585. (R)

15. *Browne, Charles*
30 escudos D, 40 escudos G,I,K,M,N,O
He is the natural brother of the former Viscount Montague, and has been a soldier for some years, but has a restless spirit and is not among the well informed of his nation. (N) He is 50 years old, has a wife and seven children, lives in Brussels and has been a pensioner since 1583. (R)

16. *Buright, Richard*
25 escudos K
He has served with honor for many years in the Spanish infantry; he is from Ireland, a fine man, and a good soldier now serving in the regiment. (K)

17. *Butler, Henry*
20 escudos K,M,N,O
He is married. (K) He is not a soldier and of little or no service. (N)

18. *Capestock, Thomas*
    20 escudos H
19. *Cawdrey, George*
    15 escudos E,H
20. *Challoner, John*
    20 escudos E,H
21. *Chamberlain, George*
    30 escudos G
22. *Chamberlain, George*
    20 escudos G,I,K,M,N,O,P
    A young man, a relative of the Duchess of Feria, at present in the college in Valladolid, he received his grant at the request of Madame de Fressin; there is no need to continue his pension. (K) At present he is studying in Rome. (N)

23. *Chambers, Anthony*
    25 escudos E,L,N,O,P
    He left England in 1585 to live in France, summoned to join Stanley after Deventer, and served in the navy for a period. (R) Pensioned by the King, he serves at present as a *teniente* in the Colonel's company. (L) He is very loyal. (N)

24. *Chambers, James*
    20 escudos G,K,M,N,O,P
    He has had long service in the infantry and cavalry, and it is important that he return to the regiment and earn his pay; he is troublesome and disturbing. (K) He entered Spanish service in November 1578, and is at present 43 years old. (R) His devotion to the King is uncertain; he does not restrain himself in various matters; he is a soldier who can serve yet he lives here idly, always complaining, as he does every day at the office of the Secretariate. (N)

25. *Chambers, William*
    15 escudos H
26. *Clement, Cesar*
    25 escudos I,K,M,N,O,P
    He was pensioned at the request of the Marquis of Burgout, whose chaplain he was for 15 escudos. Later the Duke of Parma raised it to 25 escudos; he was chaplain to Cosmo (Massei) his secretary, at present he says Mass for Don Esteban de Ybarra. (K) His father, Sir Thomas Clement [No. 27], left England 38 years ago. He was born in Louvain. (R) He is now chaplain to his Highness (the Archduke). (N)

27. *Clement, Thomas*
   30 escudos G,I,K,M,N,O,P
   He has lived most of his life outside of England, and is now
   quite old; he was pensioned by letters from Cardinal Allen
   and Don Bernardino. (K) A man of advanced years, very
   loyal, more a man of letters than a soldier; he could serve in
   other ways. (N)

28. *Coffyn, Roger*
   15 escudos G,K,N,O,P
   He is a man of little resource and no service. (N)

29. *Colvin, James*
   25 escudos H

30. *Colvin, Patrick*
   15 escudos H

31. *Coniers, George*
   25 escudos G,I,K,M,N,O,P
   A relative of the Cardinal's, at whose request he was pensioned. (K) "Very loyal and possibly of use if there is an opportunity in England; he was never a soldier, he is now past
   60 years." (N)

32. *Copley, Anthony*
   E (no amount specified)

33. *Copley, Thomas*
   40 escudos D

34. *Copley, William*
   30 escudos G,N
   A well-born gentleman, and the heir of his house, he has
   served well in the navy; pensioned by the King, he is loyal
   and could be of great service in England for his quality and
   the means at his command. (N)

35. *Court, Thomas*
   8 escudos G,I,K,M,N,P
   He is married. (K) A man of small fortune and services, but
   very loyal. (N)

36. *Covert, Thomas*
   20 escudos I,K
   He was recommended by Cardinal Allen, Don Bernardino
   and the *Veedor General* for his services in Paris; he is old and
   infirm. (K)

37. *Creech, John*
    30 escudos E,I,K
    He is from Ireland and troublesome, he was pensioned at the
    request of Patrick Sedgrave [No. 118] and was his assistant
    in that same affair; he brought letters from Rome from Cardi-
    nal de Senis of France. He is of no service not even in that
    which he is pretending to do. (K)

38. *Creech, Ralph*
    30 escudos E,I,K
    He has served for some time in the regiment of Stanley, han-
    dled the details for a surrender of a town, but did not succeed.
    He had transferred his pension into the army, and is now
    deceased. (K)

39. *Crisp, Edward*
    50 escudos G
    He requests 1400 ducats for services in the army and navy;
    he has been with the Adelantado of Castile in services of great
    importance.
    (E 2742 n.f. Petition of 24 April 1604.)

40. *Dacres, Edward*
    A, 500 florins B, 50 escudos D

41. *Dacres, Francis*
    100 escudos G, 40 escudos I,K
    A young man, the son and heir of Lord Dacres, of high qual-
    ity and large following in England, he received this pension
    before his father left England. The King has placed his father's
    pension in Rome, but it is necessary that some way of sup-
    porting this person there, or in Spain, be decided by the King.
    (K) *A marginal note by another hand:* "Lord Dacres received
    70 escudos in Rome at the embassy; after he came to live
    here the Archduke paid him the same; at present he is dis-
    turbed over the small account made of him, and wishes his
    son to live with him." (K)

42. *Danforth, John*
    15 escudos H

43. *Darbishire, Robert*
    20 escudos E,H
    The prior of the English Carthusians in Malines expresses
    gratitude to the Archduke for saving their community on two
    occasions.
    (A.G.R., P.E.A. 1869 n.f. letter of August 1597)

44. *Deane, Gilbert*
   10 escudos G,K. Deceased. (K)

45. *Denis, Gabriel*
   25 escudos D, 35 escudos G, 40 escudos I,K,N,O,P
   He has 25 escudos by order of the King, and 15 by order of
   Parma. He was a confidant of Don Juan on English affairs. A
   noble gentleman of good family, he is useful but not in the
   wars; he is married and has grown daughters to wed. (K) He
   is 60 years of age and left England in 1561; he has served
   under Alva, Don Juan and Parma, now lives in Brussels. (R)
   "He is more of an adviser than a soldier; he is known to Secretary Prada, through whom he was pensioned." (N)

46. *Dyer, Robert*
   30 escudos H,L a captain
   He asks immunity from taxes for his family living in Brabant.
   (A.G.R., P.E.A. 1869 n.f. letter of March 1597)

47. *Eaton, James*
   40 escudos G
   He has entered the service after Deventer, but has had difficulty in having his patent recognized for over a year.
   (A.G.R., P.E.A. 1830/3 letter of April 1588)

48. *Evans, Thomas*
   10 escudos I,K

49. *Eustace, Oliver*
   40 escudos K,N
   A troublesome Irishman, he has held a company in Stanley's
   regiment, but was dismissed for poor conduct, and he has not
   improved since then. (K) He is retained for occasional services; he was a captain in England. (N)

50. *Farnsley, Samuel*
   20 escudos G,I,K,M,N,O,P
   He was recommended by the King and is married. (K) A
   man of low estate, who does no services. (N)

51. *Fenn, John*
   25 escudos E,K,M,O,P
   He has been pensioned for a time in Stanley's regiment and
   later because of his age and a request of the Vicar General was
   transferred; he is now old and feeble, but a man of distinction. (K)

52. *Finglass, Thomas*
    40 escudos I, a captain

53. *Fincham, William*
    35 escudos G,K
    A well-born gentleman but of little service in wars; he received
    his pension through Cardinal Allen and Don Bernardino; now
    deceased. (K)

54. *Flood, Henry*
    30 escudos L, a captain
    Order to raise his pension to 40 escudos.
    (A.G.R., S.E.G. vol. 20 f. 23 entry of 30 April 1601)

55. *Foljambe, Godfrey*
    35 escudos G, 40 escudos I,O

56. *Ford, Richard*
    15 escudos O

57. *Franceschi, Jacomo* (Giacomo)
    No amount specified F,H,I
    The *teniente colonel* of the regiment 1590–1596, then dis-
    missed. Archduke orders a pension for 60 escudos.
    (A.G.R., S.E.G. liv. 20 f. 11 entry for 10 April 1601)

58. *Franceschi, Tomaso*
    20 escudos H,L
    The brother of Stanley's deputy, he is now a *teniente* in Colo-
    nel Patton's regiment; he should not have this pension. (L)

59. *Funlan, Lawrence*
    40 escudos F, a captain

60. *Gage, Richard*
    20 escudos D,G,I,K,N,O,P,Q
    He lost a brother in the King's service, and it was then ordered
    that he be given his brother's pension; he has served for a
    time in Naples. He is well born and very Catholic, a man of
    good deeds but slight intelligence. (K) "He is not interested
    in the King's service for he is more inclined to be a religious
    than a soldier." (N) "The sonne of Mr. Gage of Sussex,
    lodged in the English cloister at Bruxelles and there brought
    up by the English priests of that house; he is extraordinarily
    maintained and attended." (Q)

61. *Gaston, Henry*
    30 escudos I

62. *Gaston, James*
   15 escudos H, 40 escudos L, an *alférez*

63. *Gates, Thomas*
   25 escudos I,M

64. *Gervaise, Henry*
   20 escudos E,H, 40 escudos L
   Served as a captain with Colonel Bostock and lost his company, after being captured by the Dutch; he asks a license to
   go to Spain.
      (A.G.R., S.E.G. vol. 20 f. 23 entry of 12 June 1602)
   Captain Gervaise does not wish to be transferred to Milan,
   but to return to the Low Countries.
      (E 804/123. Letter of the Council of State ca. July
   1603)
   He has served 17 years in the Low Countries, and wishes
   14 months back payments.
      (E 1746 n.f. Petition of 24 July 1604)

65. *Gifford, Richard*
   30 escudos H

66. *Giles, Hugh*
   12 escudos H

67. *Gips, Andrew*
   12 escudos H

68. *Green, John*
   20 escudos H,L

69. *Green, Richard*
   20 escudos E,L

70. *Greenfield, Thomas*
   25 escudos H,L
   He has left England in 1589 and served in the regiment. He
   is 40 years of age, and has a wife in Brussels. (R)

71. *Halsey, Edward*
   20 escudos L

72. *Hazelwood, Henry*
   20 escudos G, 25 escudos I

73. *Heath, Thomas*
   25 escudos G,K,N,O,P
   He is the nephew of the Archbishop of York, the former
   Chancellor of England in the days when his Majesty was in
   England. He lost his possessions for the faith and was recom-

mended for his pension by Hugh Owen. He is well deserving and has volunteered to serve with Colonel Stanley. (ᴋ) A well-born gentleman and a loyal soldier. (ɴ) Approves Thomas Heath for service.

(E 593 f. 97. Letter of Philip II to Parma 27 Feb. 1587)

74. *Herbert, George*
20 escudos ɢ,ɪ,ᴋ
Pensioned by order of the King, a man of good parts, he is now 63 years of age and in prison in England. (ᴋ) First reached the Low Countries in 1586, he has now returned to Brussels. (ʀ)

75. *Herel, Richard*
20 escudos ʜ

76. *Hesketh, Richard*
25 escudos ʜ

77. *Hill, James*
30 escudos ɢ,ɪ,ᴋ
He was pensioned at the request of the Duke of Guise, and in his service until the Duke was murdered at Blois, at present he serves the Duke of Maine. Recommended by Bernardino de Mendoza, he has served well by sending important information. He is well born and lost his property for the faith. Since he is not employed as before he can be discharged. (ᴋ)

78. *Hopkins, Richard*
30 escudos ɢ,ɪ,ᴋ
He has lived 25 years outside of England, more a man of letters than a soldier, well born and of good conduct; now deceased. (ᴋ)

79. *Horton, Henry*
30 escudos ᴋ,ɴ
He was pensioned at the request of the Duke of Lorraine, in whose province he lives. He is married and does not serve. (ᴋ) A loyal man but not a soldier. (ɴ)

80. *Hoskins, Ralph*
15 escudos ɪ,ᴋ,ɴ,ᴏ,ᴘ
It cannot be learned at whose request he was pensioned, he is married, of little quality and has other means of support. (ᴋ)

81. *Hungerford, Anne* (Dormer)
100 escudos ᴅ, 80 escudos ɢ,ɪ,ᴋ, 125 escudos ɴ,ᴏ,ᴘ

A member of the Scottish faction and the sister of the Duchess of Feria. In the days of Alva she received 50 escudos; later it was increased after letters from the King and the dowager Empress. (ᴋ)
Anne Hungerford has lost a rent of 600 escudos a year, Parma should now assist her.

    (E 587/94. Letter of Philip II 31 Jan. 1583)
Asks assistance of the Council to recovering back payments of 3,000 escudos.

    (E 2765 n.f. Petition of 22 April 1603)

82. *Ingleby, David*
    40 escudos ᴍ,ɴ
The son-in-law of the Earl of Westmorland, and the second son of a prominent gentleman, at first he seemed to be very much against the Scot; he appears at present to be wavering a little, as he is discontented over the lack of pay; he will occasionally be of use in England. (ɴ) He is aged 48, left England two years ago and lives with his wife, Anne, and their daughter Ursula; Sybille Banks is her maid, Anne White and Mary Hanke are their servants. (ʀ)

83. *Jessop, William*
    15 escudos ʜ

84. *Kemp, William*
    20 escudos ʟ
Recommends Kemp to secure service.

    (E 588/137. Letter of King 23 June 1584)
Enrollment of a pension of 20 escudos.

    (A.H.N. Estado 251 n.f. entry for 27 July 1589)
Petition for back pay for George Kemp, uncle of William, who has served since 1564.

    (*Ibid.* Entry for 21 Aug. 1589)

85. *Knight, Richard*
    20 escudos ʟ
An Irishman, who now serves in the regiment, formerly his pension was in the army. (ʟ)

86. *Knot, William, "Doctor"*
    30 escudos ᴅ, 20 escudos ɢ, 25 escudos ɪ

87. *Langton, Nicholas*
    25 escudos ʜ,ʟ
A priest who serves the regiment. (ʟ)

88. *Lee, John*
    1 5 escudos O,P
    Recommends help to Lee.
    (E 187 n.f. Letter of Andres de Prada, 19 Oct. 1601)
    He left England in 1594, wishes back pay.
    (A.H.N. Estado 254 f. 19, entry of 8 April 1602)

89. *Legh, Edward*
    1 2 escudos H

90. *Ligons, Ralph*
    20 escudos D, 35 escudos G,I,K,N,O,P
    He was given 20 escudos by the Duke of Alva and later
    raised to 35 by the Duke of Parma; a former confidant of the
    King of Scots; he is now elderly, troublesome, and very close
    to the Duchess of Feria; he guides her sister here, he is a man
    of affairs, a soldier and well born. (K) He was thought to be
    too devoted to the King of Scots, but Father Baldwin says
    that he has now changed. (N)

91. *Lingen, Edmond*
    1 5 escudos E,H

92. *Lovell, Thomas*
    2 5 escudos I,K,M,N
    Well born and the heir of his house, he is a young student at
    present, and of little or no service; he can be discharged. (K)

93. *Lydge, James*
    1 5 escudos H,L,M
    He is married and lives in Brussels and is never with the regi-
    ment. (L) The son of Thomas Lydge, he was born in Here-
    ford in 1572 and left England in 1588. Originally given a
    pension by Parma, he has served as an archer in the bodyguard
    of Duke Ernest and was then placed in the regiment. He was
    instructed in the faith by his mother and reconciled in Malines
    by the Prior of the Carthusians. (R)

94. *Lynne, Roger*
    30 escudos K
    Deceased, came with Mompesson [No. 97]. (K)

95. *Markenfeld, Thomas*
    1 8 escudos D, 35 escudos G
    Pension ordered for Markenfeld.
    (E 587/82 letter of 7 Feb. 1583)

96. *Middleton, William*
   35 escudos G, 40 escudos I,K
   He has been a long time outside of England for his faith and
   has endured much in the King's service. Moreover, the King
   owes him money for the artillery he made in the days of the
   Commendador Mayor. He is well born, a fine man, and he
   endures great poverty together with his wife and children. (K)

97. *Mompesson, Lawrence*
   35 escudos K,M,N,O,P
   He left England with Roger Lynne [No. 94] because of suspicions that he was corresponding with Spain. Two priests
   who had come from Spain were arrested in their houses. They
   are well deserving people. (K) He left England in 1591 and
   has lived with his wife and two daughters in Antwerp for three
   years and after that, in Brussels. (R) He is not a soldier, but
   loyal and well born; he will be of service if there is an opportunity in England. (N) English ambassador in Brussels asks
   Cornwallis to assist Mompesson in gaining the arrears of his
   pension.
   (Winwood, *Memorials* vol. ii pp. 234–35, letter of 22
   June 1606)

98. *Mockett, Timothy*
   40 escudos D,G,I,K,N
   He has been here for more than 24 years; he is troublesome
   and of the Scottish faction; he was pensioned on the King's
   orders. He is now over age and married to the sister of Governor Baptiste Duboys. (K) He is believed to be loyal. (N)
   He is sixty years of age, his family lives in Louvain. (R)
   Isabelle Duboys, widow of Timothy Mockett asks help. Her
   husband served 34 years in Italy and Flanders; he died of
   fever at the seige of Ostend, leaving a wife and three children.

   (E 2742 n.f. petition of 17 Aug. 1604)

99. *Morgan, Thomas*
   55 escudos G,I

100. *Neville, Charles,* The Earl of Westmorland
   100 escudos D, 200 escudos G,I,K,M,N
   His pension of 100 escudos is by royal order since the days
   of Alva, 100 were added by Parma, "when it was a question
   of England," (K) He is commonly believed to be of the Scottish faction, a person of great quality and little usefulness to

whom nothing of importance can be entrusted; were he faithful he would be of use." (N)
Archduke orders his pension restored which was lost in a
reform by Count Mansfeldt.

  (A.G.R., S.E.G. vol. 16 f. 78. Entry of 22 May 1596)

101. *Norton, Richard*
  A 28 escudos D

102. *Owen, Francis*
  20 escudos I,K
  A relative of the Duchess of Feria, at whose request he was
  pensioned, he has served a long time, first in the Burgundian
  infantry and lately with the Spanish. He was recovering from
  a wound for a long time and for this reason his pension was
  transferred. He can now return to duty, he is an excellent
  soldier and highly honored. (K)

103. *Owen, Hugh*
  A, 20 escudos B, 25 escudos D, 60 escudos G,K,O,P

104. *Owen, John*
  20 escudos, I,K
  The nephew of Hugh Owen, the same comment as under
  Lovell [No. 92]. (K)

105. *Owen, Richard*
  15 escudos E,H
  He serves in the company of M. Meynarts. (H)

106. *Owen, Robert*
  30 escudos G, 25 escudos I,K
  The brother of Hugh Owen, he received his pension before
  he became a priest; he lives in France and enjoys a canonry.
  (K)

107. *Paget, Charles*
  75 escudos G, 70 escudos I,K,N
  By royal order he was pensioned with 50 gold escudos a
  month in Paris, and later transferred here; he was given 70 escudos as the monetary equivalent. He is a son of Lord Paget
  and troublesome. (K) He corresponds with the Queen of
  England and some of her Council. His own letters show that
  he is willing to gain a pardon; he is completely dedicated to
  the Scottish faction, and left for France six months ago, but
  his place has not been filled, as far as is known. (N)
  Order for back pay for one year.

(E 597/162. Letter of 21 Aug. 1589)
Order of Don Martin de Idiaquez for Paget's back pay.

(A.H.N. Estado 251 n.f. Entry for 10 April 1591)
License to go to France for six months from Cardinal Andrew.

(A.G.R., S.E.G. vol. 19 f. 22. Entry for 1 May 1599)

108. *Pansforth, John*
35 escudos G,I,K
He is troublesome and in the Scottish faction, but a gentleman of quality who was pensioned at the request of Madame de Fressin; he is quite old and spends his days in church. (K)

109. *Parsley, Ralph*
25 escudos G, 20 escudos I,K
He received his pension at the request of Mrs. Hungerford, whose secretary he was at 15 escudos; later, by the King's order it was raised to 20 escudos. For six years he was in the household of the Duchess of Feria. Deceased. (K)
Pension of Parsley is to be raised to 20 escudos.

(E 597/81. Letter of 31 June 1589)

110. *Persons, George*
30 escudos G,I,K,N,O
The brother of Father Persons, at whose request he was pensioned. He is married and has children, the royal letters directing that he be paid at the castle in Antwerp were ineffective; he is deserving of help in his own right aside from his brother's merits. He now has a patent from the king for his army pension. (K) He is very loyal, and can serve in matters requiring discretion, which he understands; he is not a soldier, nor was he one. (N)
The arrears of Persons's pension should be paid.

(A.H.N. Estado 251 n.f. Entry for 3 April 1590 and 15 Aug. 1592)
The pension of George Persons is to be renewed.

(*Ibid.* Estado 253 n.f. Entry for 30 March 1594)
The Spanish ambassador to the Court at Brussels is asked to help George Persons and his family who are in need.

(E 627/52 undated petition [*ca.*1610])

111. *Petit, John*
25 escudos E,I,K,M,N
A *teniente*, he served in Stanley's regiment for some years, but

it is not known how he transferred to the army. He is young, troublesome, but can return to the regiment and serve. (K)
He is well born and loyal. (N)

112. *Pilson, Richard*
15 escudos (not listed with Stanley's force)
He has served in the army under Don Cristobal de Mondragon, and in the navy; the Governor is asked to find new employment for him.
(A.H.N. Estado 251 n.f. Entry for 3 April 1590)

113. *Poley, George*
20 escudos G, 15 escudos H

114. *Raynsford, Edward*
25 escudos K,M,N
He came three years ago from England for his religion, has never served in the wars, but will be useful otherwise; he is loyal. (K)

115. *Reynolds, John*
20 escudos G,I,K,M,N,O,P
He was recommended by Cardinal Farnese. (K) A fine person and loyal; he is not a soldier but will be useful in other ways. (N) He is seventy-four years old and left England 28 years ago, has lived in Rome for three years, otherwise he remained in the territory of the King. (R)

116. *Rigsley, Francis*
30 escudos G,I,K,M,N,O,P
He was pensioned by the recommendation of Don Bernardino de Mendoza and served for a long time in the cavalry with distinction; he is very loyal. (K)
Asks immunity from taxes of the city of Bruges.
(A.G.R., P.E.A. 1869 n.f. Petition of 29 Nov. 1595)

117. *Sandford, Humphrey*
20 escudos D

118. *Sedgrave, Patrick*
35 escudos G,I,K
Recommended by the Duke of Lorraine, he has continued to pretend to negotiate the secret surrender of an important town, in which affair he has accomplished nothing in four years. (K)

119. *Shelton, Humphrey*
30 escudos G,I,K,M,N
A gentleman of quality and merit, he has lived 30 years out-

side of his native land. He was pensioned at the request of
Cardinal Allen and has remained in Rouen at that Cardinal's
request to conduct a correspondence with England. He is now
elderly and stays in Rouen which he cannot leave. (K) He is
not a soldier, and at present, he is seventy-five years old. (N)

120. *Skinner, Anthony*
　　　35 escudos I,K
　　　A gentleman of good birth, he was pensioned through the
　　　request of Cardinal Allen. "Not being paid he fled to Eng-
　　　land to seek aid among his friends." He was captured and
　　　condemned, but now it is understood that he lives at home;
　　　there is no reason to retain his name any further. (K)

121. *Sliford, Richard*
　　　15 escudos I,K,M,N,P
　　　He served for a time with Stanley but then his pension was
　　　transferred to the army, and thus he should be discharged
　　　here or made to return. He was imprisoned on suspicion, but
　　　is now free. (K) He left England in June 1589, was
　　　wounded at Nymegan, and is now 45 years old. (R) He
　　　is a lackey and of low estate, who goes about causing trouble,
　　　not believed to be loyal. (N)

122. *Smith, John*
　　　20 escudos E,H,L

123. *Smith, William*
　　　20 escudos G,K, 35 escudos M,N
　　　He is 45 years old and entered the Archduke's service in
　　　September 1596, is now serving at Audemarde. (R) A
　　　captain of great bravery and reputation among the soldiers;
　　　he will be of service anywhere especially in England. He is
　　　very loyal and does not mingle with the factions. (N)

124. *Somerset, George*
　　　35 escudos I,K
　　　He lives in Lorraine, with same comment as for Fincham
　　　[No. 53] (K)

125. *Stanyhurst, John*
　　　20 escudos E,H
　　　He never stays with the regiment; every day he is at the door
　　　of the treasurer demanding his pay. He is restless and be-
　　　lieved to be willing to serve with the "re-grouped" Irish. (H)

126. *Stanyhurst, Richard*
    40 escudos, 30 escudos H, 40 escudos M, 30 escudos N,
    50 escudos P
    A gentleman from Ireland, very loyal to the King, not a
    soldier but very useful in other ways. (N)

127. *Stanyhurst, Walter*
    25 escudos G,H, 30 escudos L, 25 escudos M,N
    The brother of Richard, lives in Paris, he is believed to be
    loyal, and it is said that he wishes to enter the clergy. (N)

128. *Stanley, Edward*
    40 escudos F,M,N
    A captain, the brother of the Colonel is a man loyal to his
    duty. (N)

128A. *Stanley, Edward*
    40 escudos F
    A captain, the first cousin of the Colonel, had a company
    1593–95. [He does not appear elsewhere on the lists.]

129. *Stanley, John*
    30 escudos H

130. *Stanley, Peter*
    20 escudos L

131. *Stanley, William,* Colonel
    200 escudos a month in every description of the regiment
    from *ca.* 1587 to 1596. His patent was transferred to the
    army after the regiment was "re-formed."

132. *Stocker, George*
    30 escudos G,I,K,M,N,O,P
    He has lived many years outside of England, and has per-
    formed many confidential services in which he was sent se-
    cretly to England shortly before the coming of the Armada.
    He was captured and tortured many times, after which he re-
    mained crippled. He and two others made a notable escape
    from prison. He is a fine man and useful. (K) He is one of
    those who took arms against the Queen in 1569. (N) He
    is 55 years old, in Spanish service since 1570, he returned
    to England on orders from Parma. He was imprisoned in the
    Tower and the Bridewell. He now lives in Brussels. (R)

133. *Stonor, John*
    25 escudos G, 30 escudos I,K,M,N,O
    He is a troublesome member of the Scottish faction, is mar-

ried and has never served in the regiment. (K) He is 37 years old. After suffering imprisonment in England, he se-cured letters of recommendation from Don Bernardino de Mendoza to Parma in 1582. Cardinal Allen let him live in the college at Rheims "for three or four years." Recom-mended again to Parma by the Duke of Guise, his pension began in 1586. His family in England had been reduced to almost complete ruin for their help to Father Campion and Father Persons, as "they even secured a printing press for the printing of their books." At the moment he lives in Louvain with a household of five. (R) A gentleman of good birth and very intimate with Charles Paget [No. 107], his connection with the Scottish faction is uncertain; he would be useful if he were loyal, but he is not a soldier. (N)

134. *Talbot, Walter*
20 escudos H

135. *Taylor, Thomas*
20 escudos G,I,K,M,N,O
He is seventy-six years old and lives in Brussels. (R) One of those who took arms against the queen in 1569, a good man and loyal, he is now nearly 80 years old. (N)

136. *Throckmorton, Clement*
20 escudos H,L

137. *Throckmorton, George*
30 escudos G, 35 escudos H
An order to raise his pension to 40 escudos.
(A.G.R., S.E.G. vol. 20 f. 24. Entry of 30 April 1601)

138. *Throckmorton, Thomas*
55 escudos G,I,K
"Thomas Throckmorton has come here at the request of Cardinal Allen but after his arrival he found him deceased. He does not wish to return to Flanders but to transfer his pension to Milan where he can conveniently correspond with England. I have found him well informed about the affairs of his country, and his compatriots have a high opinion of him. He is a useful man in good health and I believe not over forty years of age."
(E 965 n.f. Letter of the Duke of Sessa to the King, Rome, 2 March 1595)
He lost his brother in England for his dealings with Don Bernardino de Mendoza. He was formerly given 40 gold

escudos in Paris; he was well born and deserving, now deceased. (K)

139. *Thwynge, Ingram*
    30 escudos G,I,K,M,N
    He has served in the regiment with distinction, he has been employed on secret missions, he is aging and can do little in warfare, but is ideal for other important duties. (K) He is 60 years old, unmarried and lives in Brussels in the house of James Tipping. (R) He is well born and one of those who took arms against the Queen in 1596; he is loyal but elderly. (N)

140. *Tirrell, Robert*
    30 escudos G,I,K,M,N,O,P
    He was recommended by Pope Gregory XIII; he is a gentleman of good family, loyal to his nation, crippled. (K) He is 46 years old, has lived outside of England for 28 years, now lives in the house of James Tipping. (R) He is loyal, but has not been a soldier, and can be useful in other ways. (N)

141. *Tobin, James*
    15 escudos E,H

142. *Townley, Charles*
    30 escudos G, 20 escudos I,K
    He is well born and of good family, a relative of Cardinal Allen. He fled to England for the same reason as Anthony Skinner [No. 120] and can be discharged. (K)

143. *Tregian, Francis*
    30 escudos L
    Pensioned at the request of Cardinal Allen, some time ago he returned from Rome, but his place here is under litigation. (L)
    The order of the Archduke to confer the pension at 30 escudos.
    (A.G.R., S.E.G. vol 17 f. 84ᵛ. Entry of 8 Nov. 1596)

144. *Tresham, William*
    40 escudos G,K,L,N
    A man of good family who served for a time as a captain in Westmorland's regiment. He was discharged with 25 escudos but was later raised to 40; he is in the Scottish faction and troublesome. (K) He is forty-eight years old and left England in 1581. He served for a time on "voyages" to France and Spain. He now lives here with one French servant. (R)

He has asked for a complete discharge; he is poorly disposed, and corresponds with the Council in England as is proved by his own letters. He remains here complaining and speaking ill of the King's service. (NQ)

145. *Trevillan, John*
20 escudos G,I,K,M,N,O,P
He is well born, a fine man but now crippled by wounds. (K) A native of Cornwall, 60 years old, has served with M. de la Motte for six years and then in Naples under Don Luis de Velasco; he entered Parma's forces in 1586. (R) He has served in Naples and Gravelines. (N) Parma is directed to employ Trevillan.

(E 591 / 101. Order of Philip II, 28 July 1586)

146. *Tunstall, Robert*
25 escudos G,I,K,M,N
Recommended by Cardinal Allen and Don Bernardino, he fled his country for services rendered to the Queen of Scots; he is a strong man who can serve more, but at present he does not, for he is one of the unruly. (K)

147. *Versteghen, Richard*
30 escudos G,I,K,N,O,P
He was recommended by Cardinal Allen and Don Bernardino. From Antwerp he corresponds with the Jesuits in England and Father Persons in Spain on the English mission. He has also prepared *avisos* for the King's service when he had orders for them in the time of Parma. A fine man suitable for many varied services of importance, and his absence will be a notable loss in Antwerp. (K) He is very loyal, but not a soldier; his pension is arranged by the royal order. (N) Archduke Ernest is ordered to renew his pension.

(A.H.N. Estado 253 n.f. Entry of 30 March 1594)
Asks arrears of his pension.

(E 1744 n.f. Petition of 8 October 1602)

148. *Viliers, Edward*
40 escudos F, a captain

149. *Walpole, Thomas*
20 escudos H

150. *Ward, William*
40 escudos H,L,P

A captain of a company in the regiment, his pay is too high. (L) He is forty years old, and he came to France in 1585 with his wife Mary on recommendation of Don Bernardino and entered Parma's service. After Deventer he was appointed *alférez* in Stanley's regiment. His wife lived in Antwerp with their three children until last year, now lives in Brussels, "at times he handles the affairs of the regiment here." (R)

151. *Williams, Louis*
20 escudos H

152. *Williams, Richard*
20 escudos H

153. *Winslade, Tristram*
25 escudos N,O,P
He is forty-five years old and has served twenty-three years with the King's forces in Flanders, Ireland and the armada against England. He returned to Flanders recently with the Archduke. (R) A well-born gentleman, pensioned by order of the King, he is loyal and has endured much suffering. (N)

154. *Wiseman, Edmund*
25 escudos (not listed with the regiment)
Parma is ordered to employ Wiseman in his forces.

(A.H.N. Estado 251d, f. 3. Entry of 20 August 1587)

155. *Worsely, John*
30 escudos I,K,M,N,O,P
He received his pension through letters from Mendoza in England and also for certain offers of service on the Isle of Wight, where he was born of a good family. He is a soldier, but he is married with many young children. He can not serve unless he is given a position. (K) He has served for 14 years by order of the Duke of Parma, he now lives at Louvain. (R) A useful, loyal soldier. (N)

156. *Worthington, Thomas*
25 escudos E,H,L, 40 escudos M,N,P
A priest who serves the regiment. (K) A well-born gentleman, loyal and of use on occasions. (N)

157. *Zouche, Richard*
35 escudos I,K,N
He was pensioned for his services at the surrender of Zutphen,

where he was a *teniente*, he is well born and is now in sanctuary in Mons after killing a man. (ᴋ) He was one of those
who surrendered Alost, but he is in disgrace and has not received a pardon from the Archduke. He is a soldier who
could be of service at times, but his judgments are not well
regulated. (ɴ)

SOURCE MATERIALS

A. THE MANUSCRIPT SOURCES

SINCE THE MOST valuable collection for the study of Spain's interest in English Catholic affairs is the *Sección de Estado* reposing in the Archivo General de Simancas, the pertinent material sifted from the following *legajos* can be described in detail:

833–44, "Papeles de Negociaciones de Inglaterra"
584–626, "Correspondencia de Flanders y Consultas de Officio"
938–73, "Correspondencia de Roma, Negociaciones y Consultas"
K 1426–7, K 1447–9, K 1590/95, K 1602–9, K 1630–1, K 1665, K 1674, "Correspondencia de Francia, Cartas y Consultas"
2584–91, "Negociaciones del Norte"
2557–72, "Despachos para Inglaterra"
2511–15, "Consultas de Inglaterra de Officio"
2023–24, "Consultas Originales de Officio de Flandes"
1743–44, "Negocios de partes de Flandes"
2224/1–26, "Despachos para Flandes"
2288–91, "Cartas de Flandes"
2741–42, "Negocios de Partes de España"
2763–66, "Negocios de la Secretaria de Estado del Norte"
1855–57, 1874–76, "Consultas, cartas y papeles de Italia"
164–91, 2626–27, "Consultas de officio de Castilla"

In the Archivo Historico Nacional (Madrid) there is a secondary *Estado* collection where there are copies of executive orders of the Council. The following *libros* were useful: 250–66, 292–95.

In the Archives of Saint Alban's College in Valladolid are original papers concerning the founding of that institution, as well as the surviving documents relating to St. Gregory's in Seville and the hospice at San Lucar de Barrameda:

Miscelanea: Serie II, legajos 1, 13, 16; Serie IV, legajo 1.
Sevilla: legajos 17B and 17C

In the Archivo General de Indias in Seville, the complete file of Robert Frost's case is in *Sección de Santa Fe*, legajo 1.

In Rome the Archivio Segredo di Vaticano contains the reports from various Nuncios in Spain, France and Flanders, which can be supplemented by the diplomatic correspondence of the Borghese collection.

Nunziatura di Spagna: Tomos 9–52, 320–23.
Nunziatura di Fiandra: 3–II, 8, 10, 11, 48.
Nunziatura di Francia: 15–16, 48–49.
Fondo Borghese: Serie II, 448ab, Series III, 124g2 and 94C.

Also in Rome is the Archivum Romanum Societatis Jesu in which are collected reports received by the Jesuit Superiors on the order's activities in Spain, Flanders and England, as well as the minutes of the replies and orders despatched to those areas. The series is not complete but scattered through the following classifications were many useful details: *"Epistolae Receptae"* and *"Registrum Epistolarum R. P. Generalis"* for Hispania (including Castilla and Toletano), Flandro-Belgica, Anglia. Also in this archive is a separate collection known as the Fondo Gesuitico. Volume 691 contains letters from English Jesuits.

In Brussels the Archives Générales du Royaume have considerable material on the Governor's decisions over particular requests of the English *émigrés* and on local military affairs: The Papiers d'États et d'Audience: Registres 1400/1, 1036–47; Laisses 362–67, 405/2–3, 1970/1, 1869, 1976/1. The Secretairie d'État et de Guerre: Registres 8, 10, 15–20. Laisses: 124–25, 133, 300, 422, 423, 488, 500, 513.

In London The Public Record Office provides the important state paper collection which has been extensively described in the *Calendars*. Where the original is cited in the text, the following series were involved:

S.P. 12, State Papers Domestic, Elizabeth.
S.P. 94, State Papers, Spain.
S.P. 78, State Papers, France.

The British Museum also offered collections of contemporary English and Spanish documents. Of special significance were:

Cotton MS Caligula C III, Vespasian C VII, VIII, XIII.
Egerton MS vols. 1507–08.
Harleian MS vols. 295, 7042.
Lansdowne MS vols. 87, 96, 103, 512.
Yelverton MS vol. 33.

The Westminster Cathedral Archive contains unusually interesting letters by various Elizabethan Catholic clergy and laity.

Series A Collected Correspondence, volumes 1–7
Series E Miscellaneous Documents, vol. 2, Letters received by Thomas Fitzherbert.

In Stonyhurst College (Lancs.) is a valuable collection of letters, some of them early copies, on English Jesuit affairs, which were first collected by Father Greene in Rome in the 17th century.

MS "Collectanea Patris Greene," vols. B, M. P.
MS "Anglia," vols. 36–37.

In the Lambeth Palace Library, MS volumes 650–1 contain the Anthony Bacon papers that relate to Spain.

B. Contemporary Books

Allen, William: *The copie of a letter written by M. doctor Allen: concerning the yeelding up, of the citie of Daventrie . . .* (Antwerp, 1587) Chetham Society, vol. xxv, 1851.
Anon. *A Short Admonition or warning, upon the detestable treason where with Sir William Stanley and Rowland Yorke have betraied and delivered for monie unto the Spaniards the towne of Deventer and Sconce of Zutphen.* (London, 1587)
Creswell, Joseph: *Quis diues saluus. How a rich man may be saued . . . Translated into English by N. T.* (Saint Omer, 1618)
———, *Exemplar Litterarum missarum e Germania ad D. Gulielmum Consilarium Regium.* (Rome, 1592)
———, *Historia de la Vida y Martyrio que padescio en Inglaterra . . . el P. Henrico Valpolo . . . con el martyrio de otros quatro sacerdotes.* (Madrid, 1596)
———, *A proclamation published under the name of Iames king of Great Brittany. With a brief & moderate answer therunto.* (Saint Omer, 1611)

Doleman, R. (pseud.) *A conference about the next succession to the Crowne of Ingland* . . . (Antwerp, 1594)

Ecclesal, Thomas: *Relacion de un sacerdote Ingles en la qual le da cuenta de la Venida de S. M. a Valladolid y al colegio de los Ingleses.* (Madrid, 1592)

Fitzherbert, Thomas: *A Defence of the catholyke cause, contayning a treatise in confutation of sundry untruthes and slanders* . . . (Rome, 1602)

———, *An Apology of T. F. in defence of himself and other Catholykes falsely charged with a fayned conspiracy* . . . (Rome, 1602)

G. B.: *A Briefe Discoverie of Doctor Allen's seditious drifts contrived in a Pamphlet written by him, concerning the yeeldinge up of the towne of Deventer in Overisel unto the King of Spaine by Sir William Stanley.* (London, 1588)

Owen, Lewis: *The Running Register: Recording a True Relation of the State of the English Colleges, Seminaries and Cloysters in all forraine parts* . . . (London, 1626)

Persons, Robert: *Relacion de algunos Martyrios* . . . *y de otras cosas tocantes a nuestra y Catolica religion.* (Madrid, 1590)

———, *A Relation of the King of Spaines receiuing in Valladolid and in the Inglish College of the same town.* (Antwerp, 1592)

———, *A brief Apologie, or Defence of the Catholike ecclesiastical hierarchie & Subordination in England* . . . (Antwerp, 1601)

———, *A Manifestation of the great folly and bad spirit of certayne in England calling themselves secular priestes.* (Antwerp, 1602)

———, *Newes from Spain and Holland: conteyning An Information of Inglish affayres in Spayne with a conference theruppon in Amsterdame of Holland.* (Antwerp, 1593)

———, Philopater, Andreas (pseud.) *Elizabetae Reginae angliae edictum, Promulgatum Londini, 29 Nouemb. anni MDXCI, . . . responsio* . . . (Antwerp, 1593)

Rivers, Francis (Francisco de Ribera) *A Relation of the Solemnitie wherewith the Catholike Princes K. Philip III and Quene Margaret were receyved in the English College of Valladolid . . . written in Spanish by Don Ant. Ortiz* . . . (London, 1601)

Yepez, Diego de, *Historia Particular de la persecucion de Inglaterra, y de los martirios mas insignes que en ella ha auido* . . . (Madrid, 1599)

C. BIBLIOGRAPHICAL NOTE

Chapter One

THERE HAVE BEEN NO specific studies of the Elizabethan exiles and their relationship to the Spanish Court; however, several monographs have offered other aspects of their activities. For the late Msgr. Peter Guilday's projected study of *The English Catholic Refugees on the Continent, 1558–1795* there appeared only the first volume entitled *The English Colleges and Convents in the Catholic Low Countries* (London, 1914). This was largely concerned with the domestic histories of English exile religious communities. Published in the same year was Fr. Robert Lechat's *Les Refugiés Anglais dans les Pays-bas espagnols durant le règne d'Elisabeth* (Louvain, 1914) which drew its most valuable sources from local archives and correlated them with English printed sources. Arnold Oscar Meyer's, *England und die katholische Kirche unter Elizabeth und den Stuarts* (Rome, 1911 and translation, London, 1916), based on significant material in the *Nunziature* collection in the Vatican explored the development of Papal policy toward England. Far more important for its analysis of the first English exiles were the scholarly investigations of P. O. de Törne in *Don Juan d'Autriche et les projets de Conquête de l'Angleterre, 1568–78* (2 vols., Helsingfors, 1915–28) and his earlier monograph on Pope Gregory's ambitious Secretary of State, *Ptolemée Gallio, Cardinal de Côme* (Paris, 1907). T. F. Knox's lengthy introduction to the *Letters and Memorials of William Allen* (London, 1882) pieced together many of the details of that leading exile's career although much new material is now available to reinterpret his conclusions. Far more out of date both in historical method and documentation is M. A. Tierney's edition of Charles Dodd (Hugh Tootel), *The Church History of England from 1500 to the year 1688* (London, 1839–43).

Fr. John Hungerford Pollen's studies of Catholicism in Elizabethan England had the additional merit of using continental archives to give much new information on the background of the English Jesuit mission. His scholarly *Unpublished Documents Relating to the English Martyrs, 1584–1603* (*Catholic Record Society*, vol. v, 1908) contains a thorough study of Father Henry Walpole. At present Fr. Leo Hicks' many articles have provided a significant contribution to the political and religious activities of the English exiles. His introduction to the first volume of the *Letters and Memorials of Father Robert Persons, S.J.* (Catholic Record Society, vol. xxxix, 1942) contains a scholarly biography of that famous leader of the English Jesuits on the continent.

Chapter Two

Little has been done on Englefield's career aside from the appearance of the jejune article in the Dictionary of National Biography. T. B. Trappes-Lomax has traced the ownership of his estates after their forfeiture in "The Englefields and their contribution to the Survival of the Faith in Berkshire, Wiltshire, Hampshire and Leicestershire" in *Biographical Studies,* vol. 1 (1951), pp. 131–48. Professor Joel Hurstfield in "Corruption and Reform under Edward VI and Mary: the example of Wardship" *E.H.R.,* lxviii (1953), pp. 22–36, clears up certain aspects of his tenure as Master of the Court of Wards.

Chapter Three

Professor A. H. Dodd has made a detailed survey of Owen's activities from the evidence available in non-Spanish sources in "Two Welsh Catholic Émigrés discuss the Accession of James I," *Bulletin of the Board of Celtic Studies,* vol. viii (1937), pp. 344–58, and "A Spy's Report, 1604," *Ibid.,* vol. ix (1938), pp. 154–67, as well as "The Correspondence of the Owens of Plas Du, 1573–1604," *Transactions of the Caernarvonshire Historical Society,* vol. 1 (1939), pp. 47–54. The editor of the letter of Robert Persons discovered a portion of Owen's correspondence with a secretary of Parma in the *Carte Farnesiane* in the Archivio di Stato of Naples (*C.R.S.,* vol. xxxix, p. 246 note). W. Ll. Williams, "Welsh Catholics on the Continent," *Transactions of the Cymmrodorion Society,* 1901–2, pp. 46–144 is in need of revision.

Chapter Four

The article on Jane Dormer in the *Dictionary of National Biography* is inadequate. J. Stevenson edited *The Life of Jane Dormer, Duchess of Feria by Henry Clifford* (London, 1887), which is a *vie édifiante* by a former chaplain of her household. New information on the English embassy of her husband is available in M. Fernandez Alvarez, *Tres Ambassadores de Felipe II en Inglaterra* (Madrid, 1951), and in the two volumes of the *Calendar of State Papers, Spanish,* edited by Royall Tyler for the reign of Queen Mary (London, 1953–54).

Chapter Five

The first biography of Stanley was composed by Thomas Heywood for his introduction to an edition of *The Copie of a Letter
written by M. Doctor Allen: Concerning the yielding up of the
citie of Daventrie* for the Chetham Society (vol. xxv, 1851). Together with the history of the Stanley family available in G. Ormer-
od's *History of the County Palatine and city of Chester* (3 vols.,
London, 1875–82), Heywood's account is the basis for the account in the *Dictionary of National Biography*. Louis Antheunis:
"Un Refugié Catholique aux Pays Bas, Sir William Stanley, 1548–
1630," *Revue d'Histoire Ecclesiastique*, vol. xix (1923), pp.
352–69, has dealt extensively with his life in Malines after 1603.
Leo Hicks: "Allen and Deventer, 1587," *The Month* (Old
series, vol. clxiii, 1934), pp. 507–17 examines several misunderstandings about the relationship of the two Englishmen. The activities of Stanley in the Leicester expedition can be traced in Hojo
Brugman's edition of *Correspondentie van Robert Dudley* (3 vols.,
Utrecht, 1931), and John Bruce's selection in *Robert Dudley,
Earl of Leicester, Correspondence during his government of the
Low Countries,* (Camden Society, vol. xxvii, 1844). The best
survey of the meagre literature on the Spanish military establishment
in the Low Countries is in Lucienne Van Meerbeech *Les Sources de
l'Histoire Administrative de l'Armée Espagnole des Pays Bas au
XVIe et XVIIe Siècle* (Bruxelles, Musée Royal de l'Armée,
1939). L. Van der Essen's monumental biography of *Alexandre
Farnése, Prince de Parme* (5 vols., Brussels, 1933–37) provides
a thorough study of the war during Stanley's first years in Spanish
service.

Chapter Six

The biographical sketches of Creswell available in the *Dictionary
of National Biography*, the sixth volume of H. Foley's *Records of
the English Province of the Society of Jesus*, and Joseph Gillow's
*A Literary and Biographical History . . . of the English Cath-
olics* (5 vols., London, 1885–1903) are incomplete and misleading. While the general history of the seminaries has been surveyed
in Guilday's *The English Colleges* (cited in Chapter One above),
the lengthy introductions to the late Msgr. Henson's *The English
College in Madrid, 1611–1767*, and *The Register of the English
College at Valladolid* (Catholic Record Society, vols. xxix and xxx,
1929, 1930) are the most important studies to date. Fr. Leo Hicks
has probed extensively the founding of the colleges in "Father Per-

sons and the Seminaries in Spain," *The Month* (old series, vol. clvii, 1931), pp. 193–204, 410–17, 497–506; vol. clviii (1931), pp. 26–35, 143–52, 234–44. The first years of the college of St. Gregory at Seville are more difficult to trace. A brief *Annales*, composed in 1610 by Robert Persons giving his recollections of the early events, was edited by J. H. Pollen in the Catholic Record Society, vol. xiv, pp. 1–24. There are two *Annales* of differing merit for St. Alban's, both ascribed to one of the first members of its faculty, John Blackfan. The most reliable is the concise autograph version by Blackfan edited for the first time in the introduction to Henson's *The Register*. A second version erroneously ascribed to Blackfan, but actually a rambling and selective chronicle compiled later by four other different authors, was published as the *Annales Collegii Sancti Albani in oppido Valisoleti* (Roehampton, 1899).

INDEX

Note: The census of pensioners (Appendix III) contains additional names which have not appeared previously in the text.

Index

Ybarra, Diego de, 67
Ybarra, Esteban de, 57, 89, 164
Ybarra, Juan de, 198
Yepez, Diego de, 206–07, 223
Yonger, James, 74–75, 112, 189
Yorke, Sir Rowland, 138

Zafra, 98–99, 103, 111
Zapata, Don Hieronimo, 39
Zouche, Richard, 34, 263–64
Zubiaur, Pedro de, 67
Zúñiga, Baltazar de, 38, 60–61, 165–67
Zúñiga, Pedro de, 87, 178
Zutphen, 134, 135, 138

THE SPANISH ELIZABETHANS is set in Linotype Eldorado, 12 point, which was designed by W. A. Dwiggins after the letter used by a Spanish printer, A. de Sancha, in Madrid around 1774. "The name of the face was chosen as an echo of Spanish adventures in the western world."

The book was designed by
J. Richard Palmer